THE GOLDEN AGE
OF
OHIO STATE
BASKETBALL

1960-1971

THE GOLDEN AGE

OF

OHIO STATE

BASKETBALL

1960-1971

Lee Caryer

Photo on front left: Jerry Lucas drives against Indiana's Walter Bellamy in 1960. —Brockway and Emmons Sports Photos

Photo on front right: Jim Cleamons scores against Marquette in the 1971 Mid-East Regional. —Ohio State University Archives

Back: Gary Gearhart, Larry Siegfried, Howie Nourse, Coach Fred Taylor, Mel Nowell and John Havlicek celebrate the 1960 NCAA championship. — Ohio State Archives

Middle section photos: all photos labled [1]—Brockway & Emmons Sports Photos. All photos labled [2]—Ohio State University Archives

Companion Press
P.O. Box 351
Shippensburg, PA 17257-0351

ISBN 1-56043-490-2

For Worldwide Distribution
Printed in the U.S.A.

Table of Contents

Acknowledgements

Without the help of many people, this book could not have been written.

Not only did Basketball Hall of Fame member Fred Taylor develop the entire Golden Age, he gave selflessly of his time to see that it was reported accurately. He relived the time and reviewed initial drafts of the chapters.

Assistant coaches Jack Graf, Frank Truitt and Bob Burkholder all participated, as well as nearly 40 players. The Appendix has a list of all basketball lettermen at Ohio State 1960-1971, with an asterisk designating those who were interviewed at least once.

Sadly Gary Bradds and Bruce Schnabel have passed away. Fortunately Bradds' father Donald, wife Eileen and son David and Schnabel's wife Jennifer contributed their thoughts.

Jack Graf, Frank Truitt, Rich Hoyt, Larry Siegfried, John Havlicek, Doug McDonald, Don DeVoe, Tom Bowman, Dick Ricketts, Jim Shaffer, Al Rowley, Bill Hosket, Steve Howell, Craig Barclay, Jim Cleamons, Bob Siekmann and Denny Meadors all commented on at least one chapter as it was being developed.

People who were involved with the program, or competed against the school or the players, added depth with their observations. They include Rick Barry, Mike Bordner, Chance Brockway, Jimmy Crum, Jud Heathcote, Marv Homan, the late Jack Moore, Dr. Bob Murphy, Johnny Orr, Billy Packer and John Wooden.

The Ohio State Sports Information Department and the Columbus Public Library were invaluable sources of data, as were my personal collection of basketball magazines, particularly *SPORT* and

Sports Illustrated issues. I am glad those magazines were kept separate from my baseball cards, long since damaged by moisture. Back issues of *The Columbus Journal, The Columbus Citizen-Journal* and *The Columbus Dispatch* were essential, as was the assistance of the NCAA Research Department. John Havlicek's autobiography, *HONDO — Celtic Man in Motion,* was a rich source of insight and background and is quoted with his permission.

Mary Havener's typing was indispensable. Several friends, including Larry Bolden, Chuck Cole, Chip Heim, Chuck Underwood and Jim Woods, helped in various ways.

Without the help of The Ohio State Athletic Department, the book could not have been distributed to fans interested in college basketball.

Thank you all.

Preface

Ohio State's 1991 basketball season was a great one, for at least two reasons.

First, judged solely on its own merits, a Big Ten co-championship with a 27-4 record is an exceptional accomplishment. Plus a No. 1 seed in the NCAA, Big Ten Player of the Year and All-America honors for Jim Jackson, National Coach of the Year recognition for Randy Ayers ... a great season.

There is a second reason why the 1991 season was great. It encouraged Buckeye fans to relive the Golden Age of Ohio State basketball, the era from 1960 to 1971 when the team won seven championships in twelve years. Writers went back to that time repeatedly, to answer such questions as: When did Ohio State last win a Big Ten championship? (1971) Last go to the Final Four? (1968) Last play in the final game? (1962) Last go undefeated in the Big Ten? (1961) Last win the NCAA tournament? (1960).

Good teams often have similarities, and there were several comparisons of the 1991 champions to past winners.

"One thing which was always true of our championship teams," recalls Coach Fred Taylor, "was that the seniors played better than they ever had. It wasn't always higher scoring. In 1971 Jim Cleamons scored less as a senior than he had earlier in his career, but he did so many other things so well that he was Big Ten Most Valuable Player and a No. 1 NBA draft choice." For the 1991 Buckeyes, Perry Carter played well and Treg Lee showed remarkable improvement.

Watching Jim Jackson make four straight baskets to beat Purdue, then penetrate and pass to Treg Lee to beat Indiana, then score 26 points to edge Minnesota, brought Lucas, Havlicek, Hosket, Cleamons and other heroes to mind. To use Coach Taylor's phrase, they had "no fear of failure." They combined great ability with the strength of character to step forward at critical times, when the team needed them the most.

Jamaal Brown is called "a program player" by Randy Ayers. Fred Taylor could have been talking about Jamaal when he told his former players "you guys were role players before there was such a term." Mark Baker causes the defense nightmares like few players in Ohio State history, but Jim Cleamons comes to mind. Chris Jent selflessly stepped back to be a substitute in 1991 so the team could step forward. In 1960, senior co-captain Dick Furry did the same thing.

Even Randy Ayers has many similarities to Fred Taylor. Both worked their way up at Ohio State, rather than coming from other schools. Both were in their early 30's, and in their second year in charge, when they first won Big Ten titles. They shared the advantage of being able to easily relate to their players, and the disadvantage of coaching against men with much more experience. Both played inside in college, and had coaching philosophies which reflected that experience. Both stressed the importance of an education and took (or take) the high road in recruiting.

With Buckeye fans hoping that the 1991 season will be the start of another "Golden Age" of Buckeye basketball, this is a good time to take a close look at the last one. What happened? What do the coaches and players remember? How good were the best players? What lessons did today's adults learn while winning championships years ago?

In writing this book, my thinking was that if the coaches and players talked about what they remembered from the time, and these recollections were supplemented with what newspaper and magazines were saying at the time, the result would be of interest to a broad range of Ohio State fans. Fans of the time would want to relive the experience, especially if they could find out things they never knew before. Fans who never saw Jerry Lucas or Gary Bradds would want to discover how good they were. Everyone who saw John Havlicek in the NBA would be curious about him. Many fans would want to know what the men were doing now.

I had the opportunity to speak with 57 people who have first hand knowledge of Ohio State basketball from 1960-71, to ask them questions a fan wanted to know. I spoke with a minimum of three coaches and seven players from each of the twelve teams. They spoke very candidly, about the joy of the successes and the eventual value of the disappointments.

My goal through this was that the reader would feel like he, or she, had made the same journey: asked the questions which came to mind, combed through the old stats and quotes and tied up loose ends to his or her personal satisfaction. If I succeeded, the reader will conclude "What a remarkable group of men. College basketball served them well, helping them grow from young men into productive adults. They served college basketball well too."

I
Shaping the Future

Since joining the conference in 1913, Ohio State has won 14 Big Ten championships. During the 12 year period from 1960 to 1971, the Buckeyes earned seven of those titles.

Several coaches and dozens of players contributed significantly to the championships won during "The Golden Age of Ohio State basketball." This is their book. However as wide spread as the credit must be for the accomplishments during this time, one man stands first in line when the accolades are distributed. One man recruited the players, planned the practices, decided the strategy, supervised the coaches and, in fact, was responsible for every decision made during that time. The man is Fred R. Taylor.

Taylor played on the sixth Big Ten champion at Ohio State, the 1950 team which won 22 of 26 games. Without question the history of OSU basketball predates Head Coach Fred Taylor by several decades. It includes people like Robin Freeman, Paul Ebert, Frank Howard, Dick Schnittker, Bill Hosket Sr., Jimmy Hull and many, many more. However the "Golden Age" began with the NCAA championship team in 1960, Taylor's second year as coach. Every player on that team was recruited by him so he is the logical place to begin.

Taylor was born and raised in Zanesville, Ohio, graduating from high school in 1942. He remembers some things as very different from today.

"Neither my father, John Frederick, nor my mother, Blanche, graduated from high school. In fact when I was in high school I don't remember any emphasis from the teachers on going to college and getting a degree. Because my parents had both quit school in about

1

the eighth grade to help support their families, they had to work very hard. I remember noticing that, but I didn't necessarily appreciate it at the time. I do remember my father getting up very early every morning to build a fire in the furnace, so my sister Mary and I wouldn't have to get up to a cold house.

"The fondest memory of my childhood was the Saturday nights. Dad worked at the Quality Furniture store until 8:00. He would get a red pop, a white pop and a beer to split with my mother. Then the four of us would sit and listen to the radio.

"My athletic career at Zanesville was not exactly legendary," recalls Taylor. "We didn't have a baseball team at the high school, so I just played sand lot ball. Three times I tried out for the basketball team and three times I was cut. My senior year just before the state tournament one of our players was kicked off the squad and I got the tenth uniform. I didn't play enough to letter."

In the fall of 1942 Taylor entered Ohio State University. In March, 1943 he left school to enter the Air Corps and became a basketball and baseball talent while serving at bases in Denver, Colorado; Greensboro, North Carolina; and Alexandria, Louisiana. "Roland Wenzel, who played three sports at Capital University and is now in their Hall of Fame, was my first basketball coach. We got together right after I washed out of flight school, along with 36,000 other guys.

"There's no doubt my service experience enabled me to play athletics at Ohio State when I went back to college. Our camp commander at Alexandria was very sports oriented; he used to arrange training flights to the game sites. We won the baseball championship one year, though Camp Livingston had a pitcher named Kirby Higby, a star with the Brooklyn Dodgers before the service. The best we ever did in basketball was runner-up. We lost to the 2nd Air Force out of Lincoln, Nebraska. They had Goose Tatum (long time leader and dribbling wizard of the Harlem Globetrotters) and we couldn't do much about him. There were a lot of college players on those teams, and we played some college teams too. For example 'Bones' McKinney, who became the coach at Wake Forest, played for North Carolina at that time."

After 36 months in the service, honed athletically by better competition than the colleges offered at that time, Taylor returned to Ohio State for possibly the greatest college career ever by an athlete who did not letter in high school.

2

In basketball he was a frequently used substitute on a 10-10 team in 1948 and a 14-7 team in 1949. By 1950 he joined four three year starters — Dick Schnittker, Bob Donham, Gene Brown and Bob Burkholder — as the starting center. That team won the Big Ten with an 11-1 record, despite missing their star forward Schnittker for several games while he played end for the football team in the Rose Bowl. They were second ranked in the nation to Bradley.

The 1950 Buckeyes played City College of New York, coached by legendary coach Nat Holman, in the NCAA tournament. CCNY has been selected by *The Sporting News* as the 15th best college team of all time, but OSU was even at halftime, 40-40. "That was a lot of points for that time," says Fred Taylor today. "In the 1990's a comparable score might be 55-55."

The second half was more conservatively played. All-American Dick Schnittker fouled out of the game for the only time in his college career with the Bucks trailing 55-54 and two minutes to play. ("Thinking back to that game today," Bob Burkholder says, "in the lobby before the game my father could have taken a bet that Schnittker would foul out." Rather a strange wager. Or was it?) The 56-55 final score allowed CCNY to go on to win the NCAA. Having already won the National Invitational Tournament by defeating Bradley, they had accomplished something no college team had done before or has done since — win both tournaments in the same season.

City College of New York would be disgraced due to the involvement of their players in the 1951 gambling scandal which centered around Madison Square Garden. CCNY players admitted point shaving in three games in 1950-51, and later investigation revealed grades had been changed to allow admission of athletes to the academically prestigious school. Nothing was proven about improprieties in the 1950 season, but Ohio State players will always wonder about their game.

After the tough loss to CCNY, Ohio State won the consolation game against Holy Cross and its star Bob Cousy, 72-52, to finish 22-4. A pleasant end to a great season. Today Fred Taylor recalls "Bob Donham, who later played for the Boston Celtics, did a great job guarding Cousy for us." Ironically Donham and Cousy played together in Boston for four years, 1951-54, and Donham had a better field goal percentage every year. Of course it was Cousy's play making that put him into the Basketball Hall of Fame.

On the baseball diamond, playing first base for Floyd Stahl, Taylor made All-American in 1950, but the team did not have similar success.

"We had good players," recalls Taylor, "and Floyd ran good practices, getting us ready for every situation, but we didn't seem to really come together like the basketball team did."

After graduation Fred Taylor wanted to go into coaching basketball immediately, but things didn't work out. "I thought I'd get the basketball coaching job at Upper Arlington, but they decided they wanted somebody with experience. Then the Superintendent of Schools in Lima interviewed me and promised me the job at what is now Lima Senior. He said it was all set, he just had to get board approval. Then I got a penny postcard in the mail saying the board wanted someone with experience. I remember thinking 'anyone in the post office could have read this'. I felt like a failure.

"When coaching fell through I turned to baseball, and signed with the Washington Senators. Eileen and I had been married in 1947, we had bought our first car — a new 1949 Chevrolet Business Coupe, $1,599.40. I needed a job."

Taylor spent part of the 1950 season and all of 1951 with Chattanooga of the Southern Association. In 1951 he hit .296 and batted in 103 runs. He divided the 1952 season between Washington in the American League and Charleston in the American Association.

"At Washington I played behind Mickey Vernon," recalls Taylor. "He was good — he won two American League batting titles. I could see I'd have to be 50% better to replace an established player like he was. A coach or manager has to look at it that way."

In 1953 he was sold to Beaumont in the Texas League and hit 22 home runs with 88 runs batted in. Impressive numbers, but the end of a baseball career.

"The club president was a nice guy," recalls Taylor, "and he had written into my contract that I would receive 25% of the purchase price if I was sold to a team at a higher level. When my contract was sold for $10,000, that meant I would get $2,500. For comparison, the minimum major league contract at that time was $5,000. But I had to make the team to receive the bonus, so it was still a gamble.

"During the time I was playing baseball professionally I had been spending the winters in Columbus, helping Floyd Stahl with the basketball team. Floyd had been an excellent high school basketball coach in high school, but had been baseball coach at Harvard for eight years and at Ohio State for four years. Except for one year at Harvard, he had been away from basketball for a long time, so while

4

he was re-learning I was learning. I guess I was like today's graduate assistant.

"There was a very warm day in February and Floyd asked me to meet him at the OSU Golf Course for a round of golf. When he got there he didn't have his clubs, and said 'I'll just walk with you for a while'.

"Funny how you remember things," says Taylor, "but I remember really stepping on my tee shot on the first tee. It was a beauty. When we walked down the fairway he said 'How would you like a full time job with the University, as freshman basketball coach?' I promptly stuck my six iron in the ground I was so excited.

"They had never had a full-time freshman basketball coach at Ohio State. The job had just been done by one of the assistant football coaches after their season was over. Since it was a new job, I didn't know when it might be open again. It had certainly been a life long ambition of mine to coach basketball at Ohio State. A big factor, too, was that my mother was terminally ill with cancer. She died in 1954. Plus Eileen and I had a couple of kids, we liked Columbus ... it was a pretty easy decision."

For five years Taylor served as freshman coach, while Floyd Stahl and assistant Jack Graf worked with the varsity. The captain of his first freshman team was Gene Millard. "Now there was a guy who was wound pretty tight," recalls Taylor fondly. "When he played guard if the guy on one side of the floor wouldn't run the play properly, Gene would take the ball to the other side. That would teach you a lesson." Millard was varsity captain his senior year and became an excellent high school coach at Bexley, a Columbus suburb. In 1983 Bexley won the state AA championship.

Taylor even got a little varsity coaching experience during the 1954-55 season, when the football team went to the Rose Bowl and Floyd Stahl was asked to spend three weeks with them. So Graf and Taylor coached the basketball team while the head basketball coach made hotel arrangements for the football team as assistant athletic director.

After the 1958 season Floyd Stahl retired as basketball coach on April 24 to work full time in an administrative capacity for the University.

Stahl's retirement came as high school seniors were making their college decisions, so Ohio State had to select a replacement soon. A screening committee was established to interview candidates. It was chaired by Professor Roderick Barden, chairman of the athletic board, and included Professor Elliot Whitaker and Athletic Director Dick Larkins. Former OSU All-America Paul Ebert was also on the selection committee, which reviewed the credentials of over 30 candidates.

Freshman coach Fred Taylor applied. Assistant coach Jack Graf, involved with the Graf & Sons family business, did not. Taylor's most visible competition was Middletown High School head coach Paul Walker, who some thought would hope to present a package deal with his star Jerry Lucas. However Walker's influence over Lucas was not as strong in fact as it appeared to be in the media. Neither Jerry Lucas nor his parents had any thought of dictating to Ohio State.

Among the other candidates were Bob Donham, star on the 1950 OSU team and former Boston Celtic then coaching at Bowdoin College in Maine, and Jackie Moore, 33 year old coach at Columbus East. Moore, whose senior star Mel Nowell was rated second only to Lucas as a prospect in Ohio, had also coached Joe Roberts, a sophomore forward at OSU at that time.

In May, 1958, both Lucas and Nowell announced for Ohio State. June 6 Fred Taylor was offered the position of head basketball coach at Ohio State University at a salary of $8,000. When Woody Hayes had been hired as football coach in 1951 his salary was $12,500. Taylor had emerged as the best candidate through a difficult process.

"I remember the interview," he says today. "There were 12-15 on the committee and we sat in a huge circle. Rod Barden, a professor who used to own The Outdoor Store on Route 33, asked me this question: 'What would you do if the committee does not see fit to elevate you to the position of head coach?'

"Tough question. I hadn't thought a great deal about being head coach until Floyd retired, but once he did I decided I was well qualified. I said 'If I'm not chosen and the new coach would allow it, I'd like to be able to stay for one year while I look for another head coaching position elsewhere.' I didn't mean it as an ultimatum, I just wanted to be honest."

The night Taylor was hired he went to work. He and some friends went into St. John Arena, which had opened in the fall of 1956, and painted an 'O' in the center of the circle. "I just thought, 'There's one on the football field, there ought to be one on the basketball court.' So we did it."

Recruiting had been completed, so plans for the 1958-59 season could begin. Jack Graf was in place as the assistant coach, which was a good start. "Jack had been my first basketball coach at Ohio State when I was on the jayvees, and we never had a problem working together. He had great insight to the sport and had a certain ability to evaluate a situation or an individual," says Taylor today. "He often said 'Remember, we are critical of the act, not the individual.' That says something about the kind of coach he was."

Graf was an Ohio State man through and through. He had lettered in basketball in 1940-41-42 for Harold G. Olsen, serving as captain in 1942. Graf excelled as a defensive player and ball handler, but he was even better known for his football talent. He played quarterback in 1939 and 1940, then was switched to fullback in 1941 by new coach Paul Brown. The team went 6-1-1, tied for second in the conference and Graf won the *Chicago Tribune* trophy as most valuable player to his team in the Big Ten.

After receiving his Masters in Business Administration degree from Harvard University, Graf served as backfield coach for the football team 1944-5-6. He was assistant coach in basketball from 1945 to 1970 when his father died, at which time Graf left coaching to assume full responsibility for the family business.

Dr. Robert Murphy, head physician for the team from 1952-70, says "Jack was a major factor in the success of the team. He was the perfect balance to Fred's youthful exuberance." Dick Furry says "Jack Graf was a defensive genius."

Taylor's first priority was replacing himself as the freshman coach. And he couldn't have his first choice. "Bob Burkholder and I had been 'road roomies' when we played together", says Taylor. "We had an understanding that the one who got a head coaching job first would hire the other one when he could. He was head coach at Muskingum, but I knew he wanted to come to Ohio State, and I planned to ask him.

"However the selection committee had one restriction when they offered me the position of head coach — I had to hire a high school coach. Seems strange to think about now. I can't explain why I accepted that restriction, but I did.

"When I got the job I drove over to see Bob and explain why I couldn't hire him. It just wasn't the sort of message you delivered over the phone."

A local high school coach named Frank Truitt had caught Taylor's eye with his disciplined team at Columbus North. In his first year at North, Truitt had led the Polar Bears to an undefeated season before

7

snapping Middletown's 76 game win streak in the state semi-finals, 63-62. This brought the notice of everyone in the state. Though North lost the state final in double overtime 50-48 to Cleveland East Tech, the 1950 Otterbein graduate was named head coach at his alma mater on May 3, 1958.

When Fred Taylor asked about his interest in the position as OSU freshman coach, Truitt heard something he had hoped — and planned — to hear much earlier. "I accepted the Otterbein position contingent on being released if the job at Ohio State opened up," says Truitt. "It was actually written in the contract, so there was no misunderstanding. I figured Fred would get the head coaching position, and I wanted to have a shot at working for him. Otterbein understood. Things worked out well."

What foresight. Just as Lou Holtz would sign a Minnesota football contract roughly 25 years later which would allow him to resign if Notre Dame wanted him, Truitt had anticipated what he wanted to do if certain circumstances developed. His forecast was correct and he enjoyed the result.

Truitt's foresight was valuable during his seven years at Ohio State, as was his charm as a recruiter. After the players arrived, he was responsible to help them adjust to college life. "He gave the kids the most precious gift one person can give another," recalls Taylor. "He gave them time. He really cared about the players, and they knew that."

Truitt was also noted for his concentration on tactics, as illustrated by a story former Buckeye forward Jim Doughty tells about his junior year at North. "We didn't have a school bus," says Doughty, "so we always drove to games in two cars. Frank drove the starters in one, the assistant took the reserves in the other. We were driving down a highway and it was snowing pretty bad. Frank was discussing a play and he didn't think we were getting his point. So he turned off the defroster, the car fogged up and he started drawing X's and O's on the fog on the windshield. We could see what he was saying, but by then we were concentrating on what to do if the car crashed."

It didn't, but "we had lots of plays at North," concludes Doughty.

The coaching staff of Fred Taylor, Jack Graf and Frank Truitt was in place, and remained that way until Truitt took the head coaching position at Louisiana State University in the spring of 1965.

* * * *

Taylor's first year as head coach, 1958-59, the Buckeyes finished 11-11 overall, 7-7 in the Big Ten. Considering that only two starters, Larry Huston and Joe Carlson, returned from a 9-13 team, that was not a bad beginning. The season allowed the coach to make rookie mistakes and get them behind him. It allowed junior forwards Dick Furry and Joe Roberts to greatly increase playing time from their sophomore year. When the Golden Age began the next year, Furry and Roberts were ready to lead as veteran co-captains. It allowed sophomore Larry Siegfried to develop into a star in the Big Ten, and sophomore Richie Hoyt a chance to gain valuable experience as the first substitute. All four of these players would be significant contributors to Ohio State basketball in the beginning of the Golden Age.

As the 1959 season opener with Pittsburgh came closer, most fans focused on the freshman team rather than the varsity. Football Coach Woody Hayes had summarized the majority opinion in the spring when he said "If Middletown's Jerry Lucas comes to Ohio State I'm going to start watching the freshman games." The fact is the varsity was regularly beating the freshman in practice early in the year. College play was different than high school, and only Lucas was immediately effective against the varsity. But perceptions can be more important than facts.

While the freshmen were learning in practice, the varsity was getting off to a rough 1-4 start. Three straight victories over Utah, Princeton and Brigham Young, keyed by excellent efforts by Dick Furry, evened OSU's pre-conference record at 4-4.

* * * *

"I went to Columbus West High School," says Dick Furry, "where I used to bang up against Joe Roberts at East. It was nice to finally be on his side, particularly since they beat us in almost every sport.

"When it came time for college I looked at Northwestern, Illinois, Michigan, Miami (O.) and Ohio State. They were all good accounting schools, which is what I wanted. My track coach wanted me to go to Miami, but my father had played baseball at Ohio State and took me to my first OSU football game when I was nine. When the Ohio State coaches came to see me about basketball, that settled things."

The 6'6, 206 lbs. Furry was an outstanding athlete, who combined good size for the time with jumping ability which had enabled him to win a state high jump championship in track. "He doesn't know how great a player he can be," said Taylor before Furry's junior year.

9

Today John Havlicek remembers Furry as "very mature. He was a terrific jumper with a good game around the basket." Joe Roberts adds "He always wanted to be an accountant. He went after that and got it, and helped our basketball team too." Larry Siegfried says Furry was "fast, maybe close to a 10.0 100 yard dash man. Very valuable, and unselfish."

Furry recalls that "our sophomore year we were picked to win the Big Ten, with Frank Howard, Jim Laughlin, Larry Huston and Kenny Sidle." That year ended up 8-6 in the conference, 9-13 overall. Furry averaged only 3.6 ppg and shot less than 40% from the field and the foul line. He was ready to step forward as a junior, though he remembers things being different with his "new" head coach.

"When Fred was freshman coach he was one of our confidants," says Furry. "He had a different role as varsity coach. Still, he had a great deal of trust in us. He used to say 'You know how to behave. I hope you do behave so I don't have to set rules.' And even though he was in charge, he was reasonably young. He would shoot around with us, sometimes play some — we could identify with him. I imagine it was similar to the way the Ohio State players today feel about Randy Ayers."

* * * *

Four losses in the first five Big Ten games brought a quick halt to hopes for the conference season. Even though all the losses had been road games, it was unlikely Ohio State could rebound from a 1-4 record. The good news was that 6'6 Joe Roberts, with 15 points at Michigan State and 24 at Purdue, had stepped forward as a key player for the team.

* * * *

"I didn't want to go to Ohio State," recalls Joe Roberts. "Yet my senior year there we had the greatest group of guys you could ever hope to be around. All they wanted to do was win. It hadn't always been that way.

"Beginning my sophomore year at Columbus East (1954) and through my senior year I used to watch Ohio State play at the Fairgrounds. Floyd Stahl provided tickets, so I could study the teams for myself. They always had one star but mediocre teams. I wanted to go where the teams would be successful. Besides, Ohio State didn't have blacks on the team then."

Roberts' high school coach at East, Jackie Moore, said "Joe was an excellent student in high school, and did very well in college. Just a fine person. He started for us as a sophomore, and was a real leader on the 1955 and 1956 teams, both ranked No. 1 in the state during the year. The 1955 team was the best I had at East. We lost in the state semi-finals to Cincinnati Roger Bacon by one point."

"My first choice was Marquette," recalls Roberts. "Ed Hickey had won a lot of games there. He said I was all set but he was working on something about basketball in Europe at the time and things never got solidified. Georgia Tech was interested in me because I had a B+ average at East, until they found out I was black. Ohio University was interested but I found out blacks had to be off the streets at 7:00 p.m. in Athens. So I ended up at Ohio State.

"Freshman year I had knee surgery and missed the whole year. As a sophomore the team went 9-13; that was a struggle. Ohio State was strictly football — the writers wouldn't even talk to you — and the team had been expected to be pretty good. We were playing in Los Angeles, the same time the football team was in the Rose Bowl, and I was frustrated. I actually quit the team. Fred and I went on a long walk, talked it through, worked things out. I felt comfortable talking to Fred. Then my junior year, when I didn't think I was playing enough, I went to see him, we went over my stats, and I became a starter."

Concerns over race which had faced high school recruit Joe Roberts did not disappear because he was in college.

"My sophomore year we had hotel reservations in Utah. When we got there the hotel manager saw me and told Floyd Stahl 'He can't stay here.' Floyd was a nice man, so this caught him completely off guard. He said 'Joe, can you stay with your people for the night?' I said 'Floyd, this is Utah. I don't have any people here. Just give me a ticket and I'll go home.' It was finally worked out so I could stay at the hotel but I had to stay in my room and not be seen."

It had only been 11 years since Jackie Robinson had broken the color line in professional baseball. Racial unrest of the 1960's was years away. The Super Bowl wasn't even being played; Doug Williams' role as the first black quarterback to start in, and win, a Super Bowl would take place in 1988, 30 years later. Racial inequality was not discussed on the sports page — in fact it was not discussed very much at all. When people recall the 1950's as "a simpler time," that may be true because so many complex issues were suppressed — hidden behind closed doors, so to speak.

Roberts' black teammate Dave Barker, from Columbus St. Marys, simply says "Anytime we played a team from the South there were racial statements made — Georgia Tech for example." That shows considerable grace on his part, but doesn't allow the fan revisiting the era to recreate the discrimination of the time. Richie Hoyt's comment is more helpful. "I remember several times, Lexington, Kentucky in particular, when Fred would pull a couple of us aside and say 'Stay with Joe and Dave and Mel (Nowell) — never let them out of your sight'." Buckeye fans today cannot understand what life was like as a black athlete in the 1950's, but there was more to it than points and rebounds, victories and defeats.

* * * *

Consecutive home victories over Iowa and Minnesota were sparked by Larry Siegfried, high scoring sophomore who totaled 52 points. Then Indiana, second in the league behind Michigan State, came to town and set a St. John Arena scoring record which stands today, winning 122-92.

"We played a pretty decent game and got murdered," said Fred Taylor. "Indiana hit 22 of 39 shots (56%) the first half and we're still tied with them 48-48. I told our kids it's impossible. We're playing great ball. They've just got to start missing."

Actually the Hoosiers, led by sophomore center Walter Bellamy, heated up in the second half. They made 28 of 40 shots — 70% from the field. OSU was outscored 74-44 in the remarkable second half.

Wisconsin fell as Furry scored 20 points but a loss to Iowa on the road kept the Bucks from getting back to .500 in the league.

A trip to Bloomington was one of the highlights of the season as OSU avenged their 122-92 defeat with a 92-83 victory over Indiana. Co-captain Larry Huston scored 26, and Larry Siegfried scored 20, 17 in the second half. Roberts had 19, senior Jim Niehaus 15 and Furry 10. The only substitute, Howie Nourse, had a basket.

Victories over Michigan and Minnesota and a loss to Purdue left the season dead-even, 7-7 in conference, 11-11 over-all.

Not only had Furry and Roberts proven themselves as starters, sophomore Larry Siegfried had emerged as a star. He led the conference in free throw attempts, and set a Big Ten record by making 16 of 16 against Purdue. That record stood 22 years until Indiana's Ted Kitchel made all 18 against Illinois in 1981.

Siegfried led the team in field goal attempts and conversions, free throws taken and made, points, scoring average, was second in personal fouls and fourth in rebounds. The "scintillating sophomore from Shelby" had arrived.

* * * *

"Larry's senior year in high school was 1957, and I was driving a 1953 Bonneville at the time," recalls then freshman coach Fred Taylor. "I'd turn the key in the ignition and that Bonneville would automatically head north to Shelby. I saw him play a lot that year."

A reasonable course of action to be sure. Siegfried was the outstanding senior in Ohio, leading the state in scoring. He finished second to junior Jerry Lucas as the 1957 International News Service Player of the Year.

"His coach, Chuck Williams, built the team around Larry and never took him out, even if the score was 112-14," recalls Taylor. "Larry would jump center, get the tip, go get the ball, bring it up court, go into the low post, get the ball back, and score. They depended on him so much for offense they couldn't afford to have him play defense."

The system worked. Little Shelby went 21-1 before losing to Toledo Macomber in the regional finals. "They had about 3000 boys, we had 200," recalls Siegfried. Macomber then lost to Middletown in overtime.

Siegfried could have gone anywhere to college — at 6'3, 190 lbs. he was a very big, strong guard prospect for the time.

"I looked at Kentucky, Northwestern, Indiana, Vanderbilt, Wisconsin and Tennessee," he recalls, "but I wanted to be close to home so my mom and dad could watch the games, and so I could get home to hunt and fish. I was a country boy. Fred had some country in him, too. He recruited me the way it should be done, by spending time together, comparing values, goals.

"I was petrified my freshman year. I had never eaten out, never owned a top coat or a dress hat or stayed in a hotel. My family was not worldly. Sophomore year I took my first plane trip, another adjustment.

"On the court I was fine. Both freshman and sophomore years the team counted on me to do a lot of things, just like high school. Fred was coach both years, so playing varsity was not much different than playing with the freshmen. We had practiced together anyway. I was a player on the court, but a little boy off the court. I was happiest on the court; I lived in that world, the gym."

"He was intense," remembers Dick Furry. "Most of us were city kids but Larry grew up on a farm. He had a fire to play."

"You could tell Sieg could play right away," says Joe Roberts. "Some freshmen are intimidated playing the varsity, but he was competitive immediately. We used to stay after practice and play one-on-one. And he was strictly a country boy. We'd be coming back from a road game, tired, and Sieg would come up and want to tell you about sheep and goats. I'd be like 'Go away, man, we want to sleep'."

* * * *

Richie Hoyt was the other sophomore who established himself as a Big Ten player in 1959.

As a senior at Mt. Vernon Hoyt had averaged "about 28 ppg" as the scourge of the old Central Buckeye League. He was a good student, and was recruited as a football quarterback by many colleges. The Ivy League was one option, football and/or basketball presented several other choices. What to do?

"I had followed Robin Freeman growing up (Freeman, who played 1954-6, still holds the Ohio State record for best scoring average at 28.0 points per game) and had an infatuation with Ohio State basketball. When it was clear that Floyd Stahl and Fred Taylor were focused on academics I figured 'If you live in central Ohio, why not Ohio State?'

"My freshman year Larry Siegfried and I roomed together. He was even intense when it came to studying. He was either 100% focused or completely distracted — all or nothing. We struggled with the same problem, going from 'home town hero', whether Shelby or Mt. Vernon, to a team player at a big school.

"Sophomore year I worked my way into the starting line-up, then hurt my ankle and dropped back to sixth man," says Hoyt. He was also serving as Big Brother to Jerry Lucas in the Beta Theta Pi Fraternity.

"With Roberts and Furry back at forward, and John Havlicek obviously a player who would earn playing time there, Fred asked me to switch to guard and to work on ball handling that summer. I had never played guard before, but the team needed someone behind Larry and Mel Nowell," the 6'4 Hoyt recalls.

The freshmen, subject of so much discussion, were influencing the lives of the upperclassmen. That was just the start of the influence Jerry Lucas — John Havlicek — Mel Nowell — Gary Gearhart — Bob Knight would have on Ohio State basketball.

14

II

The 1958
Recruiting Class

In the movie *Butch Cassady and the Sundance Kid*, when Paul New-
man and Robert Redford are being chased relentlessly by a posse
which will not give up, Sundance keeps asking "Who *are* those
guys?" The question applies to the Ohio State freshman class of 1958-
59. Who *are* those guys, influencing the selection of a head coach and
causing veteran players to be changed from one position to another?

The recruiting class, the second best in the history of college basketball to that time according to a 1989 article by *The Sporting News*,
was essentially these five players:

Jerry Lucas: He was either —

    A. The most heavily recruited high school player, with the
possible exception of Wilt Chamberlain, to that time.

    B. The greatest high school player in the history of Ohio bas-
ketball, before or since.

    C. The best college player ever to play at Ohio State.

    D. All of the above.

The answer is D.

In the last 30 years high school fans in Ohio have seen Bill Hosket,
Ed Ratleff, Allan Hornyak, Ed Stahl, Kevin Grevey, Phil Hubbard,
Dwight Anderson, Clark Kellogg, Herb Williams, Jim Jackson and
many other superior talents. Great as they were, none compared to
Lucas as a high school player. He scored 2460 points, more than
200 higher than Chamberlain's national record. "I didn't see

(Michael) Jordan or Magic Johnson, but of those I saw play in high school the two best players were Jerry Lucas and Lew Alcindor (later Kareem Abdul-Jabbar, the leading scorer in NBA history)" says Bob Knight. Knight has observed most of the best high school players in the last three decades, and recruited people like Larry Bird, Scott May, Isiah Thomas and Damon Bailey.

John Havlicek: One of the greatest professional basketball players in the history of the National Basketball Association, he is one of only five players with 20,000 career points and 5,000 career assists. The others are Oscar Robertson, Jerry West, Kareem Abdul-Jabbar and Larry Bird. Distinguished company, and #17 of the Celtics fits right in. He wore #5 at Ohio State. Despite what sportscasters have been saying for over 30 years, *he says* his name is pronounced *Hav-ul-check*.

Mel Nowell: "The best one-on-one player in the group," according to his running mate at guard, Larry Siegfried. "He could have had a ten year NBA career if he had been drafted by the right team," says Joe Roberts, who played in the NBA and the ABA and later coached in the NBA himself.

Gary Gearhart: The quickest player on the team according to most, a great guy according to all and a practice player who made his teammates better even though he did not get the playing time he wanted during an injury-plagued career.

Bob Knight: At times the best jump shooter on the team, later one of the greatest coaches in the history of college basketball.

Nelson Miller, who would become first string catcher on the baseball team, got some aid for basketball too, and J.T. Landes of Columbus North had assistance as well.

JERRY LUCAS —

In a world where "awesome", "super" and "all-time best" are used to sell everything from sneakers to soap, it is difficult to describe the impact Jerry Lucas had on Ohio high school basketball in the 1950's. The best opportunities may be not with adjectives but with a story and a review of some of his numbers.

First the story.

Lucas grew up on the playgrounds at Middletown, playing against college players and pros while he was still in high school. "Owen Lawson and Eric Back had preceded me at Middletown and gone on to college," recalls Lucas today. They lettered at Western

Kentucky in 1956, 1957 and 1958. "They promoted our games on the outdoor courts and were able to attract many good players over the years." Those games, "6-8-10 hours a day, six days a week" caused knee problems throughout his career but advanced his development.

As word of Jerry Lucas spread, more players came to compete. As in the days of the Old West, people wanted to see who was "the fastest gun in town." But the story about Jerry's ability took place before he had become a legend. It happened when he was in junior high school.

In 1955 Lucas was in ninth grade, and was playing on the outdoor courts against a University of Dayton player named Johnny Horan. Horan graduated from Dayton in 1955 as the second leading scorer in Flyer history and played briefly in the NBA. He was 6'8 and led Dayton to a record of 50-11 in 1954 and 1955, a period when Ohio State was 21-23. Johnny Horan was an *excellent* college player, twice the most valuable player for the Flyers.

On this day in 1955 Lucas ate his lunch, shut his water off, locked him up and threw away the key, served him a Wilson sandwich ... in short, he completely dominated Horan. Impressed, Horan said, "What year is that guy?" to one of the park regulars. "Freshman," was the reply. Horan shook his head and said "What college?" "He's in junior high" was the answer.

That's the kind of player Jerry Lucas was *before* he got to high school. By age 15 had reached his full height of 6'8.

As a sophomore his Middletown team won the state tournament with a 25-0 record. He averaged 28.7 ppg and never scored less than 12 points in a game. In the six games when he scored less than 22 points the *closest* game was a 88-59 rout of Columbus East, ranked No. 1 in Ohio early in the season. The average margin of victory was 38 points in his six low scoring games. Opponents did not stop or even slow the sophomore, only the extent of the devastation limited him. If Lucas was on the court, he starred.

In one of their closest games of the year Middletown beat Cleveland East Tech 91-78 in the semi-finals in Cleveland. Lucas scored 53 points. In the championship game the Middies beat Canton McKinley 91-69, with Lucas scoring 44. Fred Taylor remembers seeing Lucas for the first time that weekend and thinking "Whoa!"

His junior year was very similar. The team won the state championship and finished 27-0. Jerry had a high game of 59 points in a 109-83 victory over Dayton Roosevelt and averaged 34.4 ppg. Games

were 32 minutes long, so that was over one point per minute —
though he sat out many of those minutes. His low game was 21
points in a one-sided 84-45 victory over Cincinnati Taft. When Toledo
Macomber took Middletown to overtime before losing 70-65 in the
state semi-finals, Lucas scored 46 points. Two came on a 25' shot to tie
the game at 61 with 0:01 in regulation after the Middies trailed by
seven points with 77 seconds to go. He had 28 in the finals as Kent
Roosevelt fell 64-54.

Lucas entered his senior year never having lost in a junior high or
high school game. During that year he scored 63 points in one game
and the Middies won 24 straight, running their consecutive victory
streak to 76 games. They were matched with Columbus North,
coached by Frank Truitt and led by future Buckeyes Jim Doughty and
J.T. Landes, in the semi-finals. Middletown was the overwhelming
favorite, even though North was undefeated. The game was tied 30
each at the half as Lucas had 12 points. At the end of the third quarter
Middletown moved ahead 48-43, and went to 52-45 early in the
fourth. Lucas dominated the boards. But North had a 16-4 spurt to
lead 61-56 with 1:10 to go. Middletown could not repeat their comeback from 1957 and fell 63-62 in the biggest upset in Ohio high school
basketball history.

Lucas made 11 of 17 shots from the field and three of five at the
line for a game high 25 points. Landes scored 23 for North. Lucas had
17 rebounds, more than twice as many as any other player. North's
ball handling and pressure defense spelled the difference in the game
— they had eight turnovers, Middletown had 17.

Asked today how he felt after the only defeat in his career to that
time, Lucas says "By then it seemed reasonable to accept defeat and
go on from there. I remember it had a devastating effect on the city. It
was like Middletown had been folded up and put into a casket."

After the tournament, two decisions were made which would
greatly influence Jerry's athletic career. He had no control over the
Cincinnati Royals exercising their territorial rights to him when he became eligible for the NBA four years in the future. The territorial draft
allowed pro teams to claim the rights to local stars to increase support
from area fans. It had been created by the Philadelphia Warriors so
they could draft a high school player named Wilt Chamberlain. The
idea was dropped after 1965, when New York claimed Bill Bradley of
Princeton, Detroit selected Bill Buntin of Michigan and Los Angeles
took Gail Goodrich of UCLA, but it enabled the Royals to control the

professional future of Jerry Lucas. At least that is the way it appeared at the time.

The other decision, more common for high school seniors, was selecting a college to attend. Lucas took unusual control in this often hectic process. "I was determined to try to have as normal a life as possible," he says today. "I decided not to talk to anyone before my senior year was over."

Jerry's father Mark, a 6'2 paper company pressman, arranged for Middletown high school coach Paul Walker and Jerry Nardiello, sports editor of the local paper, to review the more than 150 scholarship offers. The ones that appeared acceptable would be funneled to Mr. Lucas, then to Jerry. This minimized the illegal offers, but did not eliminate them.

"One scout," Mrs. Mark Lucas told *SPORT* magazine in 1962, "promised that my husband would get a $15,000-a-year job (more than twice what he was earning at the Garner Board and Carton Company), the mortgage on our house would be paid off, Jerry's brother Roy would get a scholarship to the same school, and Jerry would get a new car, an expense account and everything." Another scout pledged all of the above plus a house for Jerry when he got married.

An A student and the president of his class, Jerry had two primary criteria for his college selection. First, he had to have an academic rather than athletic scholarship. This would remove his responsibility to play and make clear his priority: an education. Second, he wanted to go to school fairly close to him, "maybe Ohio, Indiana or Kentucky." When Kentucky Coach Adolph Rupp showed up at the high school, during the season, and expected to talk with Lucas, the Wildcats were dropped from consideration.

Jerry Lucas only made three visits. The first was to Cornell, largely as a courtesy to Roy Greene, head coach at the Ivy League school. When Jerry was in junior high school Greene was coach at Middletown High School. Visits to Cincinnati, which had a superlative sophomore named Oscar Robertson, and Ohio State formed the basis for his conclusion.

"We went fishing when he was here," recalls Fred Taylor. "He caught a 10 pound catfish on a fly rod ... I remember thinking that was a good sign." Seems a wonder that Taylor, who would become famous for his game preparation, did not have the foresight to stock the lake. Maybe he did.

Two days before the national signing date Lucas called Fred Taylor at home to tell him he was coming to Ohio State. "It was a Sunday night," recalls the coach. "I remember saying 'Jerry, hold the phone away from your ear because I have to let out a yell. I did, and I think he did (move the phone)'."

Asked why he chose OSU in May, 1958, Lucas said, "For one thing, it's not too far from home, only a two-hour drive by car. My folks could come to see me. The main reason, though, was I wanted to get a good education. Fred Taylor sold me. Almost every representative who came to Middletown talked basketball first. Fred didn't. He talked education. That's what convinced me." No mention of fishing. Lucas committed before Taylor was named head coach.

Because freshmen were ineligible for varsity competition Jerry's freshman year, as they were throughout the Golden Age, his organized competition in 1958-59 consisted of games against the junior varsity before varsity games at St. John Arena. Against players who would not be playing for the varsity that night he averaged 30+ points and 20+ rebounds. He sat out much of the one-sided contests which the freshmen never lost. In two "formal" games with the Ohio State varsity late in the year Lucas scored 93 points while making 39 of 53 field goal attempts, leading the freshmen to victory. To this day, Taylor is quick to add that the varsity beat the freshmen in the first four games during the season. Even this special group of high school graduates took time to be able to compete successfully the college level. Or, as Coach Taylor says, "Those freshmen couldn't hem up a hog in a ditch defensively."

Off the court the freshman Lucas was involved in something Taylor does not remember, because he never knew about it. Despite vigorous protests by roommate John Havlicek, Jerry Lucas kept an alligator in his dorm room.

"A girl I was dating went to Florida for spring break and wanted to bring me an unusual present," says Lucas today. "She brought a baby alligator. I kept it in our room, which John didn't think was a very good idea. But I didn't want to offend her." That's the girl friend, not the alligator.

"It slept quietly under the bed most of the time, though late at night we'd take it to the shower, plug up the drains and let it swim around. I remember Bob Ferguson and Bertho Arnold, the football players, lived in our dorm and one night we invited them to visit. Bob was sitting on a bed, felt something on his foot, looked down and saw what could have been his first pair of alligator shoes. At that time it was about 2 1/2 feet long. Those guys left in a hurry and we never could get them back on our side of the dorm."

What finally happened?

"It kept growing and something had to be done. We had it for several weeks, maybe two months — never named it. I couldn't decide who to ask for advice, because the situation was rather unusual. Finally I put it in the car late at night, took it to Mirror Lake (on campus) and let somebody else decide what to do with it."

Imagine the headlines which could have appeared:

• "Lucas suspended for illegal possession of alligator."

• "Havlicek voted best one handed player ever."

• "Ferguson gains 100 yards on one foot."

After dealing with the alligator and before completing his freshman year with a 3.6 A- average, "Luke" had some free time. He and roommate Havlicek created a game of baseball played with a fraternity paddle and a plastic ball. Among the ground rules were that a ball hit over the four story dormitory was a home run. No one ever hit a home run except Lucas, who hit many. His technique was to turn the paddle sideways and hit the ball with the quarter-inch width. "Nobody else could hit the ball with the thin side of the paddle," said Havlicek. "I couldn't come close" said the man who played baseball for three years at Ohio State.

"The key to that, and a big factor in my ability to shoot a basketball, was my eyesight," says Lucas today. "Dr. Nesbitt in Middletown once told me they were 'by far the best eyes I have ever examined'. He checked my eyesight once after putting drops in — supposedly that makes vision significantly more difficult — and said it was 20-10."

If he feels his vision was responsible for his shooting ability, high school teams should drink carrot juice instead of water. He ranks first, second and third in the Buckeye record book for best field goal percentage, single season. His career mark is over 5% ahead of second place Bill Andreas. He did it with 25' jump shots, tip-ins, alley-oops, hooks with either hand and turnaround jumpers in close. He made 62.4% of his shots, converting almost twice as many as he missed.

After his freshman year everyone expected Jerry Lucas to be great. He would exceed that expectation.

JOHN HAVLICEK —

While Lucas was known throughout the country by his sophomore year at Middletown, John Havlicek had a more normal athletic career in high school. But only relative to Lucas, because the Lansing native was certainly a local legend in the Ohio Valley as a three sport star at Bridgeport High School.

John lived for sports in school. In his book *HONDO — Celtic Man in Motion* he writes about planning his 60 minute lunch period. "I knew it took 45 seconds to run home, 12 minutes to eat my lunch and 45 seconds to run back," he writes. "That gave me 45 minutes to play, and I was always wrapped up in some kind of ball."

This love of the games even took him to school early "so I could play ball. The janitor would get there around 7 o'clock to fire up the furnace. I would usually get there to meet him between 7:00 and 7:15. School didn't start until 9:00, so I would have an hour and a half or so to play. I had the place to myself. After school I would practice on the playground. Basketball began to grow on me because there was no other sport where you could play so much by yourself."

He credits Al Blatnik, supervisor of the city's Saturday morning recreation program, with first introducing him to the fundamentals of basketball ... "things like staying between your man and the basket on defense, playing defense on your toes rather than your heels, and watching the belt buckle of the man you're guarding. He pointed out that you should raise your left hand when trying to block the shot of a right-handed man, and he taught us different maneuvers to use when boxing someone out underneath the boards, such as the crossover step and the reverse pivot."

While Blatnik may have helped Havlicek decide that basketball was his favorite sport, it was never John's only sport. He was an excellent baseball player, playing second base as a freshman at Bridgeport, first base as a sophomore, third base as a junior and shortstop as a senior. He hit clean-up and, as a senior, pitched a bit. Scouts from Pittsburgh, Cleveland, Cincinnati, Baltimore and the Yankees were rebuffed because John was going to college. He played three years at Ohio State, hitting .591 on the freshman team. John would have starred on the varsity as a sophomore and junior except he missed most of the baseball season due to the NCAA basketball tournament each year. "I got to play about a month and a half each year," he recalls. "After my senior year I didn't play baseball because the basketball seniors did some barnstorming (playing games around Ohio and in neighboring states)."

Havlicek was even better at football, playing quarterback on a team known as "Big John and the Seven Dwarfs." Heavy graduation losses from his junior year left only John and one other returning starter. "We had two 130 pound guards, one tackle was 145 pounds and the other was 165. We recruited one end out of the band because we only had 26 players. I was 6'3 and 180 pounds and the biggest guy on the team."

John's senior year Bridgeport played mighty Martins Ferry, a team they had not beaten in more than 30 years. Behind his running and passing, and his three touchdowns, Bridgeport won 19-14. School was closed the following Monday for a victory parade.

Of course he was a basketball star, playing some as a freshman, regularly as a sophomore and averaging over 30 ppg as a junior. His coach was Bobby Carroll, a teammate of Fred Schaus at West Virginia. Carroll believed in up tempo play. "That was great for me," says Havlicek. "My entire basketball career has been spent playing fast break basketball."

After his junior year John began to earn a reputation for basketball — sort of. He got one recruiting letter, from West Virginia head coach Fred Schaus. He received honorable mention on an all state team, under the name "Jim Havilcheck, Bridgeport". Lucas was the top player in the state.

John's senior year Bridgeport went undefeated but, as he wrote, "The caliber of play was decent, but it wasn't as strong as in the big city areas such as Cleveland, Columbus, or Cincinnati". Bridgeport lost the first round of the state tournament when he and three other starters had the Asian flu. By now people could spell Havlicek, and he made first team All-Ohio Associated Press and second team United Press International.

While playing baseball well enough to be chosen all state in his third sport, he kept his grades at a high level and tried to make sense of "60-70" scholarship offers — many for basketball, more for football and several for the two sports combined.

Ohio State was most persistent of the football contacts, led by an alum named Ed McLain. McLain was a neighbor and part of the Woody Hayes recruiting network. John visited OSU for football in the fall of 1957, when he saw Bob White carry the ball downfield to beat Iowa and secure the Big Ten championship and a Rose Bowl trip. "I just more or less met Woody," John recalls. "There wasn't much of an exchange of words, because they had a lot of other athletes in and they had just won an important game. He said something like, 'We could have used someone like you, who could have thrown that ball around there today'. That was really nice of him to say that, I thought. He showed an interest in everyone. He knew what everyone's name was, where they were from, and what their particular ability was. But that's all there was to my first meeting with him.

"Woody also made a couple of visits to my home, and he spoke at our All-Sports banquet. He made a big impression on my parents, and on everybody, really, but my mother never did like my playing football. She was glad when I decided not to. I had made up my mind by the night Woody came to speak at the banquet, and I told him so afterward.

"'How do you know you don't want to play football?' he said. 'You haven't been away from it. You'll want to come back to it'."

"But I was persistent," says Havlicek.

"'I'll tell you what,' Hayes finally decided, 'you come to Ohio State and play basketball, and I won't bother you.' And he never did," concludes Havlicek. Of course an assistant coach may have mentioned something on occasion. Red Auerbach, long time coach and general manager of the Boston Celtics, says Hayes told him "He probably would have been the best quarterback in Ohio State history. I just couldn't get him to come out." Bob Woolf, Havlicek's agent when he played in the NBA, says Ohio State kept a locker with John's name on it in the football dressing room.

Just because Woody Hayes and football were out of the picture, Fred Taylor was not sure he would sign Havlicek. "I was thinking seriously about West Virginia, Miami of Florida and Cincinnati," John remembers.

Jerry Lucas recalls helping John decide on Ohio State. "I played with John during some all-star games, and I probably convinced him to go to Ohio State. He wasn't sure he could play there, but I convinced him he could."

Today Havlicek doesn't remember being intimidated by the athletes, but recalls feeling academic pressure. "I wasn't concerned about making the team," he says, "but I felt pressure in the classroom. Lucas was Phi Beta Kappa, Knight was brilliant, Hoyt and Furry were always 3.0+. One quarter the team had a 3.4 cumulative average. I didn't want to be the dumb bell of the team." Actually Lucas never made Phi Beta Kappa, though he did earn the equivalent in the College of Commerce, Beta Gamma Sigma.

Havlicek remembers the deciding factor as being Fred Taylor, "a low-key guy with whom I could easily identify. He never pressured me. He told me about the school and the kind of people he was trying to recruit. He assured me I could be a good player at Ohio State.

"He learned quickly just how naive I was. He called me once and said he would like to come down to my house and take me out to dinner. I misunderstood him on the phone. I couldn't really believe he was taking me to a restaurant. I simply wasn't used to anything like that. I was playing baseball the night he arrived. My mother was preparing dinner when he got there, and so he had a Havlicek dinner instead of one in a restaurant. He explained to me later that his original intention was to take me and my mother out to dinner, and I was excited to hear that."

Today Taylor recalls that night quite clearly, not because of the mix-up or the dinner but because of the conversation he had with Mrs. Havlicek while her son was playing baseball in Steubenville.

"We had a chance to talk while waiting for John, and his mother told me her real concern about Ohio State. She thought if he came to Ohio State he would have to play football. Her concern wasn't the school, but the sport. I told her 'If he comes to Ohio State and you don't want him to play football, the only way that would happen would be over my dead body.' When she said 'Why don't you stay and have dinner with us tonight?' I figured that was a good sign."

The secrets of big time recruiting — Lucas catches fish on his 48 hour visit and Havlicek comes home late from a baseball game.

His freshman year went well, though rooming with Lucas had one problem beyond the alligator. "He studied so little and got outstanding grades; I had to work, organize, and memorize to get by. It was discouraging at times." But Havlicek was a solid student, particularly after Bob Knight helped him adjust to writing college themes.

Havlicek was a regular forward on the freshman team from day one, and quickly learned the secret of existing with Frank Truitt, his freshman coach. "Frank was a great guy, and remains a good friend, but he was so intense we soon learned not to sit too close to him. He had a way of asking a question, answering it, and hitting you in the arm or in the ribs for emphasis. We all wanted to hear the answers to the questions, but we learned to sit one seat away."

When Gary Gearhart talks about John Havlicek today, the focus does not concern basketball. "I never met a more outstanding, moral person" says Hondo's former teammate.

MEL NOWELL —

Athletic stars were commonplace at Columbus East High School in the 1950's. Jim Marshall was state champion in the shot put and all state tackle before a long career in the National Football League with the Minnesota Vikings. Bernie Casey played basketball but excelled at track and football. His NFL career was spent with the San Francisco 49ers and the Los Angeles Rams, and led to a Hollywood film career. Rollie Harris and Fred Andrews went from the East High basketball court to the Harlem Globetrotters, Joe Roberts to Ohio State, Frank Wade to Bowling Green. Larry Jones played for Toledo before an outstanding career in the American Basketball Association. And Mel Nowell was the brightest star in the constellation.

"He was the best outside shooter in the history of the City League, I think," said Jack Moore before he passed away in 1991. Moore coached Nowell at East and directed City League teams throughout the 1950s, 1960s and 1970s. "He led the City League in scoring as a junior and senior, and was a good assist man too. We didn't have as many good players with Mel as we did some of the other years, and he had to carry us. He was so unselfish he felt badly about scoring so much, thought the other players might not like him. I kept telling him I wanted him to shoot more, not less.

"Mel's junior year we almost beat Middletown. Lost in overtime (72-68). We put Bernie Casey in front of Jerry Lucas and made them pass over the top. That was tough to do because Bernie was such an athlete. If they did, we had a player coming over from the weak side. It worked very well — we held Lucas to 32 points. Mel outscored him, I think he had 35.

"Mel's senior year Columbus North won one district, we won the other. We went to separate regionals. We lost to Cleveland East Tech in overtime up in Berea in the regional finals, even though Mel had about 35 points and 25 rebounds. That year every team in the finals — North, East Tech, Middletown and Zanesville — was undefeated. Imagine that. Of course North beat Middletown but lost to East Tech in the finals. Frank Truitt did a great job that year."

The 6'2 Nowell, holding the all-time City League season scoring record with 440 points, single game mark with 43, and a season's average of about 30 ppg, was the second ranked player in the state, overshadowed only by Jerry Lucas. He whittled the large list of interested schools to Indiana, Cincinnati, Miami and Ohio State by early May, at least in public. When Indiana Coach Branch McCracken approached Nowell during the Ohio-Indiana All Star tour and asked for a commitment to Indiana, Mel nodded to Jerry Lucas and replied, "See the big guy over there? I'm going where he is going."

Fred Taylor recalls asking Mel if he was ready to make a commitment during a lunch the two shared with Nowell's mother. "I asked if he was ready to make a decision," recalls Taylor, "and he said 'I have a couple more visits to make.' His mother said 'Now Melvyn, it's sinful to say that ... you know you're going to Ohio State.'"

"He came from a big, close family," remembered Coach Moore. "They'd come to watch him play and take up a whole section. His brother Jerry was an all state tackle beside Jim Marshall, and played at Miami."

The value system Mel developed from his family is clear when Jack Moore talked about his own prostrate cancer, first diagnosed in 1984. "When Mel found out, he was at the hospital all the time visiting me. That's the kind of man he is."

John Havlicek remembers Mel as "a meticulous dresser, always stylish and looking good. He loved the up tempo game." John adds "Mel gave me my nickname of 'Hondo'. He was having trouble pronouncing my last name and said I reminded him of John Wayne in the movie popular at that time."

Gary Gearhart calls Nowell "probably the best offensive guard I've ever seen, a great open court, one-on-one player. He would have been a big scorer at another school."

Bob Knight remembers "Mel Nowell, like every player on the team, had a job to do. His job was to shoot jump shots, to score, and he did it well. He was a very good player, quick with his feet and hands."

Fred Taylor remembers Nowell's greatest strength as "great body balance. He was one of the best at being able to catch the ball and being balanced and ready to shoot quickly." He also recalls that Mel liked to go one-on-one when he thought he could beat his man. "Havlicek used to say, 'Fred, Mel keeps waving me out,'" an indication that the guard wanted the forward to create room by going to the opposite side of the floor. "I'd usually say 'John, just wave back to him and stay right there.'"

GARY GEARHART —

Gary Gearhart led Dixie to the state semi-finals in Class A, small school basketball, his senior year. There were 15 boys in his graduating class. He had 18 points and eight rebounds but Dixie lost to eventual state champion Northwestern 69-55. Northwestern's star was Dean Chance, the future pro baseball pitcher.

Gearhart was a 6'2 speedster, who made first team all state while averaging 23 ppg. He would be the quickest player in the recruiting class — "I never saw a quicker player on a back door cut to the basket," says Frank Truitt today — but Ohio State was not his first choice.

"Eastern Kentucky contacted me early, their coach Ed McBrayer had like 600 career victories and I signed there. After the tournament a group of seniors in the state played a series of all star games against players from Indiana and from Kentucky. I roomed with John Havlicek and he and Lucas and Mel Nowell kept saying I should go to Ohio State. I said I couldn't, that I had signed with Eastern Kentucky.

"I later found out I could, because the rules about letters of intent, transfers and everything were much different in those days. Fred Taylor called and offered a visit strictly on the word of Luke and those guys. My selection of Ohio State was based on the friendship with those three guys during the all star games.

"Bob Knight didn't play in those games, but I got to know him when we roomed together as freshmen. He was very bright — I had to work twice as hard as he did. He slept a lot, and ate a lot of fruit which his mother sent from home. He had this little red blanket he used to carry — we called him 'Linus', after the Peanuts character."

"Gary was a good kid, but had unbelievably tough luck," recalls Taylor. "Every time he had a chance to do something he got hurt." Lucas recalls him as "a fun guy, loose and easy-going, always a friend."

Larry Siegfried, who kept Gearhart on the bench a large portion of the two years they played together, says "He was a regular, a very important part of the team. He was a constant competitor for playing time; he put pressure on Mel and I. He had a mental strength which allowed him to do the job when he played, yet never show any outward frustration from lack of playing time."

John Havlicek says Gearhart was "quick and fast, a solid player who always picked up the defensive temp. He handled a difficult situation very well."

BOB KNIGHT —

The Indiana head coach has established such a dominant presence in college basketball today that, more than any other player in Ohio State history, it is difficult to think of him as a teenager running around in short pants (weighing 180 lbs., at 6'4).

As a player his most identifiable trait was a long range jump shot with no measurable arc. Imagine a line drive just over the front of the rim, and that's almost what it looked like. Just the opposite of the rainbow jumpers of Lucas and Nowell. Yet Knight made them. When school kids of the era played HORSE anyone who made "a Bobby Knight jump shot" was almost certain to earn a letter.

"I was a pretty good high school player," says Bob Knight today. "I played varsity basketball and baseball from freshman year on, and also three years of football. Orrville was a football town, and I was probably best at baseball, but I like basketball.

"Wittenberg, Bowling Green, Kent State, Miami (O.) and Cincinnati were among the schools I considered, but I liked Coach Taylor. He was freshman coach then, but we expected him to be named head coach. There was no binding national letter of intent, so I guess we (Lucas, Havlicek, Nowell and Knight all committed to Ohio State before Taylor was named head coach) could have changed our minds.

"The other reason was Jerry Lucas," continues Knight. "He was so good that any team he was on would do well. I followed basketball as closely as anyone, but there were no camps, no AAU tournaments, no all-star games. Today the players all know each other. I had barely heard about Terry Dischinger (future Purdue star) and he was an excellent player from Indiana. But everyone knew about Lucas."

Fred Taylor thinks back to recruiting "the Dragon," a nickname which stemmed from Knight's fiery tongue. "He did everything at Orrville, much like Siegfried at Shelby. Not because he was selfish, just because he was by far the best player and the team featured him. He was a tough, aggressive kid, physically and mentally. And he was a winner.

"One other thing I remember about recruiting him is his grandmother made the best strawberry shortcake in the world," adds Taylor, licking his lips at the memory.

In his autobiography, John Havlicek has this to say about his Buckeye teammate from Orrville.

"I had never met anybody quite like him. He was a big sports fan. He knew every player and he collected sports magazines and books. He'd get his hands on anything written about sports and he knew things I had never thought of or was even aware of.

"Surprisingly, he was very lazy. He'd walk around at a snail's pace, and nobody could rush him into doing anything. The intensity he's known for today was present only on the basketball floor. He was extremely aggressive out there, and I'm surprised Joe Roberts didn't kill him, because he had to put up with him every day in practice. He'd just clobber Joe, and I don't know how Joe held himself back.

"Most of our practices were 70 percent defense, and Bobby was a bad defensive player. He couldn't play a lick. He wasn't quick and he couldn't jump. The one thing he could do was shoot. But he was smart and aggressive and he didn't make mistakes. He can recall situations about games that I played in that I have no recollection of. He could probably name every player on every team we played against, and I could never do that."

Today Havlicek adds "Bobby would wear his OSU tee shirt and khaki pants for days at a time. When you wanted to find him he'd be in his room, wrapped in his blanket reading westerns."

Jerry Lucas says "Bobby had an intensity about him, which is no surprise to fans today. He was very competitive, and had an insatiable desire for knowledge of the game of basketball. He had a strong desire to excel. After a game everyone wanted to discuss what happened; after practice Knight wanted to review every detail."

"Bob was a little short for the corner and a little slow for the Big Ten," recalls Furry, "but he was a competitor. Today he credits me with teaching him how to tie a neck tie, which was mandatory in those days."

Assistant coach Jack Graf says "Bob was not quick, and lack of lateral movement hurt his playing time. He was always a forward — when you read a reference that he played guard, consider it a joke."

Joe Roberts, as Havlicek suggested, may have thought about killing Bob Knight in practice. "He would beat me and hold me all the time," says Joe. I used to yell 'Fred, get him off me.' When that didn't work, I had to give Bob a shot in self defense. Years later, after he had established himself as a coach, I asked him 'How can a guy who played no defense in college become known as a defensive coach?'

"What did he say? Oh, you couldn't print it."

These were the starters on the best freshman team Ohio State, or almost any college, ever had. They were exceptional, individually and collectively. They regularly destroyed the varsity reserves, and were beating the varsity by the end of the season. But how good would they be on the varsity level? And how soon?

III

1960:
National Champions

At a time when freshmen routinely start their first game on campus, it is difficult to explain the mind set of the 1950s in college athletics. In their first year on the varsity, sophomores were thought of as lambs being led to the slaughter by upperclassmen. Woody Hayes then said "You lose a game for every sophomore in your starting lineup." Fortunately he changed his mind by 1968, when his sophomore dominated team won the national championship. However, that was the thinking of the time.

Still, Ohio State's sophomore class had received so much publicity that the Buckeyes were ranked No. 6 nationally by UPI. Great players dotted the teams above them. Cincinnati had Oscar Robertson, defending champion California was led by 6'10 All-American Darrall Imhoff and Jerry West anchored West Virginia. Kentucky and North Carolina rounded out the top five.

Among popular magazines of the time, *Dell Sports Basketball* selected Jerry Lucas first team All-American, with Robertson, West, Imhoff and Tony Jackson of St. John's, before his first game. They also picked OSU over Indiana and Illinois in the Big Ten. *Basketball Yearbook 1960*, however, took the more traditional approach. Their editor picked the Hoosiers, the Illini, then Ohio State in the conference, and West, Robertson, Jackson, John Egan of Providence and Ron Johnson of Minnesota as All-Americans.

Fred Taylor talked about "cautious optimism" at a late November press conference. He liked the "size, shooting, maneuvering speed

33

(quickness, rather than straight-away speed), rebounding, intelligence and attitude" of the team. He worried about their youth. "We could start three sophomores and we're in a league where sophomores don't dominate. There were only five sophomores among the top 25 scorers in the Big Ten last year ... and in the last 10 years no championship team had more than one starting." Here are some thoughts Taylor had on the players before the first game of the season, according to *Citizen-Journal* writer Kaye Kessler:

SIEGFRIED — "He scored more than we had a right to expect last year, even though he was two-teamed. He's a great competitor. We expect him to be our backcourt leader, our quarterback."

ROBERTS — "When he's right, he's very good. A good rebounder ... he treads air. We're looking for a fine year from him."

FURRY — "He's risen to the challenge of a sophomore (Havlicek) taking his job very well. He's the best jumper on the squad, has tremendous speed, tremendous potential."

LUCAS — "He's had a knee problem, but it's fine now. Everybody talks about his scoring against the varsity last year — but we'll get lots of Christmas cards from people who scored against us last year."

NOWELL — "He'll probably start. He works like the devil. I can't find fault with his shooting, he's a good feeder, good speed, good defense, good hands."

HAVLICEK — "Making a strong bid to start ... deceives you with his speed."

HOYT — "He's injury prone, but a great jump shot and will make a fine contribution."

HOWIE NOURSE, 6'7 senior center from Springfield — "He doesn't have stamina or build, but as a spot player he'll help us tremendously."

GEARHART — "A quick kid, jumps very well."

KNIGHT — "A real good shooter, hard worker, needs experience."

"Fred would say 'These guys are just puppies. They aren't dogs until they bite somebody'," recalls Frank Truitt.

Season tickets were available, $24 for 12 games, as were $2 single game tickets.

"Bones" McKinney, Fred's opponent in service basketball in the 1940s, brought a very good Wake Forest team to St. John Arena for the opener. "Bones" was disarming, and spoke with a southern drawl when he said "We know all about Fred's boys. Why I've read more about Jerry Lucas than I have about Krushchev and I just hope he takes it easy on our poah little guys."

The best of their "little guys" was 6'8, 240 lbs. Len Chappell, named All-Sophomore with Lucas by *SPORT* magazine. He had scored 2252 points in a three year Pennsylvania high school career, setting a state record with 37.7 ppg as a senior.

Future five year New York Knick Dave Budd (6'6) and Jerry Steele played the forward positions; the guards were 6' George Ritchie and a sophomore from Bethlehem, Pennsylvania named Billy Packer. About Packer "Bones" said "Just 5'10, but he'll be a great one some-day." Player or announcer? Yes.

A crowd of 9284 attended the game which began "The Golden Age". Television brought the contest to the homes of other fans, in black and white of course.

The unit of Furry-Roberts-Lucas-Siegfried-Nowell started for Ohio State, but struggled. Dick Furry recalls "I caught an elbow above my eye in practice several days before the Wake Forest game. The stitches became infected ("Sterile abscess" says Taylor today) and I missed a lot of practice. I started but I screwed everything up, having been away so much. When John went in, the team clicked."

Havlicek was sent in late in the half, and hit three quick baskets, but the Bucks still trailed 42-37 at the break. Only Nowell was scoring consistently. Wake Forest widened the lead to 47-39 early in the second half, before OSU began to come together. With all five players chipping in, a Lucas feed to Nowell gave OSU a 50-49 lead with 13 minutes to play. The game was tied at 62 when Siegfried hit a jumper and a tip-in, then Lucas got a rebound basket and a foul shot. The victory was 77-69.

None of the Bucks had shot 50%; the team finished at 36%. Lucas had 28 rebounds (a "gracious total, we thought" says Packer today) but there was disappointment that he made only six of 16 field goal attempts. He finished with 16 points, same as Roberts. Wake Forest had led most of the game, but Ohio State had escaped the opener against a Top 20 team.

Today Billy Packer, who guarded Mel Nowell and matched his counterpart with 18 points, recalls that game. "They were good, but that year we thought North Carolina was better, with Doug Moe, York Larese and Lee Shaffer. We thought we should have beaten Ohio

35

State and looked forward to playing them again. I remember Joe Roberts made a left-handed hook that just killed us that night. We might have played them in the NCAA but Duke beat North Carolina in the semi-finals of the ACC tournament and us in the finals, so Duke was the ACC representative."

Only six Buckeyes had played against Wake Forest but 15 saw court time in a 94-55 victory over Memphis State. Lucas totaled 34 points and grabbed 20 rebounds. Furry, Roberts and Siegfried joined him in double figures. Attendance was 7,009 in St. John Arena, with a capacity of 13,497. Then Pittsburgh absorbed its worst defeat in history, 94-49. In the 29 minutes and 27 seconds the starters played, the score was 79-32. Next Butler fell 99-66 and Ohio State was 4-0.

The Ohio State fans were becoming familiar with the playing styles of the sophomores. Lucas had 100 points in four games, but it seemed like he never shot the ball. Many points came on foul shots and tip-ins. Nowell had the ability to dart by his man, stop suddenly at the baseline, turn and loft a jump shot over the corner of the backboard and into the basket. This gave school boys a new shot for their HORSE games. Havlicek seemed to be basket hanging, but close inspection proved the error of that observation. Hondo played defense better than anyone on the team. However he converted from defense to offense so quickly, and worked so hard to get from one end to the other, it only *seemed* he had been down-court "cherry picking."

The offensive set was a "two guard front," common until North Carolina's Phil Ford popularized the "point guard" concept in the mid-1970's. Siegfried played right guard, called the "1" position, and Nowell left ("2"). Havlicek was the "3" at right forward and Roberts the "4" at left forward. Center Jerry Lucas was designated "5". Fred Taylor remembers "we ran most of our plays to the right side; most teams were 'right handed'." Loosely speaking, Siegfried had responsibilities similar to a "point guard," Nowell to a "shooting guard."

A trip to St. Louis to play a Top 20 team with 6'10 center Bob Nordmann resulted in an 81-74 Buck victory. Siegfried played "his finest game" according to Taylor, with 22 points, several steals and many assists. Lucas had 30 points and held Nordmann to 17. Only Furry and Knight played in relief of the starters.

Ohio State traveled to Butler and won a re-match, 96-68. The Bucks were 6-0.

Today Jerry Lucas thinks back to the pressure of those early days at Ohio State. "No doubt there was a lot of pressure," he says. "So much was expected. Much of it was self-imposed. I wanted to be a good example, a good citizen and went the extra mile to fulfill that desire. In college I had a nervous stomach before every game. Butterflies. I always wondered 'Did I work hard enough'. The nervousness was not as big a factor in the pros."

Three more road games, making five consecutive, took OSU to Utah, Brigham Young and Kentucky. By now Dick Furry, Richie Hoyt and Jerry Lucas had a regular bridge game when the team traveled. The fourth was either Fred Taylor or trainer Ernie Biggs.

Utah had a 6'10 sophomore named Billy McGill, nicknamed "The Hill," who was a challenge for Lucas. "He was really good," recalls Bob Knight. "Agile, quick spring — a big guy who could do a lot with the ball." Lucas and McGill each had 17 rebounds, Luke got 32 points, McGill 31. The Buckeyes scored 92 but gave up 97 as Utah won its seventh straight home game.

The young Bucks outscored Brigham Young 91-79 as Lucas set a BYU Fieldhouse record with 16 field goals. He took 19 shots in scoring 36 points.

On the bus after the game senior Howie Nourse referred to the ovation Jerry Lucas received after setting the fieldhouse record. Nourse said, "Hey, did you guys notice the tremendous hand I got when I went in for Lucas?" Such a sense of humor, combined with genuine athletic ability and a perfect attitude, made Nourse an important part of the team. Jimmy Crum, television announcer for the team, remembers Howie saying "If the only chance I get to play is to make him (Lucas) work in practice, I'll be happy."

"Howie Nourse," says Taylor today, "was the kind of guy every good team has to have. He was a good humor man, and an effective spot player. He was serious enough about the game, but didn't take himself too seriously."

With a 5-3 record, the next opponent did not appear to be a great Kentucky team. But they had lost only two games at home in the past three years, both to West Virginia and All-American Jerry West. So it shaped up as a tough game.

Too tough, as the Buckeyes fell to 7-2. OSU was outscored 96-93; "at that time of the year Havlicek was the only one playing defense" recalls Taylor. Kentucky starting guards Bennie Coffman and Billy Lickert poured in 55 points. Luke had 34 and the other four starters all scored in double figures, but the Bucks were learning they couldn't outscore everyone.

"Our guys were going behind Kentucky's screens," recalls Frank Truitt, "and their guards were hitting those jump shots. We told them to go over the top of the screens but they weren't doing it."

Joe Roberts remembers something else about that game. "There was a section near the center of the floor where some people were waving the Confederate flag. When Mel Nowell got into foul trouble they chanted 'Bye, bye, blackbird.' I went over to Mel to help him settle down, and they chanted 'Bye, bye Big Nigger' at me."

"After the game," remembers Taylor, "I refused to shake Adolph Rupp's hand. The newspapers down there wrote that I was a young upstart coach, but the reason was the things those Kentucky fans were saying to Joe and Mel."

Richie Hoyt still remembers that trip to Lexington for the dinner the team had the night before. "We went to the Blue Bore Restaurant and the waiter singled Joe out. He said 'We don't serve niggers here.' The whole team left."

"Those losses to Utah and Kentucky came at just the right time," recalls Joe Roberts. "Some of the guys were getting big heads."

With Lexington behind them, the No. 4 ranked Buckeyes began the Big Ten season with No. 9 Illinois and No. 8 Indiana at home. Illinois, 7-1 with only a loss to defending champion California, was demolished 97-73. OSU started well, and led 51-36 at the half. When Illinois narrowed the lead to 61-56 with 11:37 to go, Bobby (everyone called him Bobby then, no one does now) Knight started a 15 point spurt with a jumper from the corner and ended it with a three point play. Lucas (23 rebounds) and Havlicek (14) dominated the boards; Lucas (30 points) and Siegfried (26) led the scoring. Attendance was 13,163, almost a sell-out.

Indiana came to town for the Big Ten TV game on Saturday afternoon in a bad mood. A Top 10 team nationally in December, they had opened the conference 0-2 with a 79-76 home loss to Purdue and a 61-57 defeat at Northwestern. Still, the Hoosiers were talented. Coach Branch McCracken said in pre-season they had the "best physical qualifications of any team I've ever had," and the anchor was Walter Bellamy in the middle. A 6'11 junior, Walter had averaged 17.4 ppg and 15.2 rebounds per contest as a sophomore. In the corner were 6'8 senior Frank Radovich, a .542 shooter as a junior, and 6'4 LeRoy Johnson. The junior guards were 5'11 Herbie Lee and 6' Gary Long. Long later appeared in the movie *Hoosiers* in the role of a high school coach. His son Brad played Buddy, one of Gene Hackman's Hickory players.

Before a capacity crowd of 13,497 OSU won 96-95 in one of the most important games in Ohio State history, and one of the most exciting. Indiana led at the half 56-52 as Lucas missed 6:19 with a twisted ankle. They led by five with 43 seconds to play, but Ohio State's half court trap was too much for the Hoosier ball handlers. When Siegfried made his only field goal of the game to grab the victory, it was the thirteenth lead change. Mel Nowell was the leading scorer in the game with 26 points. Joe Roberts shook off a flu bug to score 14 and grab eight rebounds. John Havlicek came back from a sprained wrist against Illinois to score 21 points and grab 11 boards. And Lucas, though the target of McCracken's defense, outscored Bellamy 20 to 17 and got ten rebounds. Furry had six valuable points and Gary Gearhart, overcoming the effects of an appendectomy the first week of practice, had three.

Ohio State beat Delaware 109-38 despite the fact that Lucas was held out. Knight was leading scorer in the game with 15 points and had six rebounds, one less than game high. Delaware had been added to the schedule when a game with Cincinnati could not be finalized. *That* would have been interesting.

With Ohio State the only unbeaten conference team at 2-0, the good news was public and the bad news was private.

*   * . *   *

John Havlicek, now 6'5, had become an outstanding player. "I used to get notes from mothers saying their sons were diving on the couches at home, imitating John going after a loose ball," smiles Taylor. "I made a conscious choice to make it defensively at Ohio State," says Havlicek today. "Starting freshman year the coaches talked about our combined scoring average of 170 points in high school and I felt defense would be my opportunity."

Radio broadcaster of the time Marv Homan says "He was probably the most inspirational basketball player Ohio State ever had. He had an almost perfect basketball build, and gave 100% effort all the time. He had a marvelous temperament, was very humble and shy. He wasn't a very good shooter as a sophomore, but gained confidence as a junior."

At the time the team had all the shooting it needed. "When John started to get media attention for his defense, some of the other guys started getting turned on at that end of the court," recalls Taylor.

"John was a coach's dream," recalls freshman coach Frank Truitt. "Ask him to do anything and he did it with enthusiasm. His effort was contagious to the other players. When he went in that first game I knew he'd never come out." And he didn't, starting every game after the first one.

Before Indiana beat Syracuse 74-73 for the national championship in 1987, Coach Bob Knight asked his old friend John Havlicek to say a few words to the team. Havlicek said "Don't finish this game thinking there was something else you could have done to win. When you come back into the locker room, each of you has to be able to look at himself in the mirror and say, 'I gave it everything I have.' If you can honestly say that, you've got nothing to worry about."

Maybe not profound, but also not easy to do. Hondo never had any trouble with mirrors — he walked the talk.

* * * *

Another Buckeye was dealing with a problem outside the public eye. Only those very close to the team knew it but, in the words of Larry Siegfried, "I was at war with myself.

"In high school I was the team. As a freshman and sophomore what I wanted to do seemed to fit what the team needed, so there was no real problem. I didn't have to make sacrifices. But my junior year Fred had to blend a lot of guys who were used to being the whole team into a unit.

"In order for the team to reach its fullest potential, I had to adjust. I knew it had to be done to win, the problem was I didn't understand the emotional ramifications involved in making that decision. My awareness of this adjustment and the need for an attitude change on my part was growing faster than my emotional maturity could deal with the issue. As I look back at that experience, to be confronted with that issue was the greatest thing that could have ever happened to me. It was the beginning of the foundation that I now live by in my journey through life."

Havlicek remembers "With Larry there was always something wrong, always something to work on. That can make a tough situation. But he did what needed to be done, placed the success of the team ahead of personal goals and made the adjustment."

But there were problems. Joe Roberts remembers one practice in particular. "Fred explained a play to be run to the right side, but when Larry started to run it, the defense overreacted. Larry drove to the left for a basket. Fred wanted to explain how it went to the right, said to run it that way, Larry said something like 'I was wide open, I'm going back to Shelby' and left. Fred just called off the rest of practice and let him cool down."

Siegfried verbalized his feelings about scoring around his teammates more than he might have, because several of them began to refer to themselves as "Siegfried and the Four Gunners." As Frank Truitt says today, "The kids were very honest with each other. They would express a problem rather than keep it inside."

Truitt continues "Larry had the guts of a burglar, he'd take the ball right at the defense, then shoot, drive or pass. As a competitor I'd put him with anybody. When he saw Havlicek playing defense he got into that and became outstanding. He had this talent for getting into passing lanes and at least twice a game he'd make a steal for a basket. I used his techniques to teach others."

"He was as good a player at guard as I've seen in the Big Ten," says Bob Knight after 20 years as Indiana Head Coach. "Larry Siegfried got things done due to his ability to go all out as a competitor."

* * * *

Fred Taylor liked the defensive performance as OSU downed a good Northwestern team 81-64. Siegfried did "an exceptional job" holding Bill Cacciatore to one basket.

With a 3-0 conference record, Ohio State's first Big Ten road game was next. Purdue featured a brilliant 6'7 sophomore in Terry Dischinger and a zone defense. "Dischinger was agile, quick, strong inside and outside, could drive the ball — he was a really good player for the era," remembers Bob Knight. Jerry Lucas had a tender ankle and a bronchial condition; Joe Roberts had yet to fully recuperate from his bout with the flu.

Lucas made 11 of 13 shots for 27 points and Nowell added six of 10 for 17. OSU won 85-71. Purdue Coach Ray Eddy moved Dischinger to forward where Havlicek did a good job on him when the issue was in doubt. When the suggestion was made that Ohio State might go unbeaten in the conference, Fred Taylor said "That hasn't been done since the Whiz Kids of Illinois (12-0 in 1943)." Every team except Ohio State had at least two losses.

Michigan State was second in the conference in scoring to OSU, and the leader in rebounding, when they came to Columbus January 30. Nowell and Gearhart had missed several practices and Lucas

41

literally crawled out of bed to play. So Ohio State set a school scoring record which lasted until December, 1969 in winning 111-79.

Lucas scored 25 points and claimed 14 rebounds in 29 minutes, Howie Nourse scored 12 in relief. Havlicek scored 20 and grabbed 10 boards, Nowell scored 15 while taking only eight shots.

Michigan Coach Bill Perigo said he wished his team (0-5) was a little better so he "could see more of Ohio's fine first team" after the Wolverines lost 99-52. The score was 57-24 at the half. OSU was 6-0, followed by Minnesota at 5-3 and Illinois at 3-2, but six of their last eight games were on the road, away from now capacity St. John Arena crowds.

Richie Hoyt remembers dinner before the Northwestern game at "a beautiful old restaurant near campus." It was a benchmark for Mel Nowell, a young sophomore on his way to becoming a grizzled veteran. "Mel initially lacked confidence in himself, but he was a great observer and a quick learner. Dick Furry was always sending his steak back because it wasn't rare enough, and he did at this restaurant too. Mel was shocked, then decided to try it himself. It was part of the process for Mel, trying things and seeing how they worked. It was probably tough for him as a hometown hero, but it was fun seeing him develop from a talent to a player."

Though Buck coaches were worried about Northwestern's slow down, their zone and their crowd, the players grabbed a 33-22 lead at the half and won 77-58. Wildcat Willie Jones had scored 28 in the first game, but Havlicek limited him to 13; Siegfried held Cacciatore to eight.

Today Fred Taylor smiles when he remembers the first match-up between Willie "The Bird" Jones and John Havlicek. "'The Bird' was very good, and his moves gave John more trouble than most. During that first game Willie was scoring and John was frustrated. Then when John finally made a steal he took it down court, but missed a dunk. The ball bounced almost to half court.

"The next year when practice started we called the players together and were reviewing a variety of things as we did every preseason. I made the point that if the dunk is certain, dunk the ball; if not, we prefer the lay-up to be taken open hand facing away from the basket. From the back one of the players shouted 'You hear that John?' Everyone broke up, because we remembered the missed dunk from nine months before."

Five Bucks were in double figures at Wisconsin as the Badgers fell 106-69. Attendance was 12,187, the largest crowd at Wisconsin since 1954. By now OSU was 8-0 in Big Ten play and No. 3 nationally, behind California and Cincinnati.

Ohio State got outstanding defensive pressure from Nowell and Siegfried and beat the visiting Iowa Hawkeyes easily, 75-47. That set up a trip to Illinois, in second place at 5-3.

What should have been a major challenge was a 109-81 laugher in Huff Gym, the first time an OSU team had won there since December 13, 1945. Havlicek was incredible with 13 baskets in 17 attempts and 29 points. Lucas scored 31 points on 19 shots, and had 17 rebounds. "Plus he would start the fast break with an outlet pass before his feet hit the ground," remembers Dr. Bob Murphy. Nowell scored 17 and Roberts 14. Siegfried played strong defense and grabbed 10 rebounds. OSU shot .592 from the floor and outrebounded the Illini 58-40. The race seemed to be coming to a close; OSU was 10-0 with four games remaining, Indiana was second at 6-3.

After routing Michigan State six games earlier, the Buckeyes escaped East Lansing with a shaky 84-83 victory. A dunk by Lucas on an out of bounds play from Siegfried provided the winning points but the defensive play of Dick Furry may have been more critical. When Havlicek fouled out late in the game, Furry came in to guard Lance Olson, who already had 19 points. Three times Olson shot to give MSU the lead, three times Furry blocked it, three times OSU recovered. In a game with 11 lead changes and eight ties, Furry's defense was crucial.

A capacity crowd saw the home Buckeyes clinch the Big Ten title February 27, beating Wisconsin 93-68. All OSU starters scored in double figures and seven subs added 18 points. Field goal shooting was the key; OSU was 41 of 74 for 55.4%, led by Luke's eight of eight.

Shortly after the victory came the news that Fred Taylor's brother-in-law and sister-in-law had died in a two car crash near Pittsburgh. Fred and his wife Eileen went to Zanesville to be with their family, then he rejoined the team in Bloomington shortly before the game with Indiana. Today he says "I didn't do the kids any good that game."

Indiana forged a 52-38 halftime lead behind a 23-16 rebounding margin and won the game 99-83. It was OSU's only conference loss. Lucas (27 points, 20 rebounds) and Havlicek (25 points, 11 boards) played well, but the rest of the team struggled. It didn't help that

Taylor was away or that the Bucks had clinched the title, but the most important point is that Indiana had a very good team. They ended up 20-4, winning 12 straight after opening the Big Ten 0-3. When Branch McCracken said "You're lucky, we should be in the NCAA" he was half right. The Hoosiers did deserve to be competing with the best teams in the country. However only one team went from each conference in those days, and Ohio State won the conference. McCracken's remark would impact several future games between the two teams.

The last conference game was a visit to Minnesota, the only meeting with the Gophers and their star center 6'7 Ron Johnson. Taylor said he's "the best in the league around the basket ... Lucas is going to have to work like the devil to hold him."

The first half was tense. Gopher Marlo Miller hit six straight baskets before Gary Gearhart came in to shut him down, and OSU led only 39-38. The second half belonged to the frontline of Ohio State, and OSU won 75-66. Lucas had 23 points and 19 rebounds, both game highs, while holding Ron Johnson to 17 and 10. Roberts stormed back from a first half benching to total 18 points and 12 boards. Havlicek scored 14 as only three Bucks hit double figures.

Lucas, who only scored five points in the second half when his teammates came alive, lost the conference scoring title to Terry Dischinger of Purdue by 22 points. Both made the All-Big Ten team, along with Horace Walker of MSU, Johnson of Minnesota and Bellamy of Indiana.

Ohio State won the conference with a 13-1 record, 21-3 overall. Indiana was second at 11-3.

* * * *

During the 1960 season Ohio State was receiving national publicity, which helped their recruiting effort outside Ohio. Through the assistance of Jerry Brondfield, a 1936 alum who worked with Woody Hayes to recruit East Coast football players like Matt Snell and John Brockington for Ohio State, Fred Taylor was in contact with 6'8 Connie Hawkins of Boys High School in Brooklyn. Hawkins told newspapermen that Ohio State was among the schools he was interested in and, in fact, he visited campus.

Most basketball fans know that, early in his career, Michael Jordan was often compared to Julius "Dr. J." Erving. They were incredible leapers, wizards with the basketball, able to do things mere mortals could not imagine and capable of dunking over much taller men.

While Erving was the predecessor to Jordan, Hawkins was the original. When Erving, then in college at the University of Massachusetts, began to stand out at the summer Rucker Tournament in Harlem he was given the ultimate compliment and called "Little Hawk", after the legendary Hawkins.

The book *Raw Recruits* tells of Kentucky Coach Adolph Rupp calling a New York City writer to inquire about this Connie Hawkins who was scoring so many points in high school games. The question was, "is he white or colored?" When Rupp found out Hawkins was black, making him off limits to the Wildcats who would not sign a black player until 1970, Rupp suggested asterisks in box scores to identify the race of the players, to help simplify his recruiting.

To put it bluntly, Hawkins could do everything with a basketball but autograph it. "When he visited it was clear he was not college material," recalls Taylor.

Hawkins went to Iowa but was allegedly involved with the betting scandals and never played in college. He played in the old American Basketball League until it folded, then with the Harlem Globetrotters while he was banned from the NBA. He joined the American Basketball Association when it formed for the 1967-68 season. He led the league in scoring, was second in field goal percentage and rebounds, fourth in assists and led his Pittsburgh team to the championship. After one more year in the ABA he won a lawsuit against the NBA, joined Phoenix for the 1969-70 season and made All-NBA first team.

* * * *

At the annual appreciation banquet, emceed by Woody Hayes, the team announced an all-opponent team of Dischinger, Walker, Johnson, Bellamy as well as Northwestern's Willie Jones and Billy McGill of Utah. Hayes predicted an NCAA championship and Taylor said "Regardless of the outcome of future games, you will see the nicest bunch of kids in the country ... They're great ballplayers and they're smart — they had to be to make up for a dumb coach."

At the time 24 teams participated in the NCAA tournament. The field was limited to champions of conferences and selected independents. As Big Ten champion, Ohio State received a first round bye in the Mid-East Regional.

The regional was in Louisville, Kentucky. Ohio State's first game was against Western Kentucky, whose star sophomore guard Bobby Rascoe had just scored 27 in a 107-84 victory over nationally ranked

45

Miami (Fla.). "Our scouting report was that they may not be in good shape," recalls Taylor. "We emphasized the running game, but it wasn't working." Western Kentucky led at the half 43-37, and "by 5-6 with just a few minutes to play," says Taylor. "Then at a time-out our kids said they (Western Kentucky's players) were tiring." That was just before OSU hit a 15-4 spurt, which set up a 98-79 victory.

Lucas led the offense with 36, while Havlicek, Nowell and Siegfried all had double figures. Sieg's main contribution, however, was holding Rascoe to 16 points. Gearhart and Knight helped off the bench.

During the regionals Joe Roberts had promised the team that his wife was going to have a baby boy. "I told them I'd jump in the hotel pool with my clothes on if it was a girl," recalls the father-to-be. When a beautiful baby girl named Lori was born "I put on a cheap suit, some old shoes and dove in off the high board," recalls Roberts. It was an in-door pool, an important point since Louisville had 14 inches of snow at the time.

Roberts continued his celebration against regional final opponent eighth-ranked Georgia Tech, scoring 19 and grabbing nine boards. Lucas and Havlicek added 40 points and 26 rebounds as OSU won 86-69 to advance to what is now called The Final Four (then it was just part of the tournament). Lucas was MVP of the regional.

Joining #3 ranked OSU at the Cow Palace in San Francisco were defending champion California, ranked No. 1 with a team Coach Pete Newell said was better than the 1959 group; Oscar Robertson's Cincinnati team, ranked No. 2; and Ohio State's Friday night opponent, New York University. The Violets, 22-3, were the surprise, having beaten Jerry West's No. 6 ranked West Virginia team 82-81 and ACC champ Duke 74-59. Their star was 6'6, 210 lbs. Tom Sanders, a lean, quick inside player who would go on to a 13 year NBA career with the Boston Celtics. He averaged 21.7 ppg and 15 rebounds. Ball handler Ray Paprocky had 22 assists in the regionals and a 13.6 ppg scoring average.

Two days before the game near-disaster struck. In the words of John Havlicek from his book *HONDO — Celtic Man in Motion*, here is what happened: "I had an accident in the bathroom at the dorm. I had walked in and found that someone had left the place a mess. It was a common courtesy to leave the place clean for the next guy, but somebody had just shaved, and there was hair all over the place. I was sort of ticked off about it, and when I went over to the paper towel dispenser to get some towels I grabbed angrily and caught the ring finger and middle finger of my right hand. I required ten stitches and the fingers were very tender."

Fred Taylor was full of compassion. "Some guys make All-American and others have to cut off their fingers for publicity," he kidded. More seriously Taylor said "Sure he'll play," of the outstanding defender and 12.4 ppg scorer, "but it's hard to say how well or long. Those fingers will be sore and we don't be able to relieve the pain any without his losing his touch."

In addition Lucas had a sore throat, Roberts a thigh bruise and Siegfried a sore knee. Taylor said merely, "We're in good shape."

Today Hondo recalls rooming with Jerry Lucas in San Francisco. "When we left the hotel for practice we each had $50 with us," says Havlicek. "That was a lot of money in those days, particularly for college students. We thought we might be robbed on the street, and were afraid it would be taken out of the room. Jerry decided to leave his in the lamp, by the bulb. After practice when we got back to the room, we had forgotten about the money and turned the lamp on. Eventually we smelled something burning, and finally realized what it was. The bills were all charred and brown. It think it still spent, though." It must have. Lucas doesn't remember the incident.

As the OSU-NYU game approached, to be played at 10:30 p.m. Columbus time, the Bucks were six point favorites. California was favored by three in the later game.

Ohio State completely outplayed New York University in winning 76-54. Lucas held Sanders to eight points and scored 19. Siegfried limited Paprocky to nine points, and scored 19 himself on seven of 11 shooting. Furry came off the bench with 10 points and seven rebounds. Havlicek played a gutty game, though he only made two of eight shots.

In the post game celebration Larry Siegfried unfolded a telegram from Shelby. Signed by the merchants and school children of his hometown, the wire was over 10 feet long. Taylor announced that chief scout Frank Truitt had predicted a final score of 75-60.

After beating Cincinnati, the California Golden Bears were the final obstacle facing the young Buckeyes. Their star was Darrall Imhoff, an All-American with a 13.5 scoring average. His strength was shot blocking. He said "If you bat the ball down a man's throat on his favorite shot, he's going to choke a little and might not try it again."

Team doctor Bob Murphy recalls that California was the overwhelming favorite. "Saturday morning between games the press was polled about the game. Two writers picked us, the rest, over 45, picked Cal."

Dick Furry has another clear memory of something before tip-off. "There was a ceremony and Pete Newell was presented the Coach of the Year award. We thought Fred deserved it. We were steaming when the game started."

The championship game was shown locally on WTVN (now WSYX), and heard on WMNI, WTVN and WBNS radio. The tip-off was at midnight Saturday night.

In front of 14,500 fans, almost all rooting for the California team which had won 45 of its last 46 games, the Buckeyes were flawless. They never trailed — from Joe Roberts' driving lay-up to the final buzzer. Ohio State made 16 of 19 field goal attempts and led 37-19 at halftime. They challenged Imhoff, the shot blocker, and destroyed the outstanding California defense with their quickness and accuracy. When Cal had the ball, Coach Taylor had decided to let ball handler Bobby Wendell have room to shoot. This allowed Mel Nowell to gamble, trap, double-team and generally disrupt the Golden Bears. Nowell did his job and Wendell missed all six shots in the game.

One of the oft-told tales in Buckeye basketball history comes from the California locker room at halftime. Cal Coach Pete Newell, perplexed that Ohio State seemed to be scoring every time down court, said "We've got to get more defensive rebounds." Imhoff said "There have only been three Coach, and I got them all."

OSU didn't cool off a lot in the second half, hitting 17 of 27 shots. Havlicek was four of eight for the game, worst of the starters. MVP Lucas made seven of nine, all-tournament selection Mel Nowell hit six of seven, Roberts and Siegfried (both second team all-tournament) made five of six. Roberts even threw in a hook shot from the top of the circle. The starters were 27 of 36 — 75%. Ohio State won 75-55, a record victory margin for a final game which stood until 1968.

After the game Fred Taylor praised everyone. *Citizen-Journal* writer Kaye Kessler wrote that Fred told Lucas, who got 49 of 56 votes for MVP, "You're going to be a heckuva guy when you get a little age". Lucas replied "You look a little peaked, Coach." Taylor said "You wait a long time for something like this." Lucas replied "You only waited two years." Jerry was hard to top at any time.

Taylor took time for a serious tribute to Newell, his coaching rival. "Pete taught me how to coach basketball," said Taylor. "He's a marvelous defensive coach. I attended a clinic in Minnesota last summer and Pete spent three days with me teaching me his defense."

Thinking back to 1960 today, Gary Gearhart says "The older I've gotten the more I respect what Fred did with that team, at that age." Joe Roberts adds "We had the ultimate team concept. It started with Lucas, who didn't want to be a star."

Bob Knight has two strong memories of the 1960 team. "First is the way the coaches set everything up, prepared us and directed us," recalls the Indiana coach. "Fred Taylor was a tremendous organizer. He did an outstanding job of giving players roles they could fill. We never wasted time in practice; his approach to practice is my approach to practice today. Jack Graf did a great job with the players and Frank Truitt did an excellent job in game preparation. We had exceptional coaching.

"Second is the seniors. Co-captains Dick Furry and Joe Roberts never got the credit they deserved for what they did beyond basketball. I wasn't any big deal but they couldn't have been nicer to me. Same thing for Dave Barker, John Cedargren and Howie Nourse. They were all helpful, and very easy to be around ... good seniors."

* * * *

Later in the book, Jerry Lucas' career statistics will be compared to those of Kareem Abdul-Jabbar (then Lew Alcindor) and Bill Walton. In an effort to put Luke's accomplishments in a modern perspective, his sophomore year is contrasted with the sophomore year of Shaquille O'Neal at LSU in 1991. O'Neal far outpaced the individual accomplishments of Ralph Sampson, Patrick Erving, Hakeem Olajuwon and David Robinson at comparable stages of their careers.

	G	PPG	RPG	FG %	FT %	REB %*
Lucas	27	26.3	16.4	.637	.770	.188
(first year of varsity)						
O'Neal	28	27.6	14.7	.628	.638	.177
(second year)						

* Because the players are being compared after 31 years, and because so many changes have taken place during that time, Rebound % is used to illustrate rebounding effectiveness. In 1960 more shots were taken in the average Ohio State game (144) than the average LSU game in 1991 (139). Though Ohio State shot slightly better from the field than LSU (.497 to .495), their opponents shot worse (.388 to .424) than LSU's. Surprisingly both Ohio State and

their 1960 opponents shot free throws better than LSU and their 1991 opponents. Rebound % is an attempt to mix all those variables together by dividing the player's rebound per game average by the average number of rebounds available per game in each season.

* * * *

After a victory celebration at the Columbus Airport attended by about 10,000 fans, the Buckeyes were not through with basketball for the year. As NCAA champions they would head for Denver, to play three games against various college all-star and AAU teams. The winner of the trials would place five to seven men on the Olympic team, as the 1948 Kentucky team had done. The other five to seven players would come from the other teams. OSU had picked the perfect time to win the NCAA tournament, even granting that there is never a bad time.

The Bucks did not have practice for nearly a week. They had gone from the pressure of final exams to the intensity of the Finals to the euphoria of the victory, and needed to rest. Meanwhile some of the teams were playing in Denver, getting accustomed to the altitude and the floor.

Ohio State lost the chance to qualify as a team for the Olympics in Rome in the first game. The NAIA All-Stars, who had been practicing for two weeks in the "mile high city," beat them 76-69. The Bucks had an early 27-15 lead, and were ahead 42-39 at the half, but wore down despite an oxygen tank on the bench and frequent substitutions.

NAIA was led by 6'8 Jackie Moreland of Louisiana Tech, a major prep star who had to leave North Carolina State due to recruiting violations. He had 12 second half points. The talent on the winners was such that Zelmo Beaty of Prairie View, who would score over 17,000 points in pro ball, hardly played. In his book, Havlicek wrote "During the second half they began to play a zone, even though zones weren't permitted in the tournament. We weren't prepared for it, and lost the game."

Individual Buckeyes could still qualify for the Olympic team, and four seemed to be in contention. Havlicek, who could probably run all day five miles above sea level, had 20 points and nine rebounds; Lucas was the leading rebounder with 19 and had 13 points; Roberts had 14 points and eight boards; Siegfried scored 12.

Ohio State won the next game against a team of NCAA small college all stars easily, 89-79. The score is deceiving because the Bucks led 39-20 with 6:26 to go in the first half and Lucas sat out 15:32 in the game. All the starters were in double figures and Lucas (22 rebounds and 15 points), Havlicek (24 points, 10 rebounds) and Siegfried (seven of 14 shots for 18 points) were fighting for Olympic berths.

The last game matched the Bucks with the Phillips Oilers. OSU won the game 87-77, but by now that was not the point. Lucas, who had 58 rebounds in the tournament, almost twice as many as anyone else, *had* to be named to the Olympic team. The powerful NCAA team of Oscar Robertson — Jerry West — Terry Dischinger etc. won the tournament and would get at least five spots. Havlicek and Siegfried were competing with two Phillips stars, Burdie Haldorson and Les Lane, for remaining positions.

Siegfried guarded the 5'10 Lane and "thoroughly outplayed him" according to Havlicek. Sieg was 10 of 18 from the field and hit three straight at the foul line for 23 points; he also got five rebounds. Lane was two of eight from the field and scored five points. For the tournament Siegfried scored more (53 to 34 points), shot better and got more rebounds. Lane and a guard named Al Kelley from the Peoria AAU team (27 points, 39% from the field in three games) made the Olympic team, Siegfried did not.

Today Siegfried says "It was a disappointment, because I felt like I deserved it and had earned it. It was a matter of dealing with something that wasn't right, but it happened and you better deal with it."

Havlicek didn't have his best game at the end, making three of 14 shots for seven points, but he did have 10 rebounds. He led all forwards in rebounding with 29, more than 6'9 center Haldorson who had 27. Lucas limited Haldorson to three of 11 and nine points, but Burdie had been on the 1956 Olympic team and was named again.

The team ended up with five centers — Lucas, Bob Boozer of Peoria and formerly Kansas State, Haldorson and both Imhoff and Bellamy from the NCAA team. Interestingly Imhoff started for that team, yet Bellamy outscored him 42-18 and outrebounded him 30 to 21. Dischinger and Robertson were the only forwards named, and Oscar played a lot of guard in the Olympics. The guards were West, Lane, Kelley, Adrian Smith of the Armed Forces All-Stars who was on Kentucky's 1958 NCAA champion and Jay Arnette of the NCAA team.

The sixth NCAA selection (Imhoff or Arnette), Haldorson, Lane and Kelley were not even close to Havlicek and Siegfried in their performance at the trials. Havlicek wrote in his autobiography "Not making the 1960 Olympic basketball team is probably my most bitter

51

disappointment in sports, and I will never get over it. You only get one chance. I knew I should have been there, and I wasn't."

At the time Fred Taylor said "It appears we could have stayed at home and taken our chances on the Olympic selections from there. Granted, we are prejudiced, but we feel that two of our people were bypassed in favor of others in order to get a more equal distribution between AAU and NCAA participants. This has been an outstanding year for inter-collegiate basketball, with more excellent players than usual. We feel the committee should have taken this into considera- tion. What really hurts is when you see some of our kids completely outplay some of the others who were picked on that Olympic squad."

That Olympic team won the gold medal by overwhelming their opposition in eight straight games. The original plan to play Lucas at forward was revised because the team didn't come together until he moved into the pivot. The starting team was Lucas at center, Dis- chinger and Robertson at forwards, West and, surprise, Les Lane at guard. After the Olympics, Coach Pete Newell called Luke "The greatest player I ever coached, and the most unselfish." Jerry made 84% of his shots in Olympic competition.

Observers said it was the greatest amateur team of all time. It remained so until the 1984 Olympic team of Michael Jordan, Patrick Ewing, Sam Perkins, Wayman Tisdale, Chris Mullin, Alvin Robertson et. al. That club, coached by Bob Knight, did not have room for a player like Charles Barkley, but the selection committee took the 12 players they believed would combine for the best team. Too bad that wasn't the approach in 1960. Siegfried could have been a starter at guard and Havlicek the first forward off the bench on that 1960 team, unless Robertson moved to guard with West and Hondo slid in at for- ward. With those two on the 1960 team, that group might remain as the best of all time. But both teams won the gold, which is the most important point. Too bad John and Larry don't have the memories they deserve of that Olympic experience.

As Jerry Lucas says today, "No doubt politics kept them off the team."

*   *   *   *

One last thought on the 1960 team, and how strong it was.

A primary offense of that team was "the cutting game." Jerry Lucas played above the foul line or to the side of the foul circle and used his passing skills to find teammates breaking for the basket. If the three-point shot was available then, Luke probably would have backed up 2'-3'. Then he would have shot 50-60% from the three point line, or driven around any center who came out to contest him, or passed to Roberts, Havlicek or Furry inside or to Nowell or Siegfried from the wings. Ohio State would have had three of the best three point shooters in the country in Lucas, Nowell and Siegfried, the forwards would have been wide-open and the offense would have been even more frightening. As it was, Ohio State led the nation in team offense with 90.4 ppg for the year, and finished third in field goal percentage and rebound percentage.

Bob Knight says "The three point line would have made us impossible to play a zone defense against. We always had at least three excellent shooters on the floor."

IV
1961: Almost Two Straight

The 1960-61 Buckeyes were loaded, and everyone knew it. Jerry Lucas was the best player in the country, a comment that in retrospect seems to be an understatement. NBA scouts said he would star as a pro "right now." Captain Larry Siegfried was finding peace within himself — "Things got easier after we won the championship and the focus was on the success of the team," he says today. John Havlicek and Mel Nowell, like Siegfried, deserved serious All-America consideration but basketball writers had trouble seeing beyond Lucas.

Graduation had claimed Joe Roberts, Dick Furry and Howie Nourse, leaving one hole in the starting line-up and less depth inside. Candidates began with junior 6'4 Bob Knight, continued with senior 6'4 Richie Hoyt who had been shifted back to forward from guard, and included 6'4 sophomore Doug McDonald. The problem was considered to be about as serious as a parking ticket to J. Paul Getty.

Dell Sports Basketball picked Lucas first team All-America with four future OSU opponents — Bellamy of Indiana, Dischinger of Purdue and Dave DeBusschere of Detroit and Tom Stith of St. Bonaventure. The magazine did not mention any other Buckeyes among their top twenty players but picked OSU as their No. 1 team. Bradley, North Carolina, Utah State and Western Kentucky rounded out the first five; upcoming OSU opponents included Detroit (7), St. Bonaventure (12), St. John's (13) and Indiana (18).

SPORT magazine said Lucas "shoots and rebounds with the skill of a pro ... (he) is expected to lead the Buckeyes to their second

55

consecutive NCAA tournament championship." They had no other Ohio State players on their list of the top fifteen players but included Siegfried in their 24 man honorable mention list.

Fred Taylor's pre-season assessment included such language as "The Big Ten coaches picked us to win the league, and they haven't been right yet ... What will happen if we get injuries? ... Our schedule reads like a basketball's Who's Who ... We are going to be smaller than most teams we play and not as strong physically on the boards as we were last year ... " but he was pleased with the hard work shown in pre-season and expected improved execution based on the experience of the team.

Captain Larry Siegfried said "Lack of height, lack of height is all we've heard. Well, it's not what's on the outside, it's what's on the inside. I'll guarantee you we'll be seven-feet-two this season."

The Bucks traveled down State Route 33 to Athens to open Ohio University's new Grover Center and won, 85-64. Lucas got 20 rebounds and scored 29 points, but it was considered a less than outstanding game. This was partially due to the expectations people had for him, and partly due to the fact that he had been held out of practice at times. He says today "I was more tired in the first few games of my junior year than any I can remember." His sophomore year, the NCAA championship, the Olympic try-out, the Olympic practices, the Olympics and pre-season practice had exacted a physical and mental toll.

Siegfried and Nowell scored in double figures but no one else did. Havlicek had 10 rebounds and held Bobcat captain Bunk Adams to six of 22 field goal attempts. Adams, star of the Toledo Macomber team which defeated Siegfried's Shelby team but lost to Lucas and Middletown four years before, was the first of many outstanding scoring forwards Havlicek would encounter in the 1961 season.

At the uncertain forward slot, Knight started but made only two of eight from the field. His replacement, Richie Hoyt, drew praise with three of four from the field, three of three at the line, nine points and five rebounds.

Hoyt got the start in OSU's home opener with St. Louis, an 81-66 victory. Based on seven points, four rebounds and, as Taylor said after the game, "a good overall job ... a lot of scrap ... a good job on weakside help," he had earned the starting job for the foreseeable future.

Before the St. Louis game the OSU freshmen had been split into two teams and featured in a preliminary game for the home fans. Ray

Brown, Player of the Year in Ohio when he led Dayton Roosevelt over Cleveland East Tech 51-41 for the Class AA championship, scored 44 points in that game. The press picked him out as a star of the future. "He looked like Treg Lee, maybe even a better basketball body," recalls Taylor. "He was listed 6'5 but he was bigger than that." Brown's comments led to a story which has been handed down through generations at Ohio State. Bill Hosket, in ninth grade at Dayton Belmont at the time, remembers it today from hearing it years later. He says simply "Ask Fred about Ray Brown and the three-choice drill."

Fred Taylor tells the story. "After the game was over Ray was feeling pretty good, and told someone 'Next year that '3' position is mine.' The quote was printed. Some of us thought the '3' spot, or right forward position, was in pretty good hands with a fellow named Havlicek. John's buddies got after him, asking if he was going to transfer, how he would feel as a substitute, stuff like that.

"The next day in practice we ran what we called a three-choice drill. The situation had an offensive man driving to the basket, while the defensive man ran to catch up. The defender had to make a decision: get into position to take the charge, block the shot or 'run through the man', which literally means running in front of him to make him think you are running into him. Those are the three choices. It was done with two lines.

"When Brown got the ball on the break-out, Havlicek was in the other line. John caught up to him and simply took the ball away, making it look very easy. They went to the opposite lines and I noticed Ray 'ditching' in his line, so he wouldn't be matched against John again. Then John, who apparently had selected a place in line to be opposite Ray in the first place, also changed places with someone so he could be matched with Ray again. 'Hondo' loved a challenge."

Brown had academic problems and left Ohio State after his freshman season.

When the UPI rankings came out December 6, Ohio State got 34 of 35 first place votes. Indiana, ranked third behind Bradley, got the other one. Kansas, North Carolina and Utah State were followed in the Top Ten by future Ohio State opponents St. Bonaventure, Cincinnati, Detroit and St. John's. Still, in Columbus people were asking "What's wrong with Ohio State?" and "Why isn't Jerry Lucas shooting more?" The Bucks had won by 21 and 15 points, and something was wrong? Lucas had made four of six field goals against St. Louis but scored 23 points by making 15 of 19 free throws. No shot attempt is credited when a player is fouled in the act of shooting. Yet something was wrong. Ah, expectations.

After Ohio State blitzed Army 103-54, Wichita (5-1) presented the next challenge as well as an opportunity for a reunion. Tippy Dye, former OSU coach, captain and star, was the Athletic Director of the Shockers. Lucas outplayed future NBA center Gene Wiley and OSU had a 93-82 victory. If 20 rebounds in a game were more common today, Luke's accomplishment of 21 rebounds and 27 points might now be known as a "20-20". Havlicek hit 10 of 16 shots while holding Shocker high scorer 6'6 Ron Heller to eight of 21.

Loyola (5-0) of Chicago lost to the Buckeyes 90-65 on their own floor, despite Lucas sitting out the last 10:45. Hoyt struggled but the four other starters scored in double figures, as did Bob Knight. Sophomore Kenny Lee, second string center at 6'5, grabbed seven rebounds. Havlicek held high scoring Jerry Harkness to four baskets in 16 shots and 10 points, seven below his average. Harkness would be the star of Loyola's NCAA championship team in 1963 and play in the NBA.

After the Monday night game with Loyola, the team was scheduled to fly back to Columbus on Tuesday. However weather caused the cancellation of the TWA flight and the team took a train which arrived in Marion at 3 a.m. Wednesday. They slept a few hours and took a bus to Columbus, arriving at 10 a.m. This cut out necessary preparation time for Thursday's opponent, the sixth ranked Detroit Titans.

The visitors were 5-1, after a 20-6 mark the year before. They featured two excellent inside players in center Charlie North and Dave DeBusschere, the 6'6 All-American forward. DeBusschere would go on to a pro baseball career as a pitcher with the Chicago White Sox *and* twelve years in the NBA. He was elected to the Basketball Hall of Fame. He and Lucas would be teammates on the 1973 world championship New York Knicks team, but December 22, 1961 he was mostly John Havlicek's worry.

Detroit pulled a stratagem by playing DeBusschere at center, and caught Ohio State off guard early. He scored five quick baskets as Detroit led 19-17 with 11:49 remaining in the half. But that was pretty much it for the fine All-American; he ended with 14 points and seven rebounds. Charlie North played outside to keep Lucas away from the boards, but Lucas still had 22 rebounds and 30 points.

OSU led 42-38 at the half, and started the second period with eight start points from Lucas and Nowell. The 50-38 lead was never tested and Ohio State won 84-73.

Lucas had another "20-20" and Nowell and Siegfried combined for 34 points. Knight got the start but Hoyt played better off the bench. It was beginning to seem that no matter who opened at forward, the sub played better. And, again, Havlicek had risen to the occasion in keeping DeBusschere far below the 25.6 ppg and 20.1 rpg he averaged in 1960.

In Kaye Kessler's *Citizen-Journal* column he quoted a Fred Taylor story concerning the reputation Hondo was establishing for his defensive skill. "When we played Loyola in Chicago Stadium last Monday," said Fred, "a DePaul player was sitting in the stands. Someone asked him why he was watching the game. He said he was going to guard Marquette hot-shot Don Kojis later this week and the only reason he came was to watch Havlicek play defense."

John would have three more major challenges in the next week, as Ohio State went to New York to play in Madison Square Garden for the Eastern Collegiate Athletic Conference Holiday Festival.

For years Madison Square Garden had been known as the "Mecca" of college basketball. Some experts referred to the beginning of the modern era as December 6, 1934, when 16,188 fans watched NYU defeat Notre Dame and Westminster beat St. John's in the first regularly scheduled doubleheader in the Garden. In the minds of many of the East Coast media, winning the NCAA championship was one thing but proving yourselves in "The Gah-den" was another. "If you can make it there you can make it anywhere," says the song "New York, New York."

When Ohio State played Seton Hall (5-1), the pressure was on Havlicek again. He was assigned the Pirate's leading scorer, Art Hicks. Hicks went into the game with a 19 point average, scored five, and OSU won 97-57. Bob Knight started, was hot early, and scored 12 points. The Bucks made 22 of 35 shots in the first half, 63%, and the game was never in doubt.

Three other nationally ranked teams won their opening games. Ohio State would play 7-0 St. John's, which had easily beaten Providence, while St. Bonaventure and Utah would be matched in the other semi-final.

St. John's was a top five team, led by future NBA stars. Center LeRoy Ellis would have a 12 year NBA career. He was Luke's problem.

Kevin Loughery, a 6'3 guard, averaged over 13 ppg. Named head coach of the Miami Heat in June, 1991, Loughery scored over 11,000 points in the NBA. He was Siegfried's problem. They had help from a muscular 6'4 forward named Willie "The Bull" Hall, who averaged about 15 ppg.

But unquestionably the star of the St. John's Redmen was 6'4 Tony Jackson. He was quick and a great leaper. His coach Joe Lapchick, a veteran of 25 years with St. John's and in the NBA, said simply "Tony's the best outside jump shooter I've ever seen." Jackson would be associated with the gambling scandals and never play in the NBA, but he was a consensus first team All-American.

Before the semi-finals, Joe Lapchick was quoted as saying Ohio State had the greatest college team he had ever seen, better than the San Francisco team of Bill Russell and K.C. Jones or anyone else. Fred Taylor said "That's what makes the garden grow," adding new meaning to an old comment. The Garden was sold out at 18,496 tickets.

The Bucks trailed 38-28 at the half but put together a 13 point run early in the second period and an eight point spurt midway through to win 70-65. They "won" the second half 42-27, largely due to an effective zone press.

Tony Jackson, called "a great jump shooter; probably the toughest guy I've tried to guard" by his opponent, outplayed Havlicek ever so slightly. Today Bob Knight remembers "a fast break when Jackson took a jump shot from the side, Havlicek fouled him, knocked him over the bench, and Jackson made the shot." Jackson had 24 points versus 20 for John and 12 rebounds to 11 for the Buckeye defender. However Havlicek shot five less times and contributed several steals out of the press. Siegfried matched Loughery with eight points. The key was Lucas, who overwhelmed Ellis. Though nervous in the Seton Hall game with the incredible media attention he was generating, Jerry still had good numbers in limited action. Against St. John's he was back to his definition of normal, allowing Ellis only three baskets and nine points while scoring 23 himself. OSU outrebounded St. John's as a team by seven; Lucas had 18, Ellis nine.

When St. Bonaventure slipped past Utah, the nation's leading scorer, Tom Stith, would be Hondo's next challenge.

Stith, 6'5, was a tremendous talent. The previous year he had averaged 31.5 ppg as a junior and finished second in the nation in scoring to Oscar Robertson.

Stith would lead St. Bonaventure to a 22-3 season, make first team All-American and be selected second in the NBA draft. He had a reputation for lapses of concentration, but at times he was unstoppable.

Tom Stith hit one of those streaks against, of all people, John Havlicek. Stith scored 35 points against OSU, 28 in the second half. Afterwards Havlicek said "There goes my reputation as a great defender." Lucas compared Stith to Olympian Terry Dischinger and Taylor said "Tom Stith is greater than we thought he was. When the chips were down, he's the one the Bonnies fed the ball to. He's got great pro shooting moves." Bob Knight remembers Stith as "hard to guard inside, where he did a great job keeping people away."

The Bucks had to outscore St. Bonaventure, and did, 84-82. Lucas, despite playing with a black eye suffered in the St. John's game, scored 32 points and grabbed 21 rebounds. Siegfried controlled Whitey Martin, later the tenth man selected in the NBA draft, and outscored him 16 to five. "No guard in the country could have come up with a better job than he gave us in the second half," said Taylor. Gary Gearhart scored 11 in relief of Mel Nowell, who had a rare off night, and Havlicek had 13. Starter Bob Knight was scoreless but Richie Hoyt had four baskets off the bench.

Fred Taylor summed up the tournament by saying "This tournament did us good from the competition standpoint. You know four teams came in here unbeaten, but only one came out. We're a better club right now than a year ago. We've got more confidence in what we're trying to do." Jerry Lucas won the MVP trophy easily, though he was fifth in scoring.

Health problems, and an inability to score away from the basket, restricted Stith's NBA career.

As OSU turned its attention to the Big Ten, they were still ranked No. 1 in the nation at 9-0. Past Buckeye victims St. Bonaventure (No. 3), St. John's (4), Detroit (11), St. Louis (12) and Wichita (17) attested to the difficulty of the schedule. More than half of Ohio State's nine victories were against Top 20 teams, three of the five away from St. John Arena.

In the next three games, the Buckeyes beat Illinois, Evansville and Northwestern by an average of 29 points, then Minnesota 75-56. That set-up a televised game with Purdue, with whom they were tied for first place at 3-0.

Terry Dischinger, averaging 27.6 ppg, led the Boilermakers to Columbus. The Purdue star had set seven school records, led the Big Ten in scoring and been a starter in the United States Olympic team as a sophomore. Nationally recognized already, most picked him as first team All-American. A four sport star — football, baseball and track were the others — from Terre Haute's Garfield High School, Dischinger was similar to Lucas in many ways. Both were immediately successful on the court. They both put team success ahead of individual accomplishments. Dischinger shot more than Luke because he had less support; his team needed his scoring. Both were very bright, and enrolled on academic rather than athletic scholarships. Terry was in the rigorous chemical engineering curriculum at Purdue. However since Dischinger played high post and corner, when the two teams played he was usually one more challenge for John Havlicek.

Citizen-Journal writer Kaye Kessler summarized the game this way: "Dischinger was superb. But he had four boys going with him. Lucas was equally superb, but he had four MEN, at least two of them All-America caliber, clicking with him." Ohio State won 92-62.

Dischinger had 26 points and 11 rebounds, but Havlicek's defense limited him to only 15 shots. No other Boiler scored more than nine points. Meanwhile Sieg fired in 21 points, Nowell and Lucas 17 each, Havlicek 12 and Hoyt 10. Luke had 17 boards, Hondo 14 and Knight seven. The Bucks had a 60-30 rebound margin.

A trip to Wisconsin was next. The Badgers, having lost three players to grades, were no problem. They fell 100-68, as all Buck starters hit double figures. Hoyt, who started every Big Ten and NCAA game, scored 11 points.

John Havlicek made all nine field goal attempts at Michigan to set a single game accuracy record that still stands at Ohio State as the Bucks won 80-58. Mel Nowell also scored 18 to tie for game high scoring honors, Lucas had 17.

With a 6-0 league mark, the Bucks returned home for what shaped up as the game of the year with 3-1 Indiana. Olympic star Walter Bellamy, averaging 23 ppg, had just scored 34 against Northwestern. The other Hoosier returning starter Gary Long was at 10.3 ppg. Sophomores Tom Bolyard and Jimmy Rayl added scoring punch to the Indiana fast break style. Branch McCracken's remarks that Indiana deserved to go to the NCAA the previous year, the Buckeyes' sole Big Ten loss at Bloomington and even the 122-92 thrashing from 1959 were still on the minds of Ohio State players and coaches. The game meant a great deal in the conference race and had those other ramifications as well.

The final score was 100-65 Ohio State, but the halftime score of 46-23 provides a clearer picture of the game. The four-pointed Buckeye star was never brighter. Mel Nowell made six of eight attempts, scored 13 points and grabbed six rebounds. Larry Siegfried fired in 27 points, his season high. John Havlicek pressured Boylard into a five of 15 shooting night, hit 10 of 15 himself to total 22 points and grabbed 13 rebounds. Lucas outscored Bellamy 34 to 19 and claimed 14 boards.

Fred Taylor showed his true feelings when he said "This one meant more to me than that game in California last spring." Asked if it was Ohio State's best game of the year, he responded by saying "Is New York City big? You're darn right. I guess you could say they sorta wanted this one." He then went on to the key of the pre-game strategy, getting Lucas to shoot more. "We simply felt he could score on Bellamy and maybe get the big guy into foul trouble." Bellamy went out with four fouls at 14:16, but OSU was ahead 60-34 anyway. He came back two minutes later and played the rest of the way. Bob Knight remembers Bellamy as "better as a junior than a senior — the people around here (Bloomington, Indiana) feel that way as well."

Today Coach Taylor remembers the offensive execution in that game, and attributes the success primarily to Hondo's work as a decoy. "We had Luke set a screen for John, who broke to the ball with a vengeance, knowing he probably wouldn't get it. But that cleared out the right side for Luke and usually Siegfried, sometimes Nowell, to go two-on-two on the right half of the floor." Havlicek opened the court for his teammates and still scored 22 points.

Ohio State had gone through half of their Big Ten schedule and stood 7-0. Iowa (4-1), Purdue (5-2), Illinois (4-2), and Indiana (3-2) were the only teams with less than four losses. OSU had beaten all of them except Iowa. Then came the news that Sharm Scheuerman's Hawkeyes, 12-3 for the season, had lost four starters to grades. The race appeared to be over.

Overconfidence was not a problem at East Lansing, where Michigan State tried to take advantage of Jerry Lucas and his emphasis on his teammates. "They guarded everyone else and thought Luke still wouldn't shoot," recalls Taylor. For playing mind games with Lucas the Spartans got an 83-68 loss. But, hey, it might have worked out that way under any circumstances.

Jerry Lucas responded by making 19 of 26 field goal attempts, adding 10 of 12 free throws and scoring a school record 48 points. He claimed 21 rebounds. Coach Taylor took him out with 1:12 to play, and 46 points, but the official scorer ignored the substitution and pointed out that one more basket would break the Big Ten single game record of 47 points, held by Indiana's Don Schlundt. Lucas stayed in, Knight lobbed a pass, Lucas stuffed it and then got to sit down.

Havlicek stayed hot, making 10 of 16 field goal attempts to total 29 of 40 in the last three games (72.5%), but the other starters had only five of 22 from the floor. The strange strategy could have worked, except that Lucas rose to the occasion. Again.

Mel Nowell was the man against visiting Northwestern, making 12 of 14 shots to score 27 points in an 89-65 victory.

The Iowa Hawkeyes, hit hard by academic ineligibility of four starters, had beaten Indiana on the road and Wisconsin at home, to stand 6-1. When the Buckeyes visited Iowa City they were lucky to escape with their unbeaten rescored in tact, winning 62-61.

Coach Sharm Scheuerman had his club playing at a fever pitch. With only 6'6 Don Nelson over 6'3, Iowa outrebounded Ohio State 35-23. The Hawks led 34-24 at the half, and 59-52 with 3:36 to play. Only a 10 point Ohio State streak in the next 1:45, triggered by the zone press which had keyed the victory over St. John's, saved the day. During the run Siegfried got a rebound basket, then Havlicek hit a jump shot and made a steal. That set up two foul shots by Siegfried, who then got a steal and a lay-up. OSU led 60-59 with 2:10 to go. Knight's steal set up a Gearhart lay-up, but it was blocked. However Gearhart caught up to Iowa's Matt Szykowny, stole the ball back and scored on a lay-in to make the score 62-59. Then Don Nelson scored on a rebound basket, and Iowa regained possession at 0:19. Nelson's shot, and two Iowa tips, missed as time expired. "I died a thousand deaths on those last three," said Taylor.

Marv Homan, the radio voice of the Buckeyes, remembers having breakfast with Jerry Lucas in Iowa City. "He wanted to talk about everything but basketball," remembers Homan, also the assistant sports information director. "In the middle of one conversation he said 'Marv, there are 2065 bricks in that wall.' He had to think of several things at once most of the time." Dr. Bob Murphy says "Lucas was very comfortable talking with adults. He had questions about medicine, world events. He was an adult at 18 years of age."

Ohio State entered a potential hornet's nest at Bloomington January 20. The Hoosiers were only 4-4, but they were still steaming about Ohio State running up the score two weeks prior. They were also trying to get Coach Branch McCracken his 400th career win. Walter Bellamy wanted to salvage a disappointing year with a win over Olympic mate Jerry Lucas.

Both teams started slowly. Havlicek's free throw at 17:19 to go in the half was the first point. Lucas held Bellamy scoreless while Havlicek limited Bolyard to one basket at the half. OSU led 41-29. In the second half Indiana never got closer than three points. The final was 73-69.

The cream rose to the top for Ohio State. Nowell (27 points) and Siegfried (17) outplayed the Hoosier guards, Lucas tied Bellamy's 17 rebounds and outscored him 16 to 13, Havlicek had 11 points and the same number of rebounds. With an 11-0 record, and Purdue and Iowa having two losses each, the title was almost at hand.

Wisconsin visited St. John and fell 97-74. Ohio State led 52-26 at the half. The four returning starters had 19-14 points, Hoyt eight, sophomore Dick Reasbeck nine off the bench as fifteen Bucks played.

* * * *

California's Pete Newell had retired as a college coach after leading the United States Olympic basketball team to a gold medal. As California Athletic Director his opinions on the issues of the college game remained highly respected, so his article in *Look* magazine was noteworthy. Then. It seems dated now. He wrote:

"If the basket is not raised, preferable by two feet, no later than five years from now, I believe today's booming interest in basketball will sink in a mire of boredom ... By reaching above the rim, they (players) dunk or stuff the ball down into the basket or tap it in on a rebound. These tap-ins and dunkers require little beside reach. Yet they are worth the same two points as the two-handed set shot, the jump shot, the hook or the drive in, which call for maneuverability, coordination and marksmanship."

Imagine Michael J. Fox going "back to the future" and trying to explain slam dunk contests and the three point rule in 1961.

* * * *

Michigan State stood between Ohio State and their second Big Ten title. The Spartans had just given up 52 points to Terry Dischinger, so their part of the conference single game scoring record remained in place but Jerry Lucas was down to second in history. But Luke was named MVP of the NCAA District Four. Dischinger, Bellamy,

Siegfried and DeBusschere joined him on the first team. Havlicek was on the second team.

OSU clinched the title with a 91-83 victory after leading MSU 87-68. Senior starters Richie Hoyt and Larry Siegfried left the floor to thunderous ovations in their final home game. Lucas had another 20-20, actually 23 points, and Havlicek made 12 of 14 field goal attempts.

The Illinois "Whiz Kids" of 1943 were the last Big Ten team to go unbeaten in the conference (12-0), and those former players were on hand when OSU traveled to Champaign. However the Bucks didn't take notice of such distractions and beat the Illini 95-66 to finish 14-0. The "usual suspects" — Lucas, Nowell, Siegfried and Havlicek — all played well. Hoyt and Knight added six each.

In final Big Ten and national statistics, several Buckeyes had bad luck. Lucas was second to Dischinger in Big Ten scoring again, with six more baskets and 72 fewer foul shots in 1961. While no other Purdue players were in the top 15, Buckeyes Havlicek (No. 9), Nowell (11) and Siegfried (14) all were. Lucas ended with 230 rebounds after getting 12 at Illinois. That left him 17 short of Bellamy, who was credited with 33 in his final (home) game against Michigan. Heavy pencil, that. Though Havlicek's field goal percentage was hurt by a four of 13 night, he still finished sixth in the nation. Siegfried was perfect at the foul line but not perfect enough. He made his only attempt to end up 56 of 61 in the conference, but needed to make three to pass Sam Gee of Indiana. Gee made 46 of 50 for 92% in 1958. Larry ended up second all time. Lucas, Havlicek and Siegfried joined Nelson (Iowa), Dischinger (Purdue) and Bellamy (Indiana) on the six man All-Big Ten first team selected by the Associated Press.

As an aside, here are the NBA statistics of the six man All-Big Ten Associated Press team —

NAME	YEARS	POINTS	AVERAGE	1ST OR 2ND TEAM ALL-NBA	TITLES
Lucas	11	14,053	17.0	5	1
Havlicek	16	26,395	20.8	11	8
Siegfried	9	5,960	10.8	0	5
Dischinger	9	9,012	13.8	0	0
Nelson	14	10,898	10.3	0	5
Bellamy	14	20,941	20.1	0	0

Also, Lucas, Dischinger and Bellamy had Olympic gold medals — and Havlicek and Siegfried should have. Nelson is a highly respected NBA coach. This was arguably the best all-conference team ever chosen in any league. Imagine, the "weak-links" of the team played nine years of NBA ball.

But pro careers were in the distant future at that time. Of more immediate concern was the NCAA Mid-East Regional, in Louisville. After the Louisville Cardinals (20-7 as an independent) beat Ohio University 76-70 in the first round they became OSU's first opponents.

By sagging on Lucas with as many as three men at a time, Louisville held him to two of seven from the field and nine points. Nowell and Hoyt only had one basket each, but Havlicek made eight of 13 and Siegfried had six of 12. With four of eight for Knight and two of four by Gearhart, OSU survived a 56-55 scare. Still, it took a Havlicek 25 footer with six seconds to go and a missed free throw by Louisville at the end for OSU to advance. "I was guarded so tightly I thought I was in jail," Lucas told *Sports Illustrated.*

Today Taylor says "We were coming off exams on Thursday and played Friday, so that didn't help. Also, by then we were playing not to lose rather than playing to win. But Siegfried made a key steal, and got pushed in the back hard enough to break the neck of most people. Somehow he kept control to make the lay-up and added a foul shot. We needed that three point play, because Lucas was knocked off his feet more times that night than the rest of his college career combined."

Then, Coach Taylor cited "The best defense on Lucas we've seen this season and our lack of movement" as reasons for the low scoring performance by Ohio State. He said "It was not a game we should be particularly proud of, except we came back (down 54-49 with 2:53 to play) and won. Tomorrow is another night ... and what happened tonight is forgotten."

No, it wasn't. Lucas thought about it all day, and responded with a 30-30, 33 points and 30 rebounds, against Kentucky. OSU avenged their loss the previous year to the Wildcats with an 87-74 victory that was worse than the score indicated. The Bucks shot 59.3% from the field, Kentucky 31.9%. OSU outrebounded them 51-29; heck, Lucas outrebounded them 30-29. Havlicek had an off night, two of 10 for eight points, but joined MVP Lucas and Siegfried (20 points) on the all-tournament team. Nowell bounced back with five of seven and 13 points, a good sign with surprising St. Joseph's next in the Finals in Kansas City.

The Philadelphia school had won 15 straight, raising their record to 24-4 by beating powerful Wake Forest in the regional final. The Demon Deacons may have been looking ahead to Ohio State.

Many teams had been looking forward to Ohio State. St. Bonaventure voted to refuse a berth in the NIT, where they normally played in postseason, in hopes of a re-match. As Coach Eddie Donovan said, "I put it up to the fellows on the team. They said they would like another shot at Ohio State. I may live to regret it." St. Bonaventure lost 78-73 to Wake Forest in the Mid-East Regional semi-final.

Bradley, the 1960 NIT champion, had a locker room slogan "You must beat ... to beat Ohio State." However Cincinnati closed the season with 18 straight victories to win the Missouri Valley Conference and send Bradley back to the NIT.

So St. Joseph's, with a pressure defense which had caused 30 turnovers by Wake Forest, had the only chance to beat Ohio State on Friday night, March 24. Their leading scorer was 6'6 John Egan, not to be confused with the Providence guard of the same name. This Egan was a muscular 215 pounder, averaging 22 points and 12 rebounds a game, and was next up for Mr. Defense of the Buckeyes, John Havlicek.

Havlicek ate him alive, holding Egan to eight points on three of 15 shots. St. Joseph's Coach Jack Ramsey said "We knew Havlicek was a great player ... but (he) was even better than we thought."

Ohio State led 45-28 at the half and won 95-69. Twelve Buckeyes played and 10 scored, led by Lucas with 29 and Siegfried with 21. The team shot 63%. They were in the final game, and looked ready.

In the second semi-final Cincinnati beat Utah 82-67. The team which could not get to the final game with the great Oscar Robertson was there without him.

Most experts had expected Utah to beat Cincinnati, then lose to Ohio State in the final. Billy McGill was the eye-catching scorer who grabbed attention, almost as much as Oscar Robertson had been. Cincinnati did not have that. The Bearcats were just a bunch of hard working local kids who played defense and passed the ball to each other on offense. In short, a very dangerous foe.

Like the Ohio State team, the Bearcat players were from the neighborhood. Among the starters, only 6'9 junior center Paul Hogue, from

Knoxville, Tennessee, did not play his high school ball in the Cincinnati area.

Hogue was their most prominent player nationally, the only one expected to have a chance at an NBA career. He was the leading rebounder at 12.5 per game, and averaged 17 points. Hogue was All-Missouri Valley Conference for the second year, but he was foul prone. It as generally assumed that Lucas was too skilled for him to handle. Hogue had scored 18 points and grabbed 14 rebounds against Utah.

Co-captain Bob Wiesenhahn was a 6'4, 220 pounder, a third year starter from Cincinnati McNicholas. When Lucas and Siegfried had dominated the all state teams in high school four years prior, Wiesenhahn had been honorable mention. He was recruited more heavily for football. The Bearcats leading scorer at 17.2 ppg, he averaged over 10 rebounds and played excellent defense. He made five of seven field goal attempts in the semi-finals.

The other co-captain was Carl Bouldin, who would pitch for the Washington Senators. From Cincinnati Norwood, Bouldin was a good shooter, having led the team in free throw percentage at 80% in his first year as a starter. He had shot holes in the Utah zone the night before with 21 points.

Tom Thacker, a 6'2 sophomore forward, had gone from star of the freshman team to All-MVC with Hogue and Wiesenhahn, while leading the team in assists. The Covington, Kentucky native was an excellent athlete; despite a poor shooting touch he played pro ball for seven years.

Tony Yates was not a typical sophomore. A veteran of the Air Force, the 23 year old was two years senior to any Buckeye. An excellent defender and ball handler, Yates was a coach on the floor. In fact he would serve as assistant coach at Cincinnati and Illinois in the 70's and 80's and head coach at his alma mater for six years through 1989. He had scored 13 against Utah.

Most of the substitutes were local as well, including reserve guard Tom Sizer, Lucas' teammate at Middletown High School.

Coach Ed Jucker had served as assistant to George Smith, who became athletic director when Oscar Robertson, starting guard Ralph Davis and forward Larry Willey graduated. Those three had taken the Bearcats to two Final Fours. Jucker recalls his reaction to the promotion. "I was sick. Our tickets were all sold out for 1961. Our opponents were thirsting for revenge, and I thought 'There go 55 of our 87 points a game'."

Remembering losses in 1958 and 1959 to Pete Newell's California team, which featured controlled offense and strong defense, Jucker had completely revamped the Cincinnati style. "I decided that maybe if we gave up only 40 points a game, we wouldn't need to score much. I wanted to keep the program respectable."

After struggling to a 5-3 record and dropping out of the national polls early in the season, Jucker's system had caught on. The team was unbeaten in 21 straight as they faced Ohio State in the final. They were more than respectable, they were second in the country.

The game for the national championship, the first time two teams from the same state had met in the finals, was almost anti-climactic. The reason was a roller-coaster consolation game between St. Joseph's and Utah. It went four overtimes before St. Joseph's won 127-120. John Egan, glad to be rid of Havlicek's defense no doubt, scored 42 points while Utah's McGill had 34. After that game the fans were exhausted. The opponents for the second game were emotionally spent, as they had alternately prepared to play, then to wait longer.

The first half of the final was close, more in the up-tempo style Ohio State wanted than the slow-down Cincinnati would have liked. There were 10 ties and five lead changes. OSU had the biggest lead at 20-13 with 12:04 to play. With seven seconds to go Lucas drew Hogue's third foul, and made two shots for a 39-36 lead. But Tony Yates threw in a 40 footer at the buzzer, Cincinnati had an emotional lift and only trailed by one point as they left the floor. "That was an important shot," recalls Bob Knight.

Underdog Cincinnati outplayed Ohio State in the second half. They led 52-46 with 11:46 to play. Then the Buckeyes finally exploded, scoring ten straight points in less than three minutes. Leading 56-52, Ohio State only scored five points in the next nine minutes of regulation.

Tom Thacker shot seven for 21 for the game, but his jumper gave Cincinnati a 61-59 lead with 2:15 to go. Bobby Knight drove around Wiesenhahn on the baseline for a lay-up to tie the game at 61. Cincinnati called time-out. Knight raced to the bench and "shouted 'Why didn't you tell me I could do that? I could have done that the whole game'," recalls Frank Truitt.

Thacker missed a jump shot with 0:04 to play, Lucas rebounded and called time. Siegfried threw a seventy foot pass to Havlicek who caught it and called time. With 0:01 to play a Havlicek lob to Lucas didn't connect. Overtime, 61 all. Cincinnati had won the second half 23-22, with almost half of Ohio State's points coming in less than three minutes.

The overtime was close until the very end. Hogue, who was not called for a foul after halftime, drew Lucas' fourth and made two free throws. Havlicek made a lone free throw. Wiesenhahn got a rebound basket and Lucas hit a jump shot. Yates made a foul shot. Siegfried made one of two free throws at 0:47 and the Bearcats had the ball and a one point lead. Yates hit two free throws and Thacker a jump shot. 70-65 Cincinnati.

After the game Fred Taylor said "They simply out-hustled us. Our kids have nothing to be ashamed of, I told them that. They pleased a lot of people all year and nobody goes undefeated forever. These kids have been good winners; now they can be good losers."

The most remarkable statistic of the game was that Ohio State had only taken 50 shots, including the overtime. For the year they had averaged 67 shots per 40 minute game, 1.7 per minute. They took 1.1 per minute against Cincinnati. Without question excellent defense played a part. However OSU, led by 10 of 17 by Lucas, shot 50%. For some reason they didn't have the movement they normally did.

Individually only Lucas played well, with 27 points and 12 rebounds to Hogue's nine points and seven rebounds. Siegfried hit six of 10 for 14 points but gave Bouldin too much room. The Cincinnati guard scored 16 points. Havlicek only took five shots, making one. He scored four points while Wiesenhahn led the winners with 17 points and nine rebounds. In *HONDO* he wrote "We made that walk back through the garage and the tunnel, and at four in the morning I was still sitting there in my uniform, refusing to believe we lost. I wanted to replay the game." Nowell was three of nine from the field, scoring nine points to 13 for Yates. Hoyt and Knight combined for nine points.

Today Gary Gearhart says "Both years I thought we played badly, but maybe that's because they took us out of what we wanted to do. My junior year (1961) we were much better; senior year it was closer but we were still better." Bob Knight says "We were better in 1961, but things didn't go well. We didn't play well in the second half or overtime — sometimes those things happen."

It was the most difficult defeat of The Golden Age, probably in Ohio State basketball history.

Governor Michael DiSalle unintentionally fanned the emotion of the time by issuing proclamations designating Fred Taylor as All-American coach, the team as an All-American team and the individual players as All-Americans of the century. He sent UC players and coaches letters of congratulations. Members of the Bearcat Booster Club wanted DiSalle impeached; UC students hung him in effigy. When State Auditor James Rhodes defeated DiSalle roughly 3-2 in November, 1962, it is safe to say Rhodes didn't lose any ground in the Queen City. Mark Twain wrote "I'd like to be in Cincinnati when the world ends, because it will happen 10 years later here." UC fans got the word on DiSalle — fairly or unfairly — much more quickly than that.

While John Havlicek buried his sorrows on the baseball field, Jerry Lucas dropped out of school. April 9 he began practicing with a group of AAU All-Stars for a trip to Russia to play various USSR junior national teams. The team, coached by National AAU champion Cleveland Piper coach John McClendon, included Les Lane from the 1960 Olympic team. They left New York April 18 and returned May 10.

V

1962: Tough Finish

"The trip to Russia was a wonderful cultural experience," recalls Jerry Lucas. "I learned for myself that people are people, that there were many similarities between Russian and American people. The farther we got from Moscow, the farther from the iron fist of the Kremlin, the friendlier the people got. We could converse, talk with them.

"I didn't go for the basketball," he says today. He had played 20 straight months, and needed a mental break from the game. Some Ohio State officials advised him not to go. "But I didn't know if I'd ever have an opportunity like that again.

"Our trip was taken just after Yuri Gagarin became the first man to orbit the earth." That took place April 12, 1961. "One game we played an entire section was roped off. He was announced just before the game started, and sat right in the middle of that section, without any of the other seats occupied." Some memories last a lifetime.

When he returned from Russia, Lucas was 30 pounds under weight. He stayed away from basketball. "I was dreading the start of the season," he recalls. But he finally got a break from the sport, and by the start of practice in October was "working harder than ever" according to Fred Taylor.

The national pollsters, looking at the NCAA final as a mistake, had OSU first and Cincinnati second. *Sports Illustrated* said "Ohio State will be the first Big Ten team to win three consecutive titles since Wisconsin did it in 1914. Once some of the newcomers adjust to the style of the 'big three' veterans — Jerry Lucas, John Havlicek and Mel Nowell — this edition of the Buckeyes may be stronger than

73

the national champions of two years ago … Fred Taylor has four first-class reserves and seven good sophomores to choose from in filling out a starting five. This is the best depth Taylor has ever had." SI predicted Bob Knight would start at forward and saw a three way struggle between senior Gary Gearhart, junior Dick Reasbeck and sophomore LeRoy Frazier at guard.

Taylor was more decisive. The five seniors would start the opener with Florida State "barring brain-lock by the coaching staff or injury." THE recruiting class started the season as a unit. Gearhart was evaluated as "very fast, quick … he's shooting better and will help in defense," Knight as having had "more consecutive good practices this year than the total for his career previously."

Meanwhile the football team had finished their season with eight victories and one tie. In the UPI poll they had a slight lead over un-beaten Alabama. It was the first time in the history of the rating that the football and basketball teams of the same school ranked first in the country at the same time.

Florida State threw a Louisville-type collapsing defense at Lucas, holding him to seven shots and 11 points. But OSU responded, par-ticularly Captain John Havlicek who hit 10 of 12 shots for 22 points, and the Bucks won 72-57. Guards Nowell, Gearhart and Reasbeck combined for 26 points. Knight scored four and junior Doug Mc-Donald chipped in seven.

More football news. First, the Cleveland Browns drafted John Havlicek in the seventh round. Browns Coach Paul Brown said "he could be a great football player." Since John had not played since high school, could this be serious? Yes, since there were 20 rounds the Browns could have taken him much later and gotten the same publicity. "I always liked football and I'll certainly talk to anybody about playing after college," said Hondo.

Of matters more relevant to the "the Horseshoe", the Buckeye football team slipped to second in the final UPI ranking. They got 15 first place votes and 311 points to 18 and 318 for Alabama. More im-portant, the Faculty Council voted 28-25 not to accept the Rose Bowl bid to play UCLA. The vote was taken because the Bowl pact between the Pacific Eight and the Big Ten had run out. A new pact would be signed but for 1961 there was no formal agreement binding the con-ference champions to appear. Each champion was invited individual-ly and the Faculty Council cited "over emphasis" as the reason for rejecting the offer. This set off riots, hurt football recruiting for years, caused animosity between the Athletic Department and certain teachers, may have harmed basketball recruiting and was bigger news nationally than the success of the Buckeye basketball team.

After Ohio State won a Wednesday game in Pittsburgh, Wichita (4-0) came to Columbus for a Friday game. Then the Buckeyes had to fly to Winston-Salem for a Saturday game with No. 5 ranked Wake Forest, which still wanted to prove something from their loss to OSU in the 1960 season. "There had been a schedule mix-up, and we told the kids it was critical to put Wichita away early so we could rest," recalls Taylor. "We got off to a good start, something like 41-11, and rested our starters for long stretches. The players rose to the occasion."

Lucas and Havlicek led the scoring, with help from sophomore Gary Bradds (15 points, seven rebounds). Doug McDonald, who replaced Knight in the starting line-up, made three of six shots and got five rebounds. OSU won 85-62.

* * * *

Doug McDonald had been third team All-Ohio his senior year at Fostoria. "It was a small, rural community but we had a good team," he recalls. "I think we were about No. 7 in the state," in Class AA, the large school category. "We had two players bigger than I was" says McDonald, who played for OSU at 6'5, 203 lbs., "so I got to play all over the court."

He actually visited Ohio State twice, and neither was very positive. "I was the guest of Indiana when they played at St. John Arena," says McDonald, recalling the 122-92 rout, "then I came for an official visit to Ohio State as well. I'll never forget eating Waldorf salad in the Student Union with Fred Taylor and flipping a wedge of lettuce right out of the bowl onto the table. What a klutz."

"I went to the University of Georgia, where Red Lawson was coach, because I wasn't sure I could play at Ohio State." McDonald's senior year in high school was the year Lucas and his classmates received so much publicity as Ohio State's freshman class. "But I got homesick after a week and called Fred to see if I could come to State. He said I should talk with the Georgia people, but if it was all right with them he'd like to have me at Ohio State. They said it was OK to leave — they didn't want me if I didn't want to be there. Rules about transferring were different then, so I went to Ohio State after all."

McDonald's freshman year was spent banging heads with the varsity, and his sophomore year mostly sitting on the bench. Still he played in 22 games, and learned about life in college sports by rooming with Larry Siegfried on the road. His junior year he found the perfect roommate — one with food. "John Havlicek had a refrigerator and I had a television. Plus his father was a butcher so we had plenty of meat. We were on the first floor in the dorm, but had to move to the 10th because people kept raiding the refrigerator."

Also as a junior he was seriously competing with Bobby Knight for the forward spot beside Havlicek. The first two games McDonald was the first sub at forward, after that he was the starter. Throughout the year they practiced against each other every night. As much as Knight wanted to play, there was no animosity toward McDonald, who took away what would have been his starting position. Mc-Donald says "Bob Knight is a perfect gentleman. My parents, and my wife's parents, think the sun rises and sets on Bob Knight."

* * * *

With Wichita out of the way, Taylor turned his attention to powerful Wake Forest. He had already forgotten the incident which almost prevented the game from being played.

"Bones McKinney had called me to explain that our team was going to have to stay on campus," says Taylor today. "We had some black players" — Nowell, Jim Doughty and Gene Lane — "and Bones said none of the hotels in the area would permit us to stay." College kids spend their lives "on campus", so what was the big deal? The reason — prejudice, which was intolerable. "I said, 'Bones, if you can't get us a hotel we will cancel the game'. He called back a short time later and we stayed at a Howard Johnson Motel."

Jack Graf remembers the bus ride to the game. "Jim Doughty and Gene Lane were sitting together in the front of the bus, and Doughty noticed that the white guys were sitting in the back. He said 'If people around here see our bus, they're going to think we're freedom riders'."

Billy Packer, now CBS basketball color man, then star senior guard at Wake Forest, remembers the game. "We thought we were better as sophomores and couldn't wait to play again. But Havlicek had become a great, great player. He guarded Len Chappell, who was 6'8 and John seemed to be just as big. He was the best coordinated big athlete I've ever encountered ... relentless ... a fierce competitor. We thought he was even better than Lucas. I thought that he and Doug Moe (of North Carolina, later head coach of the Denver Nuggets) were the best players I ever played against."

Havlicek held Chappell to six of 17 from the field and 15 points, while scoring 18 himself. He outrebounded the Deacon star 11 to 10, and led Ohio State to an 84-62 victory. Lucas, meanwhile, had a 23 point — 20 rebound night and Nowell outscored Packer in a head-up battle, 19-8.

"It was a shocking experience," recalls Packer. "We thought we would win but there was no question when they beat us at home. It took a lot out of our team — we ended December below .500. Nowell was a very good college player," feels Packer. "Quick, heady, sound defender ... Very few holes in his game. Because I said Havlicek was better takes nothing away from Lucas. He was great. A two handed rebounder with a controlled outlet pass, he was extremely unselfish and intelligent. He was a pure shooter, either facing or with his back to the basket. I would call him a small (Bill) Walton."

Packer speaks from first hand experience when he says he felt Havlicek was better than Lucas in college. However the average "expert" assumes that conclusion based on a comparison of NBA careers. Lucas was very good in the NBA, a five time all star. Hondo was a remarkable pro, and played in more NBA games than anyone except Jabbar and Elvin Hayes. Yes, he was an All-American, but as for college, Lucas was the one. As Dick Reasbeck says today, "Lucas never got the credit he deserved. Sure he was All-American, Player of the Year and everything but he was even better than people realized." Bob Knight observes "Jerry Lucas is still the best player that ever played in the Big Ten."

One week after the impressive win at Wake Forest, Loyola of Chicago came to town with a 5-0 mark on an average score of 95-61. Junior Jerry Harkness and four sophomores — John Egan, Ron Miller, Vic Rouse and Les Hunter — would combine to win the NCAA tournament one year later.

This year they were not quite ready for Havlicek and Lucas. John made 12 of 16 shots from the field, all six at the line, had 30 points for a new career high, and 14 rebounds. Lucas made six of eight baskets, all eight free throws for 20 points and got 18 rebounds. Nowell chipped in 17 points, Gearhart had nine points and several steals and the visitors received an education, 92-72.

A trip to St. Louis provided Ohio State's sixth game in the first two and one half weeks of the season. OSU was outrebounded by five and only shot 45% from the floor, but Luke and Hondo were the high scorers in a 61-48 victory. This time Gearhart had five steals. He and McDonald were clearly improving the Ohio State defense.

Fred Taylor wrote a column for *Newsweek* and rated the nation's top five as follows: Ohio State, Cincinnati, Southern California, Providence, Purdue. As the issue was hitting the newsstands, Wichita beat visiting Cincinnati 52-51 to end the Bearcats' 27 game winning streak.

After two seasons filled with pulled muscles, sprains and illnesses, Gary Gearhart seemed to be a fixture at the guard position beside Mel Nowell. He didn't supply the firepower of a Siegfried, but there were other scorers. His five points a game were sufficient, since he was making 45% of his shots and playing aggressive defense. Besides, junior Dick Reasbeck could come off the bench firing if necessary.

The Buckeyes cast Penn State aside 92-49 and headed for the West Coast. They were entered in the eight team Los Angeles Classic, which included five teams in the Top 11 in the country. First round opponent Washington (5-1) was ranked 29th and the other top teams — USC ranked fifth, West Virginia sixth, Purdue ninth and Utah eleventh — were in the opposite bracket.

Neither team shot well in the opener but Ohio State outlasted Washington 59-49. Gary Gearhart was undercut on a fast break lay-up attempt and missed the last 6:14. Reasbeck came in and scored nine points, third high behind Lucas (20) and Havlicek (12). That put the Bucks in the semi-finals against UCLA.

John Wooden was the coach at UCLA, as he had been for 15 years. Neither he nor anyone else expected much of his team. In pre-season he had said "We're a running club. Of course we don't always bring the ball with us when we run. And I have a guard (future All-American, NBA player and Bruin Coach Walt Hazzard) who's an excellent passer. He may not throw the ball where someone can catch it but he throws it beautifully." One writer had written "The Bruins had no height, no center, no muscle, no poise, no experience, no substitutes and no chance." The pessimism seemed well founded. The Bruins were 4-5 on the year.

After "setting basketball back 30 years (with the way we played against Washington)" according to their coach, Ohio State ran their offense nearly perfectly against UCLA. "They ran the offense sharply and read the cues so well," recalls Taylor today.

Ohio State set a tournament scoring record in their 105-84 victory, and Jerry Lucas shattered the tournament rebounding record by five with 30. He scored 30 points as well, to go 30-30. How does that look compared to a double-double today? After the game John Wooden sought out Lucas and said "I want to tell you that you are the most unselfish athlete I have ever seen." To the press Wooden elaborated. "Our team played its very finest, but Lucas was magnificent. It was *a pleasure to lose to such a man*. I have never said such a thing before. I never expect to again."

How can a man score 30 points and be called unselfish? He only took 13 shots, making 11. Four of his shots were tip-ins. He added eight straight foul shots. As for 30 rebounds in a 40 minute game, Fred Taylor remembers Jerry's ability on the boards. "He had great timing, as everyone knows, and his hands were big and strong. He hardly ever touched a ball without holding on to it. The other thing was his ability to jump again — bounce. If the ball hit the rim a second time he would land on the floor and jump back up very quickly. Some players don't jump back up at all."

Havlicek, Nowell and Reasbeck, starting for the injured Gearhart, each added 17. It was a performance for the ages.

Yet Ohio State freshman coach Frank Truitt saw something from the Bruins which impressed him. "After the game," recalls Truitt, "I went up to Coach Wooden and said 'Your team is very well organized. Some day you will coach an NCAA championship team'. He said, 'Oh no, I'll never be that lucky'."

Truitt was more correct than he ever imagined. The 1961-62 UCLA team ended December 4-7, but they won 14 of their next 16 games and easily won the NCAA Western Regionals. They lost to Cincinnati in 1962 but Wooden and various UCLA teams won 10 championships in the 12 seasons from 1964-1975.

In the other bracket Southern California had beaten Terry Dischinger's Purdue 80-63 and Billy McGill's Utah team 85-65, establishing themselves as a formidable opponent in the final.

The key to the Trojans was John Rudometkin, a 6'6 senior of Russian parents who was breaking scoring records at USC. As a junior he averaged 28.9 points and 12 rebounds for his 21-8 team, causing *SPORT* to have him first team pre-season All-America along with Lucas, Dischinger, McGill and Walker of Bradley. That put him ahead of DeBusschere (Detroit), Chappell (Wake Forest), Hogue (Cincinnati) and Nelson (Iowa). And a fellow named Havlicek, who couldn't wait to guard the star. This was Hondo's idea of fun.

But Fred Taylor surprised — and deeply disappointed — his defensive ace by assigning Rudometkin to Lucas and putting Havlicek on rugged 6'5 Ken Stanley. "John didn't like it, but I thought we matched up better that way," recalls Taylor.

The strategy worked. Ohio State won 76-66 and Lucas outplayed Rudometkin. Both shot 26 times but Jerry made 16 in scoring 38, the West Coast star made eight for 18 points. With a twinkle in his eye after the game Lucas asked Taylor "Did I finally shoot enough?" After grinning a "Yes," the coach began to talk about the many shots Luke had passed up.

Havlicek bounced back from his disappointment to score 17 points and grab 10 rebounds. Still it wasn't fair. What had poor Ken Stanley done to deserve this? Having Hondo guard you is bad enough, but when he's mad? That's not right. Stanley cast up 10 shots, made none and had one point. Obviously Havlicek had reacted to a decision he did not like exactly as a coach would wish. As his freshman coach Frank Truitt says "He did exactly what we asked, and he did it with enthusiasm."

"John had such a reputation as a defensive player by then," recalls Taylor, "that schools were printing in their media guides how many points their stars had scored against John Havlicek. When John would see one he'd often say 'He only got ___ points against me, the rest came after I went out of the game.' He was right, but that didn't stop anyone from kidding him." Just like nine months after the missed dunk.

Fortunately Havlicek and Lucas did not need a great deal of help against USC. McDonald was scoreless and Nowell shot one of eight. Reasbeck started but neither he nor Nowell could deal with 6'2 guard Chris Appel, who scored 25. Gary Gearhart, the top defensive guard, played a little and appeared to be healing after his bruised knee in the Washington game.

Still, the Buckeyes had now won a major tournament on each coast and Lucas had another MVP trophy. Havlicek was robbed of an all tournament selection. Taylor summed things up by saying "I don't really like these tournaments coming before the real season we play basketball — the Big Ten schedule — but I'll have to admit this one really prepared us for the league." And the league began at Northwestern, one week later.

Since the tournament was over December 30, Fred Taylor had thought it would be good for the basketball team to be able to see the Rose Bowl on New Year's Day. Unfortunately the fallout from the Faculty Council decision wouldn't allow it. "Ed Weaver said 'If the football team can't go to the Rose Bowl, by God you guys aren't going either'" recalls Fred Taylor. "Hey, we didn't vote against them."

After 10 pre-season games 6' Dick Reasbeck had moved to fourth on the team in scoring with 66 points. Since he only played in nine, his average was 7.3 points per game. Given his improved ball handling and Gearhart's experience as a first line substitute, Taylor decided to start the Martin's Ferry junior in the Big Ten opener.

* * * *

"I almost didn't go to Ohio State," says Reasbeck today. "I was leaning toward Duquesne. They had a great tradition and really wanted me." That's easy to understand, as he was second team All-Ohio while attending Bellaire St. John High School.

"In the Ohio All-Star game at Troy I played with Ken Glenn and Jim Stone (All-Ohioans from Cleveland East Tech) and was high scorer. Frank Truitt came into the locker room and said 'You're going to Ohio State'. Then John (Havlicek) called.

"I knew John in high school. I had a '56 Chevy and later drove us back and forth from college.

"This area (the Ohio Valley) is so sports minded. The rivalries between the little communities is unreal it's so intense. The Ohio River separates us from West Virginia, and that intensifies the rivalry. Lose a game to a school from there and you hear about it for a year. I never thought about going there (University of West Virginia). I did play against Jerry West in an outdoor league in the summer. Scored 28 points against him." Reasbeck pauses, waiting to deliver the punchline. "He scored 44 on me."

Today Reasbeck recalls that "Siegfried taught me a lot. He was sort of a 'Valley player'." That's high praise from other Valley players or from Fred Taylor, and means someone will never be intimidated and will always compete. Havlicek, Reasbeck and later Allan Hornyak set that standard for "Valley players" at Ohio State.

Dick roomed with Bob Knight in 1961-62. "Bob was a hard guy to get to know, he was more or less a loner. The room was full of those Zane Grey westerns, and he read them all the time. When a test came up he'd start reading the material two nights before and get an 'A'.

"One night," Reasbeck chuckles, "I had twisted my ankle and was on crutches. I woke him up to take me to the bathroom. He complained about it, but he did it."

* * * *

As the Big Ten season was opening, *Sports Illustrated* selected its "Sportsman of the Year". Jerry Lucas, also cited as being amateur basketball's finest player, received a Grecian amphora, the classic symbol of excellence of mind and body. Being selected over Roger Maris, who had just hit 61 home-runs, and other professional and amateur athletes was a great honor. (The issue sold for a quarter.)

Ohio State had no trouble at Northwestern, beating the Wildcats 85-62. Havlicek fired in 27 and everybody played. Back in Columbus, Gary Gearhart's wife Kay had a son.

Today Frank Truitt remembers that game for "the most beautiful play I ever saw in basketball. Gary Gearhart and Mel Nowell had a 2-on-1 fast break. Gary passed to Mel, and got the ball back. Gary dribbled and passed to Mel, who gave it right back for an easy lay-up. What team work."

Ohio State rolled over Michigan 89-64 and Minnesota 90-76.

"After we beat Minnesota Saturday night we tried to fly to Chicago but couldn't land," recalls Taylor. "We flew back to Minneapolis, and later caught a flight to Detroit. From Detroit we took a bus to Columbus, and arrived on campus about 5:00 a.m. Monday morning. The kids got very little sleep, then went to class. Meanwhile Purdue was practicing and resting all weekend. On top of that we put in a new defense to try to stop Dischinger, which we called 'an area pick-up'. They played him at center and either forward at various times. To give him a different look we had Luke guard him in the low post, John guard him in one corner or the high post, and Doug (Mc-Donald) take him in the other corner. Almost a match-up man-to-man."

As Taylor puts it, "the kids were great." They held Terry Dischinger to nine points and beat Purdue 91-65. Lucas had a typically remarkable game with 32 points and 25 rebounds. Havlicek had 16 points and 12 rebounds, and two reserves, back from injuries, were impressive. Gary Gearhart made three of six shots from the field and three of four free throws for nine points. He was now healthy again, and was an excellent substitute at guard. Jim Doughty, sidelined with a torn knee ligament after the Northwestern game just when he appeared ready to contend for Doug McDonald's starting forward position, scored ten points and grabbed five rebounds.

* * * *

Jim Doughty had been a 6'3 junior center on Frank Truitt's Columbus North team which beat Middletown. He was strong, well-built
and an excellent leaper. He had seven rebounds and 12 points in that
state semi-final victory. In addition to his athletic ability he was "easy
to coach", according to Truitt, had a "great sense of humor" says Mc-
Donald and "had the biggest smile in the world", in the words of Jim
Shaffer, a freshman in 1962.

"Since I grew up in Columbus and played for Frank at North, they
didn't have to do a whole lot to recruit me," remembers Doughty.

Jim had played freshman ball at Ohio State in 1960 with Doug Mc-
Donald and Dick Reasbeck, but had academic problems and was out
of school in 1961. "In high school the teachers took it easy on me because I was an athlete. I didn't have to study much and wasn't ready
for college," he says.

For all his athletic ability, Doughty did not have a very good
shooting touch. "I was a better shooter in high school than in college," he recalls. "I used glasses in high school but in college they got
knocked around and bent. Contacts were new at that time — mine
were about the size of a quarter. When I looked at direct light I was
temporarily blinded, and that could happen in the middle of a shot.
Goggles would have been good, but nobody used them then."

Doughty recalls rooming with Dick Reasbeck and sophomore
Gene Lane on road trips.

"Reasbeck," according to Doughty, "was a late sleeper."

One word with "the little man from the Valley", as television announcer Jimmy Crum referred to Reasbeck, and it is obvious that
"late sleeper" is a code.

"Jim Doughty had small hands, smaller than mine, but he could
jump," says Reasbeck. "When we roomed together he worried about
me when I stayed out late. At Minnesota one year I was out until 6:30
a.m. and I had to get the janitor to let me in." Late sleeper? "Jumpin'
Jim" was just covering for his roommate.

"Gene Lane was a tremendous reader," says Doughty of the 6'8
All-Ohioan from Cleveland East Tech who could have helped future
teams if he had stayed at OSU. "He used to read a paperback in two
hours. Ernie Biggs, our trainer, kept us from getting in trouble with
Fred several times. One time Gene and I ordered burgers and fries
from room service. Right after they arrived Ernie knocked on the
door with a scheduling change. We put the food in the closet because

83

we weren't supposed to have food in the room. When Ernie left he casually said 'Enjoy the hamburgers'. Then in Iowa City we went to a place called the Salt & Pepper Club, and got back late. As we were sneaking in we ran into Ernie. He just said 'You fellows have a good time?' He never said anything to Fred, or at least Fred never said anything to us."

* * * *

The following Monday Purdue and Ohio State had a rematch at West Lafayette. Unfortunately Gary Gearhart, who had just reclaimed his starting guard position with excellent play off the bench and in practice, was hurt again. A severe ankle sprain was expected to keep him out for two or three weeks. Gearhart just couldn't shake the injury hex throughout his career.

Purdue concentrated on the Ohio State big guns, holding Lucas to 13 and Havlicek to eight, but the other Buckeye starters came through in a 94-73 victory. Mel Nowell scored a season high 29 points, McDonald had his best of the year so far with 19 and Reasbeck had his second best total of 11. Purdue's Terry Dischinger scored a sub-par (for him) 23 points on five of 14 shooting. He only had one basket while playing 20 minutes in the second half. Havlicek had come up with yet another "incredible" effort as a defensive stopper, according to Taylor.

WLW-C broadcast many of the Buckeye games, initially in black and white and more and more in color. It cost $2,500 — $3,000 to air the game, and almost another $1,000 to do it in color, according to *Columbus Citizen-Journal* TV-Radio Editor Jo Reed. WLW-C showed the Northwestern game February 3 in color and Ohio State celebrated with a 97-61 victory to go 16-0, 6-0 in the conference.

Iowa was sent home with an 89-63 black eye.

Jerry Lucas made 14 of 15 field goal attempts to set the Big Ten standard and scored 34 points as OSU overwhelmed visiting Minnesota 91-66. He raised his NCAA leading field goal percentage to 66.3%, having made 14 of 17 in the first game with the Gophers. Minnesota Coach John Kundla said "That Lucas could score a million if he wanted to. He didn't take a single shot outside where he can really kill you. I honestly thought we played a pretty good game, but those guys made us look terrible. They're so darn strong it's awful."

The Bucks were sloppy at Michigan but had enough for a 72-57 victory in stretching their Big Ten win streak to 24 games. OSU stood

84

9-0 in the conference, and stayed at No. 1 in UPI for a record 25th week.

Michigan State stayed within ten points of Ohio State, the only team to do that so far this year, but still lost at home 80-72. Their strategy was to collapse on Lucas, recalling his 48 points a year ago. He still had a 20-20 game in points and rebounds. Doug McDonald took advantage of increased operating room and scored 24 points.

February 20 Lt. Col. John Glenn from New Concord, Ohio circled the earth three times in space capsule Friendship 7, the first American to orbit. Television beamed the flight to 135 million Americans. Zanesville native Fred Taylor said "I always said Muskingum County was out of this world."

The Buckeyes made Illinois (6-4) think they were lost in space, 102-79. All the starters scored in double figures topped by Reasbeck's 18 on nine of 11 from the field. Havlicek, who had been slowed by sore knees, said simply "They felt good" after 17 points and nine rebounds. Gary Bradds (14 points) and Jim Doughty (seven) were the leaders as the bench had 31 points. Unfortunately Gary Gearhart, who had been practicing, still wasn't ready for game action.

A victory at Iowa City 72-62 meant their third straight outright conference title, as the Buckeyes went 12-0. Wisconsin was 9-3 and each team had only two games remaining. Lucas, Havlicek and Nowell, who had meant so much to those title teams, keyed the victory.

As Ohio State prepared to travel to Wisconsin to play out the schedule, they were leading the league in scoring with 87.7 points per game and defense, allowing 66.7 points per contest. The winning margin was 21 points per game. Lucas led the league and the nation in field goal percentage, Havlicek was sixth in the nation and fourth — behind Luke, Nelson and Dischinger — in the Big Ten.

When Taylor's titlists arrived in Madison Friday March 2 the temperature was 29 degrees below zero, a chilly reception to be sure. That night in Hershey, Pennsylvania Wilt Chamberlain scored 100 points in Philadelphia's 169-157 defeat of the New York Knicks. The man to whom Lucas was so often compared as a high school player made 36 of 63 field goal attempts and 28 of 32 foul shots. Not likely Jerry would break that mark — it took several weeks for him to shoot 63 times from the field.

On March 3, before a capacity crowd of 13,472, Wisconsin played the game of their lives and overwhelmed Ohio State 86-67. The high scoring Badgers, who entered the game fifth in the nation in scoring, 85.5 ppg to sixth place Ohio State's 85.3, were led by 6' sophomore Don Hearden. A 10.9 ppg scorer before the game, Hearden had 29 points on 14 of 23 shooting. All-league forward Ken Siebel added 22 points as well. Not only were the champions unable to stop the home team from scoring, they couldn't hit the side of a barn from inside themselves.

Jerry Lucas was way below his high standard with eight of 18 shooting, while Mel Nowell had nine of 21. John Havlicek had a three of 15 game; McDonald and Reasbeck combined for one of eight. Gearhart and Doughty were the only subs to score, they were three of 12. From the floor the team shot 32%.

In his autobiography John Havlicek wrote "The thing I remember most is that after the game people just came pouring out of the stands to celebrate, and when it was over Lucas had in his hand five watches he had picked up off the floor. People had clapped so hard their watches had flown off." And the people were so excited they didn't notice.

The greatness of the Ohio State team was clear even in defeat. When Taylor took them out at 1:23 to play, Lucas, Havlicek and Nowell went to the Wisconsin bench to congratulate Coach John Erickson. He later said "They were every bit as graceful in defeat as they had been in victory." Havlicek immediately began to focus on the future. "Maybe we can duplicate last year's record of 27-1," he said. "That should be good enough." Indeed, that would take them through to another NCAA championship.

Three UPI voters selected Cincinnati (24-2) as the best team in the country, but Ohio State (22-1) stayed first with the other 32 voters. Wisconsin shot to No. 16. Past OSU foes Wake Forest (No. 8), Loyola (No. 9) and UCLA (No. 12) continued to move up.

Newspaper Enterprise Association released their 1962 All-America team, selected by NBA scouts, and announced the 1962 class of seniors the best of all time. Jerry Lucas made the first team and was proclaimed "probably the finest all around college basketball player in history." The evaluation continued "He has everything — size, speed, shots, desire. His only possible weakness is a tendency to pass up a shot because he's selfless." Terry Dischinger of Purdue, Billy McGill of Utah, Chet Walker of Bradley and Len Chappell of Wake Forest rounded out the first team.

Two Midwest players who would have great NBA careers, John Havlicek and Detroit's Dave Debusschere, led the second team which included Paul Hogue, Cincinnati center, USC star John Rudometkin and Jack Foley of Holy Cross.

As the Big Ten finalé with Indiana approached, the conference champions had more on their mind than the NCAA tournament. Every game with Indiana was a little special, since the 122-92 defeat three years before. This was the only game with the Hoosiers all year. The players and coaches were determined to bounce back after the Wisconsin loss. Finally there was the Big Ten scoring race, which held a great deal of interest considering no Ohio State player was involved.

After 13 games Terry Dischinger of Purdue and Indiana's Jimmy Rayl were tied with 429 points in 13 conference games, 33.0 ppg. The Buckeyes had long respected Dischinger as a talented foe who looked to score because his team needed that from him. "I was a fan of his," says 1960 Olympic teammate Jerry Lucas today. "We appreciated his skills and abilities, and felt he never got due credit. He was a great athlete and a fine person — 'our kind of guy', we thought."

"The kids sent Terry a telegram," recalls Coach Taylor, "which said something like 'we'll watch Rayl here, you make sure to take care of your game'. They wanted Terry to know Rayl wouldn't have a big game here." Like the 56 points he had scored against Minnesota.

Before a capacity crowd at St. John Arena, the Buckeyes blew out the Hoosiers 90-65. This group of seniors never lost a game at St. John, and they won the last game more convincingly than the final score suggested. They led 41-24 at the half, and increased the margin to 79-40 when Taylor began removing the seniors to well deserved ovations. To this point Rayl had only scored 13 points against the man-to-man defense of, at various times, Mel Nowell, Dick Reasbeck and Gary Gearhart. Coach Branch McCracken played his regulars the entire game, in hopes of helping Rayl score more. The Indiana junior ended with 25 for the game, making 10 of 25 shots. Terry Dischinger scored 30 points to earn his third straight scoring title.

Mel Nowell led all Buckeyes in his last home game with 22 points. Jerry Lucas took only nine shots but had 20 points, to go with 30 rebounds (19 in the first half!). John Havlicek scored only 10 points but grabbed 11 rebounds and harassed Hoosier Tom Bolyard into a six of 16 shooting game. Bob Knight had eight points, while Gearhart finished with two. The game brought tears to the eyes of many fans and maybe a few players. Everyone had forgotten Wisconsin, while remembering so much of the rest of a glorious three years. It was a time to look back, for a short while, before the NCAA tournament.

The team went right into final exams after Indiana, and squeezed in practice time as they could. Finals were particularly difficult for John Havlicek that quarter, since he was completing a 22 hour load he had taken during the height of the basketball season. "Certain required courses were not offered in the spring, and I was determined to graduate in four years," he explains simply today.

The same day Western Kentucky beat Detroit 90-81 to advance to play OSU in the Mid-East Regionals in Iowa City, Cincinnati and Bradley met in a play-off of their Missouri Valley Conference co-championship. The game, played in Evansville, Indiana, determined which team went to the NCAA and which to the National Invitational Tournament. Cincinnati won 61-46.

For the second straight year OSU was unanimously selected No. 1 by 35 UPI coaches. Fred Taylor was Coach of the Year again. Cincinnati, Kentucky, Mississippi State and Kansas State followed in the rankings.

Lucas and Havlicek made the UPI All-America first team, along with Dischinger, McGill of Utah and Chet Walker of Bradley. Mel Nowell and Doug McDonald were honorable mention. Lucas and Havlicek were All-Big Ten with Dischinger, Nelson and Rayl; Nowell was second team.

But such honors were not the primary concern of the team. The issue at hand was Coach Ed Diddle's Western Kentucky Hilltoppers, who triple teamed Jerry Lucas and shut him off early in the game. Then with 10:37 to play in the first half Luke was called for his third personal foul and was taken out of the game. He never got untracked, ending with a four of 13 shooting night. Yet Ohio State led at halftime 43-30 and won 93-73.

Sophomore Gary Bradds had his most important effort of the season, with 10 points and seven rebounds in a pressurized appearance. Doug McDonald scored 21, Havlicek 17 and the guard trio of Nowell — Reasbeck — Gearhart added 29. Fred Taylor said "The kids did just about as well as you could expect coming off of final exam week the way they did. 'Tex' (Bradds) gave us a big lift and McDonald was tremendous — it may have been his best game ever for us."

The nine point total tied Lucas' career low, which had come against Louisville's triple teaming in the Mid-East Regional semi-finals in

1961. After that 1961 game Ohio State met Kentucky in the Mid-East Regional final and Lucas scored 33 points in leading the team to an 87-74 victory. In 1962 Ohio State defeated No. 3 Kentucky 74-64 in the Mid-East Regional final. Lucas scored ... 33 points. Kentucky was in the wrong place at the wrong time for the second straight year.

Kentucky Coach Adolph Rupp said "It's awfully nice that all these people (14,500) got to see Mr. Basketball tonight," then added "the only way to stop a monster like Lucas is to graduate him."

While Lucas deserved center stage, John Havlicek was right beside him. Hondo had been the only other Buckeye in double figures with 13 points, and grabbed more rebounds (10) than anyone in the game except Jerry (who had 15). But most importantly Havlicek had shut off Kentucky's Cotton Nash. The outstanding sophomore averaged 23.8 ppg for the season but only made five of 19 shots in scoring 14 points against the Buckeyes' Secretary of Defense.

Fred Taylor said "Nash is great, but he bumped into a guy a little greater. If John ever did a better job it had to be on big Len Chappell — and I hope he can do it again." Wake Forest had won the Eastern Regional by overcoming a six point St. Joseph's lead with 1:06 to play and winning in overtime, 96-85.

It was like old home week at the NCAA Finals, played in Louisville at Freedom Hall. UCLA had won 11 of its last 12 games to face Cincinnati, which had rolled through the Mid-West Regional. Their game followed the third match-up of Lucas-Havlicek-Nowell et. al. versus Len Chappell and Billy Packer.

Wake Forest (21-8) had won 12 games in a row, and was described as "a better team than the one we beat," by Frank Truitt. "They're using their size now and they're more experienced." Chappell had led the team in scoring in every game, and had scored 50 points against Virginia. He averaged 30.3 per game, despite his low game of 15 against Havlicek in December. Packer, son of the head coach of Lehigh University, was the smallest man in the tournament at 5'10 but effectively ran the show and scored 13.7 ppg for the season.

The game started slowly for Ohio State. Packer and his back court mate Dave Wiedeman were hitting from outside so Gary Gearhart went in to provide more perimeter defense. He knocked in a jump shot to break the sixth tie of the game and give OSU a 19-17 lead at 11:16 to play. The Bucks extended that to 46-34 at the half and won 84-68.

Chappell led both teams in scoring with 27 and rebounds with 18, but Havlicek rose to the occasion. The "big man from the Valley" scored 25 points and grabbed 16 rebounds. He got plenty of help from his teammates. Lucas scored 19 and added 16 rebounds. McDonald and Reasbeck both scored in double figures, and Doughty came off the bench with eight points and five rebounds.

Wake Forest Coach Bones McKinney said "I thought Ohio State played as great a game as any college team I've ever witnessed. Any doubt in my mind that they were not great was certainly dispelled. Fred Taylor can certainly be proud of this team. They're definitely the No. 1 team and I hope Lucas' knee is OK."

THAT was the question.

"When I came down on my heel I had a very sharp pain in the knee," Lucas explained. "I was up in the air after a rebound and turned when I started to come down. Someone bumped me lightly and I came down on my heel, twisting it."

At the time Friday semi-finals were followed by Saturday final games. Lucas would have less than 24 hours to recover. Would he play? "Will the sun come up in the east?" was his answer to that question. The real question was, how well would he play?

Cincinnati had dodged UCLA 72-70 as Tom Thacker made a 25 footer with 0:03 to play to decide it. It was Thacker's only basket in seven attempts.

The 1962 Cincinnati team was a more difficult opponent for Ohio State than the 1961 version. Paul Hogue was back at center, and had added to his offensive arsenal while cutting down on his fouls. He averaged 16 points and 11.9 rebounds for the year, but scored 36 and grabbed 19 in the UCLA game. Tony Yates returned as the floor leader and Tom Thacker joined him in the back court. Both were experienced juniors and excellent defenders. Co-captains Bob Wiesenhahn and Carl Bouldin had graduated, but they were replaced by two of the best sophomores in the country. George Wilson, 6'8, had led Chicago Marshall High School to the Illinois state championship as a high school All-American. He was a rugged rebounder. Ron Bonham, 6'5, had a remarkable jump shot and was referred to by many as the best Indiana high school player since Oscar Robertson. He averaged 14.3 ppg as a sophomore.

Despite the improvement in offensive firepower, the key to the success of the Bearcats in 1962 was the same as in 1961 — defense.

The Bradley team which the Bearcats beat 61-46 to qualify for the NCAA averaged 80.6 points for the season.

Here is the way Ray Cave, basketball writer for *Sports Illustrated*, saw the match-up before it was played:

A Cincinnati-OSU final would pit the country's best defense against its finest offense. Jucker has managed to convince George Wilson that you can win recognition as a defensive player, and Wilson is much improved since December, when he was tense and overeager. Bonham, the other starting sophomore, is the team's only defensive weak spot, but he, too, has improved, and he has become the Bearcats' best shot as well. Paul Hogue is as powerful and awe-inspiring as ever. Tony Yates, at guard, could hardly get better. One sidelight of the seething feeling behind an Ohio State-Cincinnati final is that Ed Jucker is incensed because for two years Ohio State has always led the weekly national polls, because Cincinnati has no player who has made first string All-America and because Fred Taylor has twice been named Coach of the Year. Jucker thinks Hogue should be a top-ranked All-America. He is wrong there, but he does have a player who, if it were not for the absurd voting system, would be one and richly deserves it. That is Tony Yates who, though relatively unrecognized, is the best basketball technician on this team.

Finally Cincinnati has played a slightly tougher schedule than Ohio State this year, and played it well, winning its last 16 straight. It is a beautifully disciplined, formidable team. "People said we were lucky when we won last year," said Paul Hogue angrily last week. "We're going to show them who is boss."

Perhaps. But this isn't last year in Columbus either. Ohio State now has a strong bench. The team has been looking at the movies of the 1961 game and is understandably appalled at what Taylor calls "the way we just stood around." This year a man who is standing around can be quickly replaced. In 6-foot-5 Doug McDonald the Buckeyes have a much improved forward who gives them a strong man where they were weakest last season. If Cincinnati's Wilson proves too tall and tough under the backboards, Taylor is now in a position to try something that would surprise everyone. He could bring in 6-foot-8 Gary Bradds, who is sharp-elbowed and most enthusiastic, as a forward, to give Lucas some giant-size help.

Most important of all, however, is the play of Lucas. He has his ordinary games. He is, by nature, a quiet, self-effacing, cooly professional young man. His wrath is rare indeed. But he is what Adolph Rupp would call "a bad man to rile up." There is every likelihood that Lucas would take the floor against Cincinnati plenty riled up. Ohio State might need 40 points out of Lucas that night. Those 18,000 screaming people in Louisville may well see Lucas score that many. Favored or not, our choice is Ohio State.

But Lucas couldn't score 40 points, or even his average of 22. "When we went out on the floor, I knew right away he wasn't going to be as effective as usual," recalls Havlicek. Luke made only five of 17 shots, and scored 11 points. Meanwhile Paul Hogue scored 22 and took a game high 19 rebounds. Cincinnati won 71-59. Hogue won the MVP trophy, the first time Lucas had been in a college tournament — three NCAA Regionals, three NCAA Finals and two invitationals — and not been selected Most Valuable Player.

For days after the game people asked if the knee had bothered Lucas. Stoically he was the sportsman, and lied. "No, it didn't, " he would say. "Hogue bothered me, but the knee didn't." When Taylor was asked he always said "Luke says the knee didn't bother him." That is called a non-answer.

Two days after the game Ed Jucker told the UC Boosters Club luncheon "It is a credit to Lucas, an All-American off the floor as well as on, and Ohio State for not using his knee as an alibi. Lucas was certainly slowed down Saturday night. How much it bothered him no one knows."

Everyone who saw the game knew it bothered him. He played in pain, and with a fraction of normal mobility. He had dominated Hogue the year before, 27 points to nine and 12 rebounds to seven. This time he was outplayed, by one man, straight up. It had never happened before in his college career.

Now that the statute of limitations has passed, and an honest answer won't bring coast to coast cries of "poor sport", what was the impact? "It was a problem," says Lucas of the left knee, bandaged almost completely from the bottom of his shorts to the top of his sock. "I was about 30%, if that. I probably shouldn't have played. Bradds would have done a good job, maybe the players would have rallied around him."

Bradds had done a good job. He played the final half at forward and scored 15 points. Would OSU have won if Lucas had been 100%? Not necessarily, for several reasons.

Sports Illustrated later pointed out the superiority of the Cincinnati back court. For this game, at least, that was true. Mel Nowell made four of 16 from the floor. His nine points, eight by Reasbeck and two from Gearhart did not compare favorably to the 21 by Thacker and the 12 by Yates.

Havlicek had an off night from the floor, with five of 14. He scored 11 points, to Bonham's 10, and got nine rebounds. He was the victim of a coaching move by Ed Jucker which worked better than the Cincinnati coach could have hoped.

Jucker took his best shooter out of the offense. Bonham was such a threat that Havlicek had to concentrate on him, even when Bonham was outside the range of most college players. The other Bearcats then played 4-on-4 against the less physical Buckeyes, without being concerned about Havlicek's excellent weak side defensive help or his rebounding. An added benefit, which may not have been intended, was that Hondo was less effective on offense.

Since many players rest on defense in order to have energy for offense, this theory may sound strange. But Havlicek was not like most players — his energy and competitiveness were almost unlimited. While giving away 3" and 40 lbs. to Len Chappell, Havlicek scored 25 points in the semi-finals. He had 30 while chasing fleet Jerry Harkness of Loyola, and 24 against Eric Magdanz of Minnesota, fourth leading scorer in the Big Ten. If there was ever a player who rose to the challenge it was John Havlicek. He got mad when he wasn't allowed to guard John Rudometkin, the Southern California All-American. When he was challenged on defense he usually met that challenge *and* excelled on offense.

Fred Taylor was asked about the theory almost three decades after it might have helped, and said "With John it might have worked that way."

Two facts seem clear in hindsight. First, the best player in America, Jerry Lucas, was far below par. Second, he had been 100% as a junior and Ohio State had lost to a Cincinnati team which was not as difficult a test as the 1962 team. Ohio State might have lost with a healthy Jerry Lucas. "They were better in 1962," says Bob Knight, "even if Lucas had been 100%."

At the Appreciation Banquet a very emotional Jerry Lucas spoke of the burdens and responsibilities he had felt during "the greatest four years of my life," and thanked almighty God for the opportunities. Fred Taylor said "Luke always seemed to have that icy calm and nothing seemed to get him. But he's a very intense young man with a tremendous sense of appreciation for other people."

* * * *

After the season the five seniors embarked on a barnstorming tour, playing 23 exhibition games in Ohio, Pennsylvania and West Virginia. It was a fitting way to wrap up their college careers, since they had first met while touring as high school seniors.

The tour caused John Havlicek to miss the Ohio State baseball season, but he enjoyed being with his friends one last time. "We got $4,300 a piece," recalls Hondo. "The first game we made $407 each. I remember because Mel Nowell calculated $400 times 23 and bought a new Bonneville convertible."

* * * *

One of the great groups of basketball players to ever enter a university was gone. They had won a national championship, two second place trophies, three Big Ten titles, three NCAA Regional titles, a pre-season tournament title on each coast, and 78 games against six losses. They never lost a game at home, and never lost a Big Ten game when the conference race was in question. They had a winning record against every school they played except two — Utah (0-1) and, of course, Cincinnati (0-2).

Many people think the 1960 team was the best, others assume it was. There are several convincing arguments for that choice, primarily that they won the last game of the year. They were clearly the best team in the country that year, but does that mean they would have beaten the 1961 or 1962 team in a game of fantasy basketball? Maybe, maybe not.

The 1960 team was the deepest of the three. Their second team of Furry and Knight at forward, Nourse at center, and Hoyt and Gearhart at guards was a pretty good group of players. It had the most pro players, as the entire first string — Roberts, Havlicek, Lucas, Siegfried and Nowell — all played in the NBA. John Havlicek, Larry Siegfried and Bob Knight feel that future Buckeye teams were a little weaker each year. Joe Roberts says today that "Jerry Lucas was never better than his sophomore year."

But John Havlicek got better. He shot 46.1% as a sophomore, 53.9% as a junior and 52.0% as a senior, raising his scoring average every year. And Larry Siegfried was better as a senior than he had been as a junior in turmoil. Lucas shot less as a junior, so his scoring was down, but he got 28 more rebounds. The 1961 team only lost one game, went undefeated in the Big Ten, won an impressive holiday tournament in Madison Square Garden by playing three strong New York teams and swept through a more difficult schedule than either the 1960 or 1962 team had. Despite the impressive schedule, the 1961 team had the best total defense of the three teams, anchored by excellent defenders at center in Lucas, forward in Havlicek and guard in Siegfried.

It would be easy to think that the 1962 team, minus Roberts, Furry, Siegfried and Hoyt, with Mel Nowell's shooting down from previous years, was the weakest of the three. Yet Havlicek had continued to improve, Lucas increased his rebound totals again and McDonald, Reasbeck, Doughty and Bradds were excellent additions. The five man senior class was obviously most experienced in its final year. The 1962 team steam rolled its opposition. Only one victory was closer than 10 points, an 80-72 win at Michigan State. They won by 22 at NCAA semi-finalist Wake Forest, by 21 against NCAA semi-finalist UCLA and by 10 against nationally ranked USC in Los Angeles.

Maybe the 1960 team was the best, but the other two offer a strong case as well. Possibly the greatness was in the continuity of excellence for three straight years, a greatness that was never tarnished by hint of scandal or suspicion of impropriety. The worst thing that happened was probably when Lucas lied about the extent of trouble with his knee, and that was done in the name of sportsmanship.

* * * *

Statistics can be dull, but they are helpful in understanding the dominance which Jerry Lucas had over college basketball when he played.

There were four players who had a field goal percentage of over .600 for a season in 1960, 1961 or 1962. Three of them were named Jerry Lucas, as he led the nation every year. His 1960 mark of .637 was the best ever for someone taking as many shots as he did that year. It was farther ahead of the second place finish, .576 by Paul Hogue of Cincinnati, than second place was ahead of twentieth. Luke's three year mark of .624 broke the existing career record of .605 by Joe Holup of George Washington. Jerry Lucas was the best shooter in the history of college basketball when his eligibility ended.

Additionally Lucas won the NCAA individual rebounding championship twice, as a junior and a senior. He was the first player to ever win five national individual titles in a college career.

There is an old saying to the effect that "he may not be in a class by himself, but it doesn't take long to call roll." That describes Jerry Lucas: he may not have been the best shooting, scoring, rebounding center for a championship team in the history of college basketball, but he was in a small group. Here's the group, in order of championships: Lew Alcindor, UCLA, 1967-8-9, three; Bill Walton, UCLA, 1972-3, two; Jerry Lucas, OSU, 1960, one. The number of championships won is not debatable. The relative merit of individual statistics, on the other hand, is like beauty — it's in the eye of the beholder. Following is a record of the three year careers of Alcindor, Walton and Lucas.

	GAMES	PPG	FGP	RPG	W-L	NCAA FINISH
Soph. Year						
Lucas	27	26.3	.637	16.4	25-3	1
Alcindor	30	29.0	.667	15.5	30-0	1
Walton	30	21.1	.639	15.5	30-0	1
Junior Year						
Lucas	27	24.9	.623	17.4	27-1	2
Alcindor	28	26.2	.613	16.5	29-1	1
Walton	30	20.4	.650	16.9	30-0	1
Senior Year						
Lucas	28	21.7	.611	17.8	26-2	2
Alcindor	30	24.0	.635	14.7	29-1	1
Walton	27	19.3	.665	14.7	26-4	3
Career						**TITLES**
Lucas	82	24.3	.624	17.2	78-6	1
Alcindor	88	26.4	.639	15.5	88-2	3
Walton	87	20.3	.651	15.7	86-4	2

The numbers seem to say that for scoring the order was Alcindor, Lucas, Walton; for field goal percentage, Walton, Alcindor, Lucas; for rebounding Lucas, Walton, Alcindor. That would make each first, second and third in the three categories. The difference between the three players is far from clear, but no other center compares to Jerry Lucas, Lew Alcindor and Bill Walton for team and individual success for a college career.

VI

1963: The Rose Bowl Rule

The best center in college basketball, the best forward in the history of Ohio State and a second team All-Big Ten guard who started every game in the past three years had all graduated. Two other veterans were gone.

Captain Doug McDonald's response at the pre-season Agonis Club Tip-off dinner was "We hope to give you the kind of basketball you are used to. We know we're missing some players — what are their names?"

It was a good line, but how did he really feel?

"We had some apprehension going into that year. We expected to be decent, but maybe not co-champions of the Big Ten. As we played together we got more and more confident," says McDonald.

Opinions were varied about the team that lost 69% of its points and 74% of its rebounds in the graduation of Jerry Lucas, John Havlicek, Mel Nowell, Gary Gearhart and Bob Knight, and the scholastic ineligibility of former 6'8 All-Ohio center Gene Lane of Cleveland East Tech. Lane would have been a junior. The OSU Media Guide stated the team would "rate no more than a 'dark horse' label ... The Buckeyes could be very troublesome ... winning a fourth straight championship is not likely, as the team has only limited experience. Lack of a strong scoring punch and board control are other causes of concern."

Dell Sports picked eventual NCAA champion Loyola of Chicago as the best team in the Midwest and ranked Illinois, Wisconsin and Indiana 1-2-3 in the Big Ten. Regarding Ohio State, "The giants have departed but don't count the Buckeyes out of the running; the rest of the league is still wary of Coach Fred Taylor's big, strong crew, which is not without experience."

United Press International had them #25 in the country, following Big Ten teams Wisconsin (9), Illinois (13) and Indiana (20). Cincinnati, Duke, Kentucky, West Virginia and Loyola were the top five.

Sports Illustrated reported Coach Taylor had cut short a practice session and taken the team to dinner, suggesting this might take the place of post-season celebrations. But they did pick the Buckeyes #12, after Illinois (10) and in front of Indiana (19) and Michigan (honorable mention). An unnamed Big Ten coach was quoted as saying "Let me tell you one team the experts are kissing off too early — Ohio State." Comments were made about the six players expected to play the most, returning senior starters 6'5 Doug McDonald and 6' Dick Reasbeck and juniors 6'8 Gary Bradds, 6'4 Jim Doughty, 6'4 Don Flatt and 6'3 Dick Taylor, no relation to the coach.

Coach Taylor walked the tight rope, saying "This is going to be a pretty good basketball team, make no mistake about it. Don't try to compare them with our teams of the past ... but we do want to do the same thing again (win the Big Ten)."

Don DeVoe, after 19 years as a Division I head coach, remembers a confident team. "There was never any doubt in our minds we would win and we would compete for the Big Ten title. We didn't expect to miss a step. We had great confidence in Coach Taylor and ourselves. After practicing against the best every day, we expected to be tough."

During six weeks of pre-season practice, Fred Taylor, Frank Truitt and Jack Graf emphasized the need to make "one more pass than last year". That would unify the group, and result in better shots.

"Every pre-season we stressed the need for each person to carry out his offensive assignments every night," says Taylor. "One night the #2 defender on the other team has you, and you may not score much, but you can make him work and open things up for a teammate. The next time maybe the #4 defender has you and it's your night to score. Always go all out and the team never misses an opportunity from a match-up."

Taylor thought consistent effort would result in balanced scoring — "on a given night any one of these guys is going to be the leading scorer," he said in November.

As the opening game with Utah State approached, the top six Buckeyes were just as *Sports Illustrated* had forecast.

Captain Doug McDonald had been well trained for his role as team leader, having roomed with Captain Larry Siegfried as a sophomore and Captain John Havlicek as a junior. His junior year he shot 51% from the field, trailing only Lucas, Havlicek and Bradds, and averaged 7.8 ppg. His 24 points at Michigan State had probably saved that 80-72 victory; his scoring appeared to be more important this year than last. "He was a gentleman basketball player," remembers Fred Taylor. "His block out technique was flawless, in fact he did all the little things. Very unselfish."

Dick Reasbeck, a regular throughout the past Big Ten season, had improved his defense and would have more opportunities to launch the quick half-jump, half-push shot which had earned him the nickname "Shotgun". The previous year his high game was 17, but the Martins Ferry native had 49 points in one game as an All-Ohioan at Bellaire St. John. For the team to succeed, Reasbeck had to score much more than the 7.8 points of his junior year, and he was ready. He liked to shoot.

Gary "Tex" Bradds, coming off a 15 point second half against Cincinnati and a .694 field goal percentage for the year, gave fans reason for optimism. At little Greeneview High School in Jamestown, Ohio he had scored 65 points in one game. Kentucky had wanted him badly. Jerry Lucas said Gary was the best college center he had played against — better than Imhoff or Bellamy or Hogue. But Jerry was so gracious, was he serious?

Columbus North graduate 6'4 Jim Doughty had earned the other forward spot with his physical play inside. He had moved past Bob Knight to become the first forward substitute last year, but, like Bradds, had never started a college game. Still, as the center on the only team to beat Middletown when Jerry Lucas played there, he had faced challenges before.

Fifth starter would be 6'3 junior Dick Taylor from Cuyahoga Falls High School, who the coaches felt might become a defensive stopper like Siegfried had been. Erratic as a sophomore, Dick had lost 20 pounds over the summer, improved his ball handling, and was playing with increased confidence.

First sub would be Don Flatt of Brooklyn, a guard as a sophomore but now primarily a forward. He had been recruited by Jerry Brondfeld, an active recruiter for Woody Hayes in New York. When Frank Truitt called to say hello from the floor of the NCAA championship game in California in 1960, the honors student in electrical engineering decided to become a Buckeye.

The season opener was December 1 at home with Utah State, 22-7 in 1962. The Bucks trailed 34-31 at halftime, and struggled until a Jim Doughty drive put them ahead to stay at 49-48. The 62-50 victory was not accomplished by balanced scoring, but Gary Bradds had 32 points and 14 rebounds to suggest that center would not be a weak point for the team. In addition to his key drive, Doughty made a great hustle play to turn a certain breakaway basket into a traveling violation at a crucial time. He added 12 rebounds. Utah State coach LaDell Anderson was impressed by OSU's 46-43 rebound advantage, saying "We've got some big strong boys, but Ohio did the best job anybody has ever done blocking us out."

Despite an opening victory over a strong opponent, there were some causes for concern. Captain McDonald only registered five points and four rebounds, though he did hold highly regarded Wayne Estes to 10 points. Reasbeck was five of 16 from the field and ball handling errors resulted in Dick Taylor being replaced by sophomore Dick Ricketts.

Two days later St. Louis came to town, with three regulars back from the team the Bucks had defeated 61-48 last year. Gary Garrison, a 6'8 junior, burned Bradds for 13 points in the first 15 minutes but could add only nine more. Meanwhile the skinny center ("Gary never weighed more than 180 lbs. at Ohio State," recalls his father, Donald Bradds) hit 10 of 15 field goal attempts, and added 11 foul shots, to total 31 points. Doughty, with 17 points and 11 rebounds, and Reasbeck, six of 13 from the field plus six rebounds, played well. Dick Ricketts and Don Flatt chipped in off the bench in the 84-59 victory.

The Bucks blasted Virginia 70-46.

West Virginia, "a much better, stronger team than last year (24-6)" according to Coach George King, came to town December 8 for the Buckeyes' fourth game in the first week of the season. Star of the team was senior All-American guard Rod Thorn, who would play eight years in the NBA; future Mountaineer head coach Gale Catlett was a forward. *Sports Illustrated* had picked them #5 in pre-season, UPI #4. This game was a major test.

100

Emotions were so high that after three minutes and 25 seconds each team had five turnovers. Neither team shot well, 41% for OSU and 44% for West Virginia. Trailing 37-34 at the half, the Bucks came back to win 76-69 to go 4-0. Heroes were plentiful. Bradds scored 19 despite being the focus of changing defenses, and added 20 rebounds. Doughty had 17 boards as the home team won that battle 54-43. All starters had nine points or more. Of all the bright lights, though, the brightest was defensive play of Taylor and Reasbeck on Thorn, who made only nine of 23 attempts.

Texas Christian came to town December 15 and left with a 74-62 loss, so the Bucks took a 5-0 record on their first road trip. They had games at Detroit December 22, Butler December 27 and Wichita December 29.

Detroit was no problem. Dick Reasbeck scorched the nets with 12 of 17 from the field for 28 points, Bradds had 19 and Ricketts and Taylor joined them in double figures. Bradds had 16 rebounds and sophomore Tom Bowman gathered 12. OSU 101-66.

Butler was a struggle. The Buckeyes, now ranked No. 3 in the country, had to come back from a 28-20 halftime deficit to win 66-62. Gary Bradds, starting to make the All-America checklists, led both teams in scoring (24) and rebounding (16). The stage was set for a trip to Wichita State to play Coach Ralph Miller's Shockers, beaten soundly by the Lucas-Havlicek Buckeyes in the past two years. It was a trip which remains clearly in the minds of the Buckeyes today, particularly three sophomores on that team.

"The weather was bad, and the plane was grounded," remembers then sophomore Jim Shaffer. "We had to ride in a train across Kansas to get there."

"When we got there we went to eat at a buffet," recalls Tom Bowman. "We waited in line for a while, then a bell rang. All the employees got in line, wiped out the buffet and there was no food left. Fred got a refund and we ate some place else, but I never really understood what happened."

"The place was called 'The Pit', and I remember feeling like a gladiator," says Dick Ricketts. "It was packed. We came out first, and everybody held up a newspaper, like they were reading it. When they came out the place went crazy."

Wichita State was big and strong, led by future NBA stars 6'7 Dave "The Rave" Stallworth and Nate Bowman, who would be teammates on the New York Knicks' 1970 championship team. They outrebounded the Bucks 34-28, and shot 58% — far over their average. Both Bradds and Reasbeck fouled out in the 71-54 loss. Reasbeck, also nicknamed "Weiner" because he had some hot dog tendencies, departed by going to the "W" at half court and spitting on the floor. Then he walked to the bench and raised a well known salute to the crowd. It was not "We're No. 1". Nor was it wise.

"I remember standing by the court, feeling sad that we lost, and this big man grabbing me from behind and pushing me into the locker-room. It was Fred — he knew I shouldn't be hanging around," says Ricketts.

Tom Bowman remembers what happened next. Nothing. "We were afraid we wouldn't be able to get to the bus. Turned out to be no problem. Probably a good thing we lost," he recalls.

St. John Arena and a capacity crowd of 13,497 looked pretty good two nights later, even if it was New Years Eve. Gary Bradds set an Arena scoring record with 45 points as Ohio State beat Brigham Young 97-91. Doug McDonald exploded for 24 points and Doughty added 12. The Buckeye guards shot poorly, five of 23, but ran an offense which only committed eight turnovers.

As calendar 1962 ended, Big Ten opponents knew that Ohio State was indeed a power and Gary Bradds at nearly 24 ppg had become a headache of extreme proportions.

* * * *

"When Gary was two or three years old we got one of those toy baskets with a bell which sounded when the ball went through the hoop," remembers Donald Bradds, Gary's father. "He used to play by the hour, and every time that ball went through he'd jump up and clap his hands. We never got tired of hearing that sound."

And Gary never got tired of seeing the ball go through the hoop. He scored 1655 points in three seasons of varsity play at Greeneview High School in Jamestown, located in Southwestern Ohio. He holds many scoring records today for what is now called Gary Bradds Memorial Gymnasium. His senior year he had eight games of 40 or more points while averaging 33.2 ppg.

Yet despite those scoring totals, few people thought he was a player. United Press International named sixteen players to their All-Ohio Class A team in 1960 but Gary Bradds was not among them. Only two major college programs recruited him hard, Ohio State and Kentucky.

As a junior in high school Gary had started dating a freshman named Eileen Ford. They were married several years later, but Gary's desire to attend college close to Jamestown, Eileen and his family would heavily influence his selection of a school. The closest major college was Cincinnati and a UC graduate, Fred Morr, Ohio's director of natural resources, was a friend of the Bradds' family. It might have been a natural choice for Gary, and could have resulted in four consecutive national championships for the Bearcats, but it never happened.

A Cincinnati scout, who remained anonymous, explained why to *SPORT* magazine for their March, 1964 article on Bradds: "We heard this farm kid scored 60 points in a game so I went to look. He scored, but only because he was a head taller than everybody else. His coordination was unbelievably poor. Like a guy throws him an easy pass, and it goes right through his hands and off his chest. We didn't even write him a letter. But when I think how he's improved, I could jump off Newport Bridge."

Though there weren't a large number of schools after Bradds, Kentucky and Ohio State went to war for him. "Adolph Rupp took our family out to dinner several times," remembers Mr. Bradds. "They used the hard sell, compared to Ohio State."

Gary talked about that hard sell, delivered personally by Coach Rupp, the Baron of the Bluegrass. "He guaranteed I'd be a starter as a sophomore at Kentucky. And he kept on saying Lucas was so good I'd never play at Ohio State while Jerry was around. That was a big challenge. I had to see."

Gary loved challenges, and never lacked for confidence. His high school opponent Don DeVoe remembers the private side of Bradds. "He was one of the most confident people I've ever known with regard to basketball. He told me matter-of-factly that he'd be an All-American at Ohio State, and he said it before we enrolled. He fully expected to make people forget Jerry Lucas. Now he didn't show that side often — that would be bragging and Gary didn't do that no matter what his records. But he was candid with me and that is how he felt."

Fred Taylor recalls Bradds in high school. "I saw him four times, and Frank Truitt saw him several as well. He'd get off balance, but he always came up looking at the basket and clawing for the ball. We liked that."

That effort, familiar to Ohio State fans of the era, was taught to David Bradds, Gary's son, now on a basketball scholarship at the University of Dayton. "Dad used to say rebounding is all desire," recalls David. "Whoever wants it the most gets it."

When Gary decided to go to Columbus with buddy Don DeVoe, to be closer to his girl friend Eileen and to compete with Jerry Lucas, another competitor continued his efforts. Adolph Rupp asked the NCAA to investigate Ohio State's recruiting. All things considered, that's ironic. Nothing came of the investigation.

What many people have forgotten is that Bradds actually enrolled at Kentucky, and was on their campus for two days before he left without contacting Ohio State. He said to his father "If Ohio State won't take me I just won't go to school, I don't want to be at Kentucky." Ohio State took him.

On a freshman team with several all staters from bigger schools, Gary scored 26.9 ppg, shot over 58% from the field and averaged 15.7 rebounds to lead the team in all three categories. More importantly, DeVoe remembers "He was the only one of us who could score when we played against the varsity."

As a sophomore Bradds provided a legitimate back-up for Lucas, but Jerry was healthy and that meant time on the bench. The challenge was facing Luke everyday in practice. "I learned more scrimmaging against Lucas than I would have on Kentucky's first team," Bradds said at OSU.

"Gary was one of the best practice players we ever had," recalls Taylor. "When he rebounded he flew after the ball. He was so intense he actually gave Lucas a workout, and that was remarkable. In later years when he became a regular, a star, an All-American it was always 100% every practice. That's probably why he improved so much."

When Gary went into the game as a sophomore the outcome had usually been decided, it was "garbage time" and, in the words of assistant Sports Information Director Marv Homan, "he played like a man with three legs." But when he scored 15 points against Cincinnati in support of a hobbled Lucas in the NCAA final, the second guessers wondered why he hadn't been playing more.

"Jerry Lucas could do everything well. At center, he had a chance to do all those things — catch, pass, screen, shoot, rebound, drive, move without the ball, run, fake, everything. He was the best in the game at that key position so he was the center," explains Taylor. "So the question becomes, why didn't Bradds play forward?

"Gary's skills were effort, intensity and shooting in rhythm. When we tried him at forward he had trouble freeing himself on the wing and passing and driving from the wing. And he couldn't play defense out there. He had played center all his life, was improving rapidly, would be our center as a junior and senior, and both he and Lucas were benefiting from the practice against each other. Moving Gary to forward for a year would have meant losing all those benefits while asking him to do things he had not done, and was not picking up easily, and would not have to do in the future. Besides we didn't need him all year until the Cincinnati game," says Taylor. Left unsaid is the thought that OSU might not have needed him then if Lucas had not been hurt.

A review of the 61-62 season confirms the coach's point. Except for a loss to Wisconsin, which Bradds probably could not have prevented, and the final, the closest game was an eight point victory over Michigan State. Havlicek, McDonald, Doughty and Knight provided effective play at forward and Bradds was not needed. And the move could have slowed his progress at center, and possibly even allowed Luke's concentration to waver a bit during the year.

So Bradds would forever be a center at Ohio State, where he now ranks second and fourth in best single season scoring average and sixth and eighth in rebounding average. But how was he on defense? Good shot blocker?

"We never asked him to block shots," says Taylor flatly. "He was too valuable to us on the offensive end and on the boards, we couldn't risk the fouls. He had some good efforts as a defender on his own man but as a team player he had to stay in the game."

* * * *

Big Ten play started with a tough 78-76 victory over Minnesota as Bradds hit 12 of 16 field goals for 27 points ("He gets that shot off so fast you can't believe it," said Minnesota Coach John Kundla). Dick Reasbeck added 22. Doughty had 13 points and 13 rebounds as those three and Captain McDonald played all 40 minutes. Ricketts was the only sub, splitting time with Dick Taylor who shot a tough one of seven from the floor.

After that Saturday game came the trip to tiny Huff Gym to play the No. 3 ranked University of Illinois. The Illini won 88% of their games in the gym, where seats were so close to the playing floor that

105

spectator's feet were over the boundary lines. "It was the worst gym in the Big Ten," recalls Doug McDonald. Plus Coach Harry Combes had some great talent that year.

Seniors Dave Downey, at 6'5 already No. 2 among the school's all time career scorers, 6'9 Bill Burwell and 6'2 Bill Small, fresh from scoring 25 in a conference opening win against Iowa, had been considered a great recruiting class. Now they were being challenged for playing time by the Illinois sophomores. Tal Brody, a 6'2 guard, became an immediate starter and 6'10 Skip Thoren and 6'6 "Bogie" Redmon offered excellent high school reputations. Combes had said "We're shooting for a Big Ten title, and nothing less than 14-0 will please me."

The Buckeyes led 37-36 at the half behind 20 points by Bradds and eight by Reasbeck, and led 48-45 with 15 minutes to play. But a 16-2 Illinois spurt broke it open. As Illinois did a better job on Bradds (33 for the game), nobody else came through. Ricketts and McDonald were in double figures but Reasbeck and Doughty combined to shoot nine of 39. The Bucks shot 34% from the field, Illinois 47%. Since the league did not have a round robin schedule, that was the only meeting of the two teams. As one interested fan, Northwestern Coach Bill Rohr, said after the 90-78 loss, "It's a shame OSU doesn't get another shot at Illinois." (It turned out to be.)

Michigan brought a 2-0 league record, tied with Illinois, and the best field goal percentage in the league (.526) to St. John Arena the following Saturday. Their physical sophomore center Bill Buntin was averaging 33.5 ppg for league games and ranked fifth in the nation with 16.7 rebounds per game overall. Meanwhile foot problems caused Bradds to miss practice.

Sophomore guard Dick Ricketts was named to start over Dick Taylor, who had not scored against Illinois and only averaged 4.0 ppg since his fine game against West Virginia. Ricketts would stay in the line-up until he graduated.

Gary Bradds conducted a "Welcome to the Big Ten" party for Buntin, outscoring him 25 to 15 before Buntin fouled out. In all Bradds had 33 points and 15 rebounds. Reasbeck added 16 points, Ricketts 10. Both Don DeVoe, with a hustle tip-in at halftime to cut the Wolverine lead to 29-25, and Tom Bowman, with 10 rebounds, helped off the bench. All this resulted in a 68-66 victory which was more effective than artistic.

After the game Coach Taylor said "We were concentrating on our guard-center attack". This would become the key to the season, taking advantage of the shooting ability of Bradds, Reasbeck and Ricketts and the surprising strength of the two guards. The pass would be made by a guard to a forward and the guard, most often Ricketts, would go inside to screen the center. Done properly this freed Bradds for an instant at the foul line where he could catch a pass and be in rhythm to launch his remarkably accurate jump shot. The problem was having a guard strong enough to effectively screen the 6'8-6'10 man guarding Bradds. Ricketts could do it ("He was stronger than any guard I played against in three years of college or four years in the NBA," says former Buckeye Captain Bill Hosket, "except for Larry Siegfried"). Reasbeck was very strong as well. If Bradds was not open, there might be an open jumper for the other guard. If not, a forward would set a screen for the guard who originally screened for Bradds, providing a quick 12' jumper or a two on two opportunity. The strategy worked against Michigan and would be honed throughout the year.

Unfortunately the guard-center offense did not click at Iowa City and Ohio State lost 81-74 after leading at halftime, 34-27. Gary Bradds had 26 points and 14 rebounds, and Jim Doughty bounced back with 19 points and 11 boards, but the guards couldn't drop the ball in water while floating in a boat. Reasbeck was four of 21, Ricketts two of 10 and Dick Taylor zero for seven off the bench. Including 14% from the guards, Ohio State shot 32% as a team.

The loss put Ohio State two games behind the 4-0 Illini. Rugged Paul Silas, the nation's leading rebounder at 19.7 rpg and a 20.5 ppg scorer, then brought Creighton to town for a difficult non-conference game.

Bradds outscored Silas 25 points to 18, matched him with 19 rebounds and the Bucks won 78-73 to mark victory Number 100 in the career of their coach. Fred Taylor praised the team's shot selection, poise and hustle, and liked the 31 points from his starting guards and eight off the bench of DeVoe.

Northwestern came to Columbus two days later and future Wildcat Coach Rich Falk hit 12 of 19 for 32 points. He had averaged 11.4 ppg before the game started. Gary Bradds' untiring effort to score 35 in the face of changing defenses and a great game by Captain Doug McDonald were the keys to a 72-70 victory. McDonald guarded crafty Rick Lopossa and held him 10 points below his 18 point average. The Buck captain scored 12 points himself. Buck guards had 21 as only the five starters scored.

That Saturday a trip to 0-6 Purdue seemed perfectly timed to keep the Bucks on track. Only high scoring guard Mel Garland, who succeeded Terry Dischinger as their designated scorer, popping up at guard, forward or center, wherever he had an advantage over his defender, and center Bill Jones loomed as major obstacles.

Bradds held Jones to eleven, but nobody could match up with Garland. "After stopping Lopossa they tried me, but Garland was too quick," recalls McDonald. Garland had 15 of 17 from the field; his 34 points keyed a Purdue attack that scored 93 points on .645 shooting. So the Bucks outscored them, winning 97-93, despite being outshot and outrebounded. Bradds had 38, Ricketts 22 and Reasbeck 18 as they all shot over 60%. The only important negative was that Bradds missed a foul shot, stopping his streak at 31. Jimmy Rayl had the league mark with 32.

Today Fred Taylor remembers the end of the game. "The clock went out and they used a hand held stop watch. It was the longest game — I was afraid we'd keep playing until they got the lead, then it would be over."

"Fred always called that the 50 minute game," remembers Jim Shaffer. "What he doesn't remember is the cereal bowls of shrimp we all ate at the buffet at the hotel. We moved so slowly that game we probably stopped the clock ourselves."

Reasbeck smoked in 14 of 19 shots for 31 points, Bradds added 25, Doughty 16 and McDonald 12 as the Bucks blasted Wisconsin at home, 94-70.

A trip to Michigan gave talented and talkative Bill Buntin a chance to prove he could repay Bradds for outplaying him in Columbus. But Buntin's 21 points and 10 rebounds paled in comparison to Bradds' 34 markers and 14 boards; Buntin told Doug McDonald, "I think I've said too much." Reasbeck added 16. OSU 75-68.

Meanwhile at Indiana, Dave Downey scored 53 points but the Hoosiers beat Illinois 103-100. The loss dropped the Illini to 6-2 and a first place tie with the Bucks.

Ohio State was a bit flat for visiting Michigan State, but recorded an 87-77 victory. The Bucks had played well two straight games, and led 53-40 at the half. Foul trouble and a triple team on Bradds closed the margin to seven in the second half but "it goes up as a win," as the coach said. Bradds had 31 points, the guards combined for 30 and the forwards 26.

Mrs. Gary Bradds, who remarried after Gary died of cancer and is now Mrs. Eileen Bennington, remembers that Michigan State game today. "I was working on campus, and wanted to get home before coming back for the game. Gary was with the team eating their pre-game meal at the Golf Course. As I was driving by St. John Arena a car pulled out and I was in an accident. Nothing serious, but we had to wait for a policeman to come over and traffic was starting to build up. I was more anxious than he was until he found out who I was. Then he was in a big hurry. He said 'We have to get you moved before Gary and the team see you.' An accident report was one thing, but disturbing Gary Bradds before a big game, *that* was important. But Gary didn't find out about the accident until he got home, and of course they won, so it worked out."

The team had been awaiting the rematch with Iowa for over a month, and hosted the Hawkeyes February 23. Bradds had an above average game, even for him, with 40 points and 22 rebounds. Reasbeck scored an important 16. OSU won 83-70.

Fred Taylor's former players remember that he had an unusual coaching style. Rather than tell you something was wrong, he would ask a question which would lead you to realize the point he wanted to make. By thinking about his question your understanding might be better. For example, a common question was "Did you ever think we might be asking you to set that screen for a reason?" Try to answer that one. The process might be "I set the screen to free a teammate, he wasn't free, I need to set a better screen."

In Reasbeck's case, when the team flew back from Iowa City, where Dick was four for 21 in the first game, Coach Taylor had made a comment. It involved Reasbeck not getting his hand smashed in the airplane door when it closed. Since that is not a common occurrence, and Coach Taylor never made comments about a shooter missing good shots, Reasbeck had reassessed his shot selection — and been in the 50% range since.

"Fred and I argued a lot when I was at Ohio State," says Reasbeck today. "As I look back he was right every time. He was a great coach. Anybody can take one star player and form a team. He was able to take a whole group of star players and make a champion."

Northwestern held the ball but Bradds still found time for 25 points and 19 rebounds as the visitors beat their patient hosts 50-45. Could anyone beat Illinois?

March 2 Purdue came to town for the final home game for seniors Doug McDonald and Dick Reasbeck. The Boilermakers were 1-11 but they had Garland and Jones, who, like Buntin, had been claiming he would get even with Bradds. Also Bradds had an infected nail removed on Tuesday and missed practice on Wednesday. Jim Doughty had the flu and couldn't start the Saturday game.

No problem.

"Weiner" Reasbeck left in a blaze of glory, hitting 14 of 23 for 32 points, and McDonald had a solid nine point, nine rebound game. Bradds outscored Jones 29 to 17 and DeVoe had nine points and 11 rebounds in place of Doughty. Final score 95-75, Ohio State.

AND Michigan gave Illinois its third conference loss 84-81. If the Bucks won their last two games they had a fourth straight Big Ten championship in the bag. Eight straight conference victories now allowed them to control their own destiny.

Freshman coach and super scout Frank Truitt said there were two keys to victory at Minnesota. "Bradds has to get 25," he said, to no one's surprise, "and Ricketts has to get 20."

Truitt was sure Reasbeck, with 32 against Purdue and 22 in the first Minnesota game, would be guarded by Bob Bateman, who had just put the clamps on Jimmy Rayl. "Shotgun" would have trouble scoring. Bradds would get some kind of collapsing zone, but would still have to have an "average" night. Ricketts had to score.

Maybe he was nervous the first half — Ricketts made two of eight. Defense, 12 points from Bradds and eight from Reasbeck, had provided a 36-27 OSU lead. At the half Taylor encouraged Ricketts. "I said 'Don't worry when you miss shots, worry when you can't get shots. If you've got a good shot, take it'. I always liked to see him shoot because even when he missed it was close, good tipping material." Ricketts hit a jumper to start the half and ended with nine of 10 field goals in the period. His 23 for the game, with 25 from Bradds and DeVoe's solid relief job for the not yet recovered Doughty resulted in an 85-65 triumph. And a "well done" for Truitt.

Tom Bowman, a sophomore on the team, remembers that trip to Minneapolis for two reasons apart from the game.

"The night before the game some of us — 'Rick' (Ricketts) and Shaffer, probably, and maybe some others — went to this family style restaurant. We noticed this guy with OSU on his sport coat. We didn't know him, but later found out Oregon State was in town to play Minnesota in something so he was probably from there.

"Anyway, we're eating dinner and this woman walks up to the front of the room and starts taking off her clothes. She was a stripper! So after dinner we go back to our rooms and find out Fred wants to see us. He's already heard about this and wants to talk about what happened. I think someone saw that Oregon State guy and that's why it was reported. But that doesn't matter now.

"So Fred was not real mad; he seemed to believe us. He said 'Did you ever think about leaving when she started to take off her clothes?' Somebody said 'Yes, Coach, you know we did think about that.' " Taylor's approach of asking a question to make a point had backfired. Instead of saying "You should have left" he wanted them to think through what had happened. The problem was they had thought it through, and had decided to stay. The matter was dropped.

"Later Jim Shaffer, Dick Ricketts and I were together in a room in St. Paul," recalls Bowman. "We had the television on, and heard someone in our hotel was about to jump off the top of the hotel we were in. We looked out the window just in time to see a man go flying by. He crashed through the canopy and landed on the street. You don't forget something like that."

* * * *

Dick Ricketts, "Rick" to reduce confusion with teammates Dick Reasbeck and Dick Taylor, was well established long before the Minnesota game. Purdue Coach Ray Eddy had said "He's as good a sophomore as there is in this league." Yet this was the time when Dick *had* to score, in addition to the ball handling, screening, free throw shooting (.911 for the year) and defense he had provided since replacing junior Dick Taylor in the line-up. Fred Taylor had not hyped him in pre-season, but he knew "Rick" was a player the first time he saw him play in high school.

"Sometimes you know when you see a high school kid play that he can play in college. With Dick, I just knew," recalls Taylor. "Then Branch McCracken at Indiana told him he wouldn't get to play if he went to Ohio State, so he should go to Indiana. That's probably the best thing that could have happened to us. Dick said 'If I don't play then somebody else will be playing pretty well'. Then he came and played."

"He would have played if freshmen had been eligible," says buddy Jim Shaffer today. "Nowell, Reasbeck, Gearhart — he'd have been on the floor with those guys." Ricketts was 6'1, 177 lbs.

Taylor recalls another Ricketts story. "We often scrimmaged the freshmen with the varsity. Helped them learn the system, and gave us an early look at who was intimidated by the veterans and who would compete.

"Somebody took a shot and Lucas went *way* up for the tip-in. Just as he was reaching for it someone undercut him and all of a sudden he's parallel to the floor. Not only did he regain his balance to land on his feet, on the way down he reached over, grabbed the ball below the rim and tipped it in. It was all time highlight film stuff. But I wasn't thinking about highlights. I'm thinking the best player in America is going to die right in front of my eyes, and I'm halfway out on the floor when the play is over. Trying to regain my composure and slip back to my seat I hear 'Rick' say 'That was a really good shot.' I never again worried about him being intimidated!"

At tiny Belle Center, Dick played everywhere, on and off the court. He averaged 15 points as a freshman, over 26 as a sophomore and junior and 32 as a senior. He made first team All-Ohio Class A as a junior and Player of the Year as a senior. He was also quarterback in football, "all over" in baseball and a member of the 880 track team which went to the state his sophomore year.

He doesn't remember much about recruiting. "I didn't think much about colleges, I was just playing," he says. Sounds like Donald Bradds talking about his son ("Gary didn't read the papers, he just played"). "Well, there was Ohio Northern, Kentucky, Bowling Green, Indiana. Maybe Frank Truitt could remember," he said. Anyone who would put Ohio Northern and Kentucky in the same sentence obviously wasn't going to be much help.

"The first school I think of is Toledo," remembers Truitt. "They were there every time I went."

In recalling the decision, Ricketts says "It was the old question 'Do you want to be a big fish in a small pond or a small fish in the big pond?' I liked Frank Truitt and had tremendous respect for Fred Taylor, so I decided to try the big pond."

Being the youngest of six brothers probably helped him avoid the natural feeling of awe for players like Lucas and Havlicek. "Lack of intelligence may have helped too," he modestly adds. But he clearly describes the process he went through in adjusting to college. "It seems like everyone starts out with pride. When things don't go well, that pride is replaced with doubt and possibly fear. The fear causes you to work harder, so it serves a purpose.

"I knew I didn't want to fail. With a coach like Fred Taylor, and all the success he had, it wouldn't be the coach, it would be the player."

Growing up with five older brothers left an imprint on Rick in two other ways. "We played pretty rough, and never called fouls. I had to hold my own. After that, the physical play in the Big Ten never seemed too bad to me." While his teammates benefitted from that trait, at times they suffered from another one — the ability, as a freshman at least, to start something, then blend into the crowd when the coaches came. "As great a player as he was, when I think of Dick it's of a guy who could cause trouble and not get caught," says Don DeVoe.

Tom Bowman agrees, and remembers a time he and Dick got caught. "We got to know each other at the North-South All-Star game at Cuyahoga Falls when we roomed together, and formed a close friendship. One day at practice freshman year we were alone in the freshman locker room and started fighting. Not angry, but silly, like brothers. We were rolling on the floor, giggling and laughing, and Fred opened the door. We froze — how much trouble were we in? He just shook his head and walked away, never said anything."

Rick remembers himself as "not a great ball handler. I got a chance to play because of my passing ability, and because I could hit the open shot. I just didn't try to do anything I couldn't do."

Marv Homan, Buckeye broadcaster, uses different terms. "He was one of our smartest guards," says the radio voice of the entire era. "An excellent team player, in the same class as Siegfried as a competitor, solid in every area — just an outstanding guard."

"Dick was a fine, fine player," says Captain McDonald today. "He was the missing piece we needed."

Fred Taylor compares him to the captain of Indiana's 1976 NCAA championship team in one way. "He was like Quinn Buckner, in that every time he was around a loose ball, he got it." Coaches love those guys.

* * * *

As Ohio State prepared for the final game at Indiana, *Sports Illustrated* was analyzing their chances in the NCAA tournament. Speculation was that they would make the semi-finals and lose to Duke. However, due to the Rose Bowl rule, as Fred Taylor still calls it, a tie for the conference title would eliminate their chance. At that time, ties resulted in the team most recently in the tournament being prohibited from returning. Since OSU was in the NCAA in 1962, a tie with anyone meant they stayed home. Playoffs were not permitted until 1968, multiple representatives from a conference years after that.

The game figured to be difficult, and very fast paced. It was the only meeting between Indiana and Ohio State that year; unfortunately the Bucks were not scheduled with either Indiana or Illinois at home. In the two Indiana-Illinois games both teams hit the 100 point mark both times. Jimmy Rayl would finish second in league scoring at 27.0 points per game, and Tom Bolyard third at 23.7. Identical twin sophomores Tom and Dick Van Arsdale, who Taylor had tried to recruit, were already stars. The Hoosiers had plenty of scoring punch.

To help prepare his team for the pace of the Hoosier's fast break, Taylor instructed the freshmen not to dribble but to run the ball up court in practice.

Today Buckeye players remember the beginning of the game almost as clearly as the game itself.

"We had to walk a long way through the crowd to get to the court, on sawdust," says Ricketts. "Somebody tried to throw Coke on Bradds but he hit Shaffer. Jim picked the guy up off the floor and tossed him back into the crowd."

Jim Shaffer doesn't recall that entry in the "Hoosier fan toss for accuracy and distance," but does remember "fans heating pennies with their lighters, then throwing the pennies at us."

Indiana started well but Ohio State held the lead 36-34 at the half. An Indiana surge gave them the lead 52-47, but 10 straight Ohio State points made the score 57-52. The Bucks extended that to 71-60 and appeared to have the game in hand with 6:23 to go. However the delay game did not work as well as it should have. Indiana got opportunities and Tom Bolyard, "the best all-around 6'4 man in the league" according to Frank Truitt's scouting report and "a magnificent competitor" in Fred Taylor's words after the game, took control. Bolyard scored 11 straight for his team while Ohio State could only total two, closing the Buckeye lead to 73-71.

At 79 all, Ohio State had the ball with seconds remaining. Taylor set an emergency scoring play to free Bradds for a jump shot around the foul line. Reasbeck hit him with a pass ("I had a pretty good shot myself," says Dick today. "Guess I picked the wrong time to pass. Looking back I wish I'd have shot.") Bradds turned, saw a lane and drove to the basket. He was called for charging. "Think you are going to get *that* call?" winces Dick Ricketts today. Overtime.

With Bradds, Reasbeck and McDonald out with fouls, Indiana won 87-85. Yet Indiana's Branch McCracken blasted the officials while Taylor said they did "a fine job under the circumstances." Bradds ended with game high 32 points and 14 rebounds despite a continuing barrage of insults from Rayl. All five starters scored in double figures but only Captain McDonald shot well from the field. "The only way we could have gotten out of there alive was to lose," McDonald said in the locker room afterwards.

What if the delay had worked better? What if the shooting had been average? What if the Bucks had prevented Indiana's eight baskets on offensive rebounds? What if Bradds had shot the jump shot? What if Reasbeck had shot?

That kind of thinking puts people away. But the real shame is that Illinois and Ohio State, co-champions at 11-3, did not have a play-off. As Taylor says "We just wanted a chance to compete, win or lose."

Gary Bradds was the unanimous choice of his teammates as OSU MVP, and later received that honor for the Big Ten. He led the league in scoring at 30.9 ppg and finished second to Michigan's Buntin with 12.7 rebounds. He was first team All-Big Ten with Downey, Buntin, Bolyard and Rayl. Reasbeck made second team.

UPI's final rankings listed Cincinnati (23-1), first, followed by Duke (24-2), Arizona State (24-2), Loyola (24-2), Illinois (19-5), Wichita State (19-6), Mississippi State (21-5) and Ohio State (20-4), eighth.

In the NCAA tournament, Illinois barely beat Bowling Green 70-67 for the chance to play the Loyola-Mississippi State winner in the Mideast regionals final. The significance of the Loyola-MSU game is that it represented the first time the southerners had taken the floor against a team with a black player. Twice in the previous four years Mississippi State had won the Southeastern Conference and refused the NCAA invitation. This year the coach and players voted to go and the President and Board of Regents approved. However Governor Ross Barnett threatened to cut off funds to the school and dispatched a sheriff with a restraining order. The team snuck across the state line and stayed in Tennessee before flying to the tournament. Loyola won 61-51, then blasted Illinois 79-64 . In the finals Loyola beat Duke 94-75, then knocked Cincinnati out in overtime 60-58.

* * * *

It was a remarkable year for Ohio State: Big Ten co-champions, 20-4, No. 8 in the country, all despite the players who had graduated.

115

Almost as remarkable was the background of the starters on the team. Basketball was supposed to be a city game, yet the only starter from a metropolitan area was Jim Doughty of Columbus. Based on 1990 census information, Doug McDonald's Fostoria had a population of 14,983, almost twice the size of Dick Reasbeck's Martins Ferry — 7,990. Yet they were huge compared to Jamestown (Gary Bradds) at 1,794 and Belle Center (Dick Ricketts) with 796 people. First substitute Don DeVoe hailed from Port William, population 242.

Add those five towns together and their total population approximates the 26,778 people who lived in Zanesville, home of Fred Taylor. No one was mentioning Zanesville in the same sentences with New York, Chicago or Los Angeles.

Shelby, home of Larry Siegfried with a population of 9,564, and Lansing, home of John Havlicek with a population of less, had been good to the Buckeyes earlier. In the 1962-63 season small towns were almost completely responsible for the success of the Ohio State basketball team.

VII

1964: Five Straight

"They say you have to have a pair to open and Gary Bradds and Dick Ricketts look like a real good pair," said Fred Taylor in pre-season. And they were. Bradds was clearly the best center in the United States and Ricketts a proven Big Ten guard. But the other positions were a mystery. As the pre-season press guide said, success depended "upon the rapid development of sparingly used reserves and a meager sophomore contingent."

Both Associated Press and United Press International rated the Bucks seventh in the country. Bradds and Taylor weren't going to fool them again. But *Sports Illustrated* failed to include them in the top 30. Most picked them second in the conference to Michigan, where new-comer Cazzie Russell was saying "We'll probably win two NCAA titles." About Ohio State, *Basketball Yearbook 1964* said "After Bradds it doesn't look impressive. But Coach Fred Taylor's Buckeyes were counted out of the race completely last year and won."

Bradds had starred on the United States team which competed in the Pan American Games 1963. They won the gold medal by defeating Brazil in the championship game in their home country. Jimmy Crum, Channel 4 sports director and television broadcaster of Buckeye games throughout the Golden Age ("High altitude wrestling," "This is a real barn burner," "How about that?"), was in San Paulo, Brazil for that game and describes the atmosphere.

"The floor was surrounded by armed guards," says Crum. "When somebody threw a bottle of booze onto the floor from one of the highest parts of the arena, I went over to one of the guards to stand. He was very kind, and spoke some English. He pointed to his feet

117

and said 'Señor, if we have trouble, follow me.' He then pushed a lever by the floor and opened a trap door which we could use to escape."

That's one way to prepare for road games in the Big Ten.

After a solid sophomore season, including third on the team in scoring, second in field goal percentage and first in free throw percentage, the challenge for Dick Ricketts would be to increase his scoring average of 9.4 ppg. He would be most responsible to make defenses pay when they sagged on Bradds.

Jim Doughty had only played two years and had been elected co-captain with Gary Bradds. In 1963 he was second on the team in rebounding and only scored three points less than Ricketts for the year. But he could not return in 1963-64.

"After being elected co-captain," recalls Doughty, "I was honored and wanted to do a good job. I tried to be conscientious in all areas, including school. The trouble is I took too many hard courses, got in over my head and my grades suffered. With a wife and child to support I played for the Globetrotters that year (1964). I was at my basketball peak that year I missed," he says. Doughty graduated from Ohio State in 1970.

Doughty's departure made it three straight years — Ray Brown in 1962, Gene Lane 1963, and now Jim — that a quality forward was lost due to academics.

Don DeVoe had played well late in the year and would get first shot at one forward spot. Don Flatt and LeRoy Frazier were seniors — would they claim the other two open positions?

At the very least, a rugged pre-conference schedule was expected to help the team get ready for the Big Ten. Duke and Wichita State were in everyone's top five and Davidson, Utah State and St. Louis were mentioned as national powers.

Joe Carlson, co-captain of Taylor's first Ohio State team in 1959, brought Davis of California to St. John Arena to open the season and his team got blasted, 68-42. Eleven Buckeyes saw action. Butler was more trouble two days later but 31 points by Bradds and 12 of 15 shooting, for 26 points, by DeVoe led to a 74-68 Buckeye win. Next stop for the 2-0 team was the West Virginia Invitational.

On the flight to Morgantown, the DC-3 plane encountered some turbulence. Dick Otte, then covering the team for *The Columbus Dispatch*, never liked to fly and was not enjoying this flight at all. The players immediately came to his rescue, chanting, as Jim Shaffer recalls, "The plane's going to crash, the plane's going to crash." It helped the players relax, but may not have done much for Otte.

The first game of the tournament was with Duke, ranked #4 in the country. Twelve members returned from a 27-3 national semi-finalist, including high scoring Jeff Mullins. As the Bucks prepared for Duke, guard Tom Bowman sprained an ankle and became a doubtful starter. But one certain starter was Don DeVoe, who had claimed a forward position with his play to date.

* * * *

DeVoe was not exactly a "prep All-American", despite averaging over 30 ppg at Port William High School in Clinton County, Ohio. "We had eight boys in our senior class," remembers DeVoe. "It was the next to last year the school existed. That district is now part of Wilmington.

"I didn't go to college the year after high school. That was probably wise. I was only 6'3 then, and grew to almost 6'5. Spent the season playing independent ball for Martinsville Coal and Feed. Since I had grown up playing with Gary Bradds, when Frank Truitt started recruiting him, Gary told Frank about me. They offered me a partial scholarship and I grabbed it. It was a great opportunity — to play at Ohio State and go through school with my friend Gary.

"What a shock that first year was. Socially things were fine because many kids from our rural area were there. However I was not prepared academically. Frank Truitt helped me so much in that area with his weekly progress checks. Then the freshman team had 15 players on at least partial scholarship, and they all had great high school careers. Ray Brown, AA Player of the Year from Dayton Roosevelt, had a body which could have been chiseled by a sculptor. Strong, great hands, one on one skills, fade away jump shot — he had Jimmy Jackson-type ability for that era. He was astute, he just wouldn't go to class. Gene Lane, 6'8, Cleveland East Tech star, and Joel Haynes, 6'3, who broke all of OSU great Robin Freeman's scoring records in Cincinnati, and Jerry Spears of Columbus West. What a group!

"I was happy to be part of the team as a sophomore — played three minutes in five games — and really thrilled to get a full scholarship as a junior." As a senior he had become No. 3 man.

* * * *

A well played game against Duke left Taylor happy about everything but the final score. "One point (76-75) leaves you so many ways

119

to see how you could have won," he said. But the offense was solid. "We'll never score more than 75 against a team of Duke's caliber," he said. The shooting was excellent at .588 on 30 of 51. Bradds had 28 points, Ricketts 16 and DeVoe, before fouling out, ten. Bowman played hard before fouling out, and sophomore Al Peters contributed six points. The Bucks just never had an answer for Jeff Mullins, who scored 32.

In the consolation game the next night Ohio State beat St. John's 66-64 in dramatic fashion. With six seconds left the Redmen had the ball in a tie game, but Tom Bowman's defense caused a turnover and the Bucks called time. An emergency scoring play was called and, unlike in the Duke game, worked perfectly. At 0:01 on the clock Dick Ricketts jumped in the air and launched a 15' jump shot. The ball went through the hoop as the gun went off. As usual Bradds led both teams in scoring (23) and rebounding (14). Ricketts added 18 on eight of 10 from the field, DeVoe had 10 points and Bowman eight.

Powerful (3-0) Davidson was next, led by a cast of interesting characters. Lefty Driesell was 32 years old, in his fourth year as coach of the Wildcats, who had been 20-7 the previous year. Junior center Fred Hetzel had been Player of the Year in the Southern Conference as a sophomore. Co-captain Terry Holland was a starter at forward, and would become head coach of Virginia. The other forward was 6'5 Dick Snyder, a sophomore from North Canton who had caused *lots* of coaches to be confused. According to UPI he was the best quarterback in Ohio in 1961, earning first team honors over Frank Stavroff of Columbus Eastmoor. Most coaches assumed he would play football in college, and Snyder "couldn't seem to make up his mind which sport he wanted," recalls Fred Taylor, who "went after him strongly". Driesell convinced Snyder to play basketball at Davidson and it turned out to be an excellent choice, leading to a 13 year NBA career and 11,755 regular season points.

December 11, 1963 Ohio State lost at home for the first time since Purdue beat them 93-87 in 1959. They had won 50 straight. Davidson won 95-73 and dominated throughout; Snyder had 25 points. The Bucks were out-rebounded 51 to 36 and shot only 37 percent. Of some consolation were Jim Shaffer, with eight points in a starting role, and Bob Dove, six off the bench, providing production at the corner spot opposite DeVoe.

Two days later a very ordinary Missouri team made it two straight losses for the home team, shooting 51 percent to beat the Bucks 85-74. Spirits were down and Wichita State, with Dave Stallworth (28 ppg and 10 rpg) and Nate Bowman (double figures in both), was coming to Columbus next.

In their best game of the pre-Big Ten season, Ohio State blasted Wichita State 78-60. Jim Shaffer, 6'8, 230 lbs. starter at forward the last two games, moved to center where he completely outplayed Nate Bowman, 15 points to four and nine rebounds to seven. This allowed Gary Bradds to accept the challenge of guarding Stallworth. While the Wichita star had 25 points and 12 rebounds, Bradds had 28 and 16. Additionally the guards played well, Ricketts with 14 points and Bowman nine. Houston was next.

Bradds (29 points, 17 rebounds) and Shaffer (20 and 12) again controlled the boards and Ohio State beat the visiting Cougars 79-62. The spotlight now included Jim Shaffer, known as "Baby Huey" to his teammates.

* * * *

Jim Shaffer was the big man on his team at Gahanna, a suburb on the east side of Columbus. "I was the only player on the team over 6' tall," he recalls. His high game came against Columbus South in the Central District tournament when he hit 17 of 23 shots to total 42 points in a double overtime victory, 63-61. In a great clutch performance he had all 15 of Gahanna's points in the fourth quarter and four of the six in overtime. The next night future Buckeye teammate Tom Bowman and his 20-0 Linden team double and triple teamed "Shafe" to defeat Gahanna (17-5) 44-42.

"I remember Maryland, Louisville and Northwestern being interested, but if Ohio State hadn't called I probably would have gone to Ohio U. or Bowling Green. As it was, I had lunch with Jerry Lucas and John Havlicek at the Ohio Union. We had shrimp cocktail. I couldn't believe those guys took time for me," Shaffer says.

After graduating from Gahanna, Shaffer and his high school friend Harry Alexander took a most eventful vacation to Florida. "We drove down and stayed in St. Petersburg one night," recalls Shaffer. "Later in the trip we saw a newspaper article that St. Petersburg had recently had an encephalitis epidemic, but we didn't think anything about it.

"After we got back my father asked me to take our white 1961 Ford to Gandolf Ford on East Main Street to have something done. When I got there I had forgotten what he wanted to be fixed; I remember he was upset that he had to tell me again when I called. I was very tired, and crawled into the back seat to sleep while it was being fixed. (At 6'8 that still must have been better than a couple of plastic waiting room chairs.) After it was fixed I remember driving back very, very slowly. At home I slept constantly — I fell asleep while I was eating. Then I was checked into University Hospital — I remember looking out and seeing an empty Ohio Stadium. The next day I woke up with a patch on my lower back. They told me I had a spinal tap. Supposedly that is very painful, but I don't remember a thing.

"I started at Ohio State on time and began to practice. Other than being heavier than I would have been as a freshman, I really don't know if the encephalitis affected my career or not."

What memories linger from that freshman year?

"I remember early in the year they had me at forward and I was assigned to guard John Havlicek in practice. Guard him? I couldn't even find him. And late in the year, Bob Knight had been asked to speak at the athletic awards banquet at Gahanna. He called and asked it I would like to go with him. He made a friend for life with that offer."

* * * *

As December was coming to a close, Branch McCracken was becoming philosophical. In his 25th year as Indiana University basketball coach, UPI reported that he told a basketball writers luncheon problems of recruiting and alumni are "beginning to bother me. It's a lot tougher to coach now than it was 20 years ago," said McCracken. "The kind of job I want would be coach of an orphanage, where there are no parents to come around, or a state penitentiary, where the alumni never come back."

* * * *

Two road games, with opponents anxious to repay losses from the 1963 season, stood between the Buckeyes and Big Ten play. The games did not go well. First Wayne Estes scored 40 points and OSU shot only 35% as Utah State won 79-66. Then St. Louis out rebounded the visitors and won in double overtime, 91-89.

Don DeVoe remembers what happened next. "We flew back on New Years Day, and there was a terrible snow storm in Columbus. Instead of sending us home, Fred had us stay at St. John Arena for practice. A *hard* practice, but we needed it." OSU was 5-5.

Three days after that surprise practice the Bucks traveled to Wisconsin and beat the Badgers 101-85. All starters shot 50% or better, and sophomore Al Peters hit six of 14 off the bench. Bradds had 32, Ricketts 20 and Bob Dove, getting a chance to start after playing well against St. Louis, had 14.

A familiar site had greeted Taylor and the seniors as they walked past a trophy case in the Wisconsin arena. The game ball used when Wisconsin defeated Ohio State 86-67 March 3, 1962 was on display. "That gave me something to talk about with the team," recalls Taylor. "Later we made that trophy case a regular stop every time we went to Wisconsin, although eventually they got wise and took the ball out. I always wondered if they put it back each time we left."

The following week Minnesota, with a 7-3 pre-conference mark, a win over Purdue and sophomores Lou Hudson, Archie Clark and Don Yates joining veterans Mel Northway and Terry Kunze, came to St. John Arena. The Gophers excelled at the screen and roll play, and Taylor, Graf and Truitt stressed defense of that series all week in practice. Frank Truitt remembers an early play. "They ran a screen at DeVoe, and he knocked the ball away. Then he recovered it and passed ahead for an easy lay-up. I felt like that was a key to the game," Truitt says of the 85-73 victory.

Powerful Michigan blasted Ohio State in Ann Arbor 82-64 in a show of force which sent reverberations throughout the league. With 6'7, 230 lbs. center Bill Buntin and 6'5, 195 lbs. Larry Tregoning back, joined by sophomores 6'7, 220 lbs. Oliver Darden and 6'6, 218 lbs. Mr. Everything Cazzie Russell, the Wolverines were very physical. A 49-34 rebound deficit and cold early shooting were too much for OSU. "We had a dozen shots real early with no pressure and missed them all," said Taylor.

With Purdue coming to town, Taylor wanted to send his team a message to be more aggressive. Kaye Kessler, writer for *The Citizen-Journal*, reported that the players actually wore hip pads in practice. The day before the game at the weekly Rebounders lunch, Taylor was asked "Who's guarding (Dave) Schellhase?", the 6'4 sophomore who had scored 43 points against Notre Dame earlier in the week. "We're looking for volunteers," he replied. Later at practice Don DeVoe approached the coach with "that look" in his eye and said "I volunteer."

"DeVoe played Schellhase so physically I thought the kid was going to punch him," remembers Tom Bowman. Without hip pads DeVoe held the high scoring sophomore to seven shots. Yet teammate Bowman did an even better job on Mel Garland, who had blitzed the Bucks the previous year. Garland scored one point. On offense Bradds hit 20 of 30 attempts for a career high 47 points. He was joined in double figures by Ricketts and subs Shaffer and Peters in a 98-87 victory.

* * * *

From Cincinnati, Ohio State's conqueror in recent years, came a report so bizarre that it was difficult to take seriously. Having lost consecutive games to Bradley and Drake, lowering his record to 9-3 for the season and 91-10 in the last 3 1/2 years, Bearcat Coach Ed Jucker was "hanged in effigy". Apparently the best record in the country over 101 games, including two NCAA titles and a second place finish, was not good enough for the fans.

* * * *

Determined to stay close to Michigan's 5-0 mark, Ohio State traveled to Michigan State (2-3) two days after beating Purdue. Despite 48 points from Gary Bradds, and 17 from Jim Shaffer as he returned to the starting line-up, the Bucks lost a "hard fought" game, 102-99.

Ohio State led 25-19 when star guard Dick Ricketts and MSU sophomore Stan Washington were ejected from the game for fighting. Bob Dove remembers "Dick had a bruise on his cheek, from an elbow or a punch. We felt it was planned to get him out of the game — he was a key for us and Washington was a sub."

Ricketts remembers it this way: "He came off the board with the ball and I jerked it away from him. He squared to throw a punch and I grabbed him in a bear hug (to prevent a punch being thrown). It was really nothing." In any case, OSU lost a nine point lead in the final 10 minutes and the Buckeyes had their second conference loss.

Easily the biggest game of the season loomed February 3. Mighty Michigan had moved to No. 2 in the country, behind undefeated UCLA, and was on the verge of running away with the Big Ten race. Ohio State had a must win game, for themselves and the league.

Don DeVoe remembers a focused Buckeye team before the game. "Nobody talked. It was extremely quiet. Gary (Bradds) and I were taped together and never said a word to each other."

In one of the great games ever played in St. John Arena, Ohio State knocked off Michigan 86-85.

The visitors had an 18-9 lead as Bradds started cold. Three point plays by Ricketts and Bowman cut it to 18-15 but Michigan moved out to a 28-19 margin. Then Gary got going, and cut it to 35-33 Michigan. OSU led 42-41 at the half. The lead changed hands several times until Shaffer hit a jumper from the side at 11:24 to make it 60-58. State never put the game away, but stayed ahead.

Bradds came back from a one of 10 start to hit 15 of his next 19 field goal attempts, and 10 of 12 from the line for his third straight 40+ point game. DeVoe was all over the floor, and had 11 points and seven rebounds. Shaffer and Dove combined for 11 points and 11 rebounds. Ricketts had his usual solid floor game and 12 points. Tom Bowman had his first night in double figures with ten, played all 40 minutes with Bradds and Ricketts, and, in a game of big plays, two of the biggest. He had moved from shaky question mark to solid exclamation point in the OSU starting line-up.

* * * *

"I had a wonderful high school experience playing for Vince Chickerella at Linden McKinley," Tom Bowman remembers. "We were undefeated — one of the victories was over 'Baby Huey's' Gahanna team — until we lost to Canton McKinley in the regional finals." "Bullwinkle", as Bowman's teammates at OSU later called him, was second team All-Ohio AA, the first all stater from Linden.

"When I started thinking about college I considered Ohio U., and Kentucky was interested but they didn't have any blacks then. It helped that 'Chick' was assistant baseball coach at Ohio State — I felt like I knew what was really going on there. Actually it was just what Coach Taylor told me — get an education and compete for the Big Ten championship. Also Dave Barker from the 1960 NCAA championship team was student teaching at Linden, so he told me stories about the team.

"My freshman year I found out everyone else was all state too. It was a whole different ball game. I don't see how freshmen today compete on the varsity level," Tom recalls. "There were so many adjustments, and it seemed like there wasn't any time. We had to run from practice to 10th Avenue to get our dinner — the line closed at 6:00. Sometimes we didn't have time to shower.

"Not only did you have to learn the rules, but how to work them in your favor. There was a football player who was a legend at that. It used to be that you could sign for your books and they'd give them to you. He would come in 8-10 times, sign, walk out with the books and sell them. The university changed that rule — you had to bring in the course number. Yes, he signed his own name every time — maybe that's why they caught him," Bowman grins.

"'Chick' had me play sort of all over in high school, but I strictly played forward at Ohio State until after practice started my junior year. It would have been better to have had some work at guard earlier, but two things really helped. One was having John Havlicek guard me in practice as a freshman. He put so much pressure on the ball handler I either took care of the ball or lost it. The other was playing backcourt with Dick Ricketts. Not only did he know what to do on the court, he *always* did it. I never had to worry about where he would be. I had to know where he was supposed to be, and he'd be there."

Asked to remember playing with Bowman, Rick immediately recalls "The end of the Michigan game, they missed a shot inside, then a tip, and about eight hands were above the rim, going for the rebound. Just a little higher were two more — they were Tom Bowman's and he grabbed the ball. That won the game."

Actually that rebound by the 6'2, 178 lbs. leaper with 13 seconds left, 85-83 OSU, led to a foul shot. Bowman hit the shot, which did win the game since Russell made a 30' jumper at the buzzer. It was only worth two points then. OSU 86-85.

* * * *

Hoping to avoid a let down after the Monday Michigan victory OSU journeyed to Bloomington for a Saturday contest with the Van Arsdale — led Hoosiers. All eyes were on Gary Bradds, who had 137 points in the last three games and had now played 633 1/2 of a possible 650 minutes for the season. That included eight full games, and all 50 minutes in the double overtime St. Louis loss.

The Bucks won an overtime "barnburner", edging Indiana 98-96 despite Bradds, DeVoe, Shaffer, and Dove watching the end with five fouls. Gary had 40 points before departing, DeVoe 17 points and a game high 17 rebounds, and Dove added seven points off the bench. Ricketts' career high 24, including 15 in the second half, were all necessary to withstand 46 totaled by Tom and Dick Van Arsdale and 27 more by Jon McGlocklin. Tom Bowman remembers being hit in the head with a flashlight from the crowd. But this was Bloomington, and the result was much better than the previous year when an overtime loss cost an NCAA trip.

Balanced scoring by Illinois was good for 92 points, but Ohio State scored 110. Bradds had 49, to set the OSU single game scoring record which stands today, on 17/28 from the floor and 15/16 from the line. He also had a game high 21 rebounds as the Bucks dominated that category. Dove had 14 points and 13 rebounds off the bench and Ricketts was outstanding with nine baskets in 11 attempts. Bowman played excellent defense on Illinois guard Tal Brody. Too bad St. John Arena wasn't full. It hadn't even been against Michigan.

"Does he look at the basket — or does he just have a string tied to the ball?" asked Wisconsin Coach John Erickson after Bradds had 40 points in leading OSU to a 92-74 win over the visiting Badgers. Shaffer had 11 first half points to help provide a 48-33 margin at the break, and others contributed, but Gary was the story. With his sixth straight 40 point game he had broken Terry Dischinger's record for consecutive and total 40 point games in a season. He had a 10 ppg lead as leading scorer in the conference, and was first in rebounding and field goal percentage.

Looking back on that streak, tremendous credit must go to Bradds. "He was the only player I ever saw who couldn't get rid of a floor burn on his chin," according to DeVoe. "He had this big cleft chin and kept banging it on the floor. I never saw a player with his desire." Gary made 93 of 160 in the six game streak for 58%; obviously he was not forcing bad shots.

Neither was Ricketts, who shot 66% for the five games after the streak started. Rick's man couldn't double team Bradds. Everybody screened for Gary, and everybody looked for him. It was truly a team individual achievement. As Fred Taylor told his players years later, "You guys were role players before anyone knew what that was."

"I remember one time Fred said 'We need to have the shooters shoot, the rebounders rebound and the passers pass.' He said it all the time," recalls Bowman, "but I remember this one time because I had just passed to Bradds for four straight baskets. Guess Fred didn't want me thinking it was my turn to shoot," Tom laughs.

"Fred Taylor could put the pieces together and make the puzzle," concludes Bowman.

Iowa won the battle (holding Bradds to 30 points) but lost the game, 99-82. DeVoe had 23 points, including seven of seven from the field. "I loved to play there," he recalls. "The ball seemed small and the basket big." Ricketts had 18. Bowman made five of seven attempts to get 12 himself, despite being distracted by the birds he remembers flying around the ceiling.

Michigan's loss at Minnesota put OSU into a first place tie at 8-2. Then the wheels came off at Northwestern. Bradds was three of 21 and Ricketts three of 14. They shot 17% from the field and totaled only 22 points. DeVoe contributed only three points. However Jim Shaffer (23 points and nine boards), Tom Bowman (11 and seven rebounds) and Don Flatt (11 and some strong defense off the bench) came to the rescue. OSU won 72-61.

Visiting Indiana held Bradds to 15 but Ricketts and DeVoe each scored 16, plus reserve Jim Brown had seven as the Buckeyes won 73-69.

OSU went to Illinois and won 86-74 in a more typical fashion than they had in the last two games. Bradds hit 14 of 25 shots, compiling 34 points and 14 rebounds. Ricketts made seven of 10 for 17 points. Their eighth straight victory meant an 11-2 record going into the last game with Michigan State.

UPI named Bradds the College Player of the Year over Walt Hazzard of UCLA. Gary had become the best, the goal he privately set for himself when he arrived on campus with buddy Don DeVoe. Publicly he said "I consider it quite an honor."

No one questioned that he deserved the honor, no matter what he did against Michigan State. Then he did a lot against the Spartans, leading both teams with 31 points and 16 rebounds. He set a new single season Big Ten scoring record with 474 points (breaking Terry Dischinger's 459), a new season Big Ten field goal record with 175 (Buckeye Robin Freeman had that mark at 164), and a new OSU season scoring record with 735 (Freeman had 723). But he never played for points, he played for victories. "He laughed at the Northwestern fans for celebrating when he didn't score much but Ohio State won," recalls Donald Bradds, his father. Unfortunately the MSU game didn't work out.

The Spartans jumped out to a 10-1, then a 24-11 margin. The Bucks had an 11 point spurt, taking a 46-39 halftime lead. Ahead 72-66, the Bucks hit a cold streak. Then the shortest man on the court, Dick Ricketts, had a rebound basket to make it 80-79 OSU with 31 seconds left.

Spartan Pete Gent had not yet decided his future was in football (wide receiver for the Dallas Cowboys) and literature (he authored *North Dallas Forty*). He was a basketball player against Ohio State, with 23 points. His last two came on a long jump shot and 0:10 and made the final 81-80 MSU.

OSU was the best shooting team in the conference for the year, but could only make 36.5% from the field and 62.5% from the line against MSU. Bradds and Ricketts shot 22 of 50, 44%, but the rest of the team made only eight of 32, 25%. The conference title that had seemed so certain now appeared to be gone. All Michigan had to do was beat Purdue (7-6) at home and they had the outright championship.

The Buckeyes' traditional season ending banquet was held at the Ohio Union. The mood was mixed — disappointment with losing in the final game but satisfaction with an outstanding 11-3 Big Ten record. Gary Bradds was named MVP, Don DeVoe Most Improved and Dick Ricketts Captain for 1964-65.

"I'd like to think we could have more teams like this one, one every year," said Taylor. "If we have teams with the ability of this one to work together ... to work in practice as hard as this group ... if we have a squad next year with leadership such as Dick Ricketts can provide, ... winning will take care of itself."

Don DeVoe had attended the banquet with his mother and father. "After it was over we turned the car radio to the Michigan — Purdue game," he recalls. They heard Purdue give Michigan its only home loss of the season, 81-79. "Frank Truitt had been saying Purdue might win, and he was right," says DeVoe. "After that game I felt much better, knowing we were co-champions." But the "Rose Bowl Rule" would keep the No. 16 Buckeyes out of the NCAA tournament. Again.

Gary Bradds ended the season as the unanimous choice of almost 400 coaches as the National Association of Basketball Coaches "Player of the Year". He was Big Ten MVP and set four scoring marks. He led the league in field goal percentage (.535 — Ricketts ended at .515) and rebounding (13.2 per game).

In the NCAA tourney, Michigan beat defending champion Loyola 84-80 and Ohio University 69-57, then lost to Duke 91-80 in the semifinals. The Blue Devils lost 98-83 to UCLA. The Bruins and their coach John Wooden had the national championship Frank Truitt had predicted in December, 1961.

VIII

1965-1967:
Nothing Lasts Forever

The average sports fan assumes his favorite team will exceed expectations in the beginning, then rapidly improve after that. Cincinnati fans hanging Ed Jucker in effigy illustrated the mentality. However sports mirrors life, it is made up of highs and lows. The three year period from the fall of 1964 to the spring of 1967 was the low of the Golden Age of Ohio State basketball.

Maybe not a low, as the record was 36-36. It was flat, and, in comparison to the periods before and after, down. The five earlier seasons had resulted in 114 victories, 18 losses, five Big Ten championships and an .864 winning percentage. The four seasons to follow provided 75 victories, 28 losses, two championships and a .728 percentage.

Each of the seasons had successes and failures, outstanding players, and included a few cards from the "Iffy Deck" — What if this had happened? What if that had not happened? Each one had pieces of the puzzle missing, ingredients without which that team was unable to compete for the conference championship.

1964 — 1965

Another major rebuilding task was obviously necessary. Gary Bradds, Don DeVoe, Don Flatt and LeRoy Frazier had all completed their senior season. Academic problems had claimed a returning starter, again, as Tom Bowman was ineligible. With three starters and two subs gone, 62% of the points and 56% of the rebounds had to be replaced.

131

"The problem wasn't grades," recalls Bowman. "I had nearly a 3.0 average as a freshman. The problem was hours toward graduation. I had changed from Medical Counseling, with a lot of math and science, to Business, and needed a course in Spanish in summer school to have enough hours.

"Everything was going fine. The teacher kept telling me I was between a "B" and a "C". Frank Truitt was checking every two-three weeks, and hearing the same thing. Then the final grade came out — F," he says, shaking his head.

"The best way to explain it is, that was the time of the decision not to let the football team play in the Rose Bowl. Certain teachers resented athletes. When Fred or Frank asked the teacher what happened, she refused to explain and acted offended.

"Because I came from a Columbus high school, for years people used my ineligibility as a reason to explain why Fred Taylor didn't get along with blacks. I never experienced anything like that. In my case, the school may have let me down but the basketball program didn't," he concludes.

The line-up of juniors Bob Dove and Al Peters at forward with seniors Jim Shaffer (center), Dick Ricketts and Jim Brown helped OSU to a 2-1 start with victories over South Dakota and Texas Christian and a loss to St. Louis. Then one of the shortest line-ups Fred Taylor ever started — 6'6, 6'4, 6'3, 6'1, 6' — gained a 77-69 victory over the Houston Cougars. Dick Ricketts had 15 points in the second half to lead the scoring with 22 on 10 of 14 field goals. Sophomore Ron Sepic and junior Al Peters backed him with 16 each.

* * * *

"Pete's done a great job for us," said Taylor after the Houston win. His leading scorer (17.5 ppg) had 39 rebounds in four games to lead there as well. Peters stood 6'3, but liked it inside, having led New Lebanon Dixie to the state A championship as a center. That was four years after Gary Gearhart took Dixie to the state semi-finals.

Two highlights from high school involved future Buckeyes Gary Bradds and Andy Ahijevych.

"As a sophomore I had 29 points against Gary," remembers Peters. "Trouble is, he had 41 against me."

The game with Andy's Berlin Highland team was sweeter. In the tournament final All-Ohioan Peters had 21 points and Dixie won 74-62. Both future Buckeyes made all-tournament first team. "Al and

Andy spent most of their freshman year talking about that game," recalls classmate Bob Dove.

Al remembers something else that happened during the year he and Ahijevych (today his business card shows the pronunciation: A-hee-a-wich) spent as freshmen. "The first long distance phone call Andy made to his girlfriend in Sugarcreek, he thought the call was free after three minutes. I remember him running around the dorm getting change for the operator."

Back problems would plague Peters not long after his excellent start as a junior; Ahijevych had to wait until part way through the Big Ten season to become a consistent starter.

* * * *

The Bucks played poorly against Butler, winning 67-66 because of a Peters tip-in and a Sepic steal. Then they were soundly beaten 87-64 at powerful Davidson, which still had Hetzel and Snyder, and 112-71 at No. 18 ranked Brigham Young.

Jim Shaffer was back at the starting center position and his game high 18 points and 11 rebounds led OSU over Dartmouth 90-59. That brought No. 7 ranked Duke (5-1) to St. John.

Shaffer outplayed 6'10 Blue Devil center Hack Tison (21 points to 16, 15 rebounds to nine) but Bob Verga's 28 points and Jack Marin's 18 were too much. A stretch of 6:22 to begin the second half when the Bucks missed 14 straight field goals didn't help. Duke won 94-89 in double overtime, though a questionable goal tending decision would have meant a regulation victory for the home team.

That the game was so close is remarkable considering Ricketts was four of 18 from the field and Sepic seven of 23. If either had a near normal shooting night a victory over a nationally ranked team might have ...

Shaffer again had game high totals in rebounds (19) and points (23) as visiting Georgia Tech was beaten 73-68. After the game coach Whack Hyder said "Fred's going to find out how the other half like us live." Apparently he wasn't impressed.

With a 71-64 loss at Purdue, an 84-72 home defeat by Indiana and a 97-77 pasting at Minnesota, OSU began the Big Ten season 0-3. Al Peters' back injury had made him completely ineffective, and Bob Dove was struggling as his replacement. However Uniontown (PA) sophomore Ron Sepic had established himself at the other forward, pressing Captain Ricketts for the scoring leadership despite not starting the first three games.

* * * *

"The first time I heard of Ron Sepic was when I saw him on The Ed Sullivan Show," remembers classmate Al Rowley. "He, Lew Alcindor and three other guys were announced as the five best high school basketball players in the country."

"That was after Lew's sophomore year," remembers Sepic. "Edgar Lacey, who played at UCLA with Lew, and Bobby Lewis of North Carolina were there too. The fifth guy was Ian Morrison from St. Petersburg, Florida, the leading scorer in the nation at about 36 ppg. I think he went to South Carolina but had grade problems."

Other high school seniors that year, who had outstanding college and pro careers, included Jimmy Walker, Earl Monroe, Clem Haskins, Walt Frazier, Pat Riley and Louie Dampier. Sepic was at the top of an impressive group.

Certainly Sepic was a major recruit at Ohio State. "Jim Shaffer called him 'Golden Boy' to reflect his success in high school," remembers Bob Dove, "but the nickname didn't stick. Ron was just too down to earth."

Basketball, with The Ed Sullivan Show, three years as a starter at Uniontown ("Wherever we went he found people from Uniontown," recalls Dove), 48 straight victories and a Pennsylvania state championship his junior year, was only part of Sepic's high school resumé. "Woody Hayes kept recruiting me as an end even after I came to Ohio State to play basketball," says Sepic. Ron would be drafted in the 12th round by the NFL Washington Redskins in his senior year, though he never played football in college.

Sepic selected Ohio State because of Fred Taylor ("He had an air of integrity," says Ron. "He seemed like an honest man, a class man. Of course, he turned out to be that way as well."), Frank Truitt, potential opportunities in Columbus, and the distance from Uniontown. "It came down to West Virginia, which seemed too close, Duke, which seemed too far, and Ohio State. It was 200 miles away, a five hour drive then with no two lane highway. That was about the right distance."

"When I got to Ohio State the school seemed so big, it felt like a long way from home; it was scary. There were nine guys on scholarships. I wondered if I was good enough to play at this level. I feel sorry for the guys who play varsity as freshmen today.

"I remember being surprised at how physical the players were," says the former football player. "The skill level of a big man like Gary Bradds shocked me. But the varsity players took you under their wing and helped you along. There were a lot of good people, and the camaraderie helped.

"I remember thinking 'This isn't so bad' after the first Big Ten game when we played Purdue." He had 25 points and nine rebounds. "With scouting reports it became tougher quickly," remembers the 6'5, 214 lbs. athlete. "One other thing about that year. When we lost to Duke (2 OT) I remember wondering if I had made the wrong choice. That's just the way a kid thinks."

"The thing about Ron Sepic," recalls Fred Taylor, "is he had no fear of failure. He was always ready to take the big shot when the game was on the line. Some players avoid a situation where the pressure is really on, but Ron never did."

* * * *

The schedule maker generously provided back-to-back games with Wisconsin (to finish 4-10 in the league) and the Buckeyes took advantage, winning 98-86 at home and 73-71 after a trip by the trophy case in Madison. Ricketts and Sepic led the scoring, Shaffer and Sepic got help on the boards from Ahijevych.

However four straight losses, to Illinois and Iowa at home and Illinois and Michigan on the road, removed all hope of a sixth straight championship. In fact, with an 8-11 record and five games to go, a losing season seemed inevitable.

Up to this point, the highlight of the season was probably the time Andy Ahijevych was guest on The Fred Taylor Show. Andy says it was "a thrill." Jimmy Crum, the host, says it is the single public event for which he has received the most comments.

"This particular show we were taping, because we had to leave for a road game. Fred, Andy and I were on a stage, and I was leaning back in my chair. I leaned too far," says Crum, beginning to laugh at the memory, "and fell over backwards. When I saw the tape later it showed my feet straight up in the air, then my body completely off camera.

"The first thing Fred said was 'are you all right?' The second thing he said was 'I'm leaving it in the show.' Even today, people mention that to me," Jimmy says.

Ahijevych, off camera, had become a starter and played very well in the home stretch for Ohio State. He averaged 17 ppg and 10 rpg in the four victories to close the season.

Today Fred Taylor recalls visiting with Andy and his mother. "Andy was born in a German detention camp and his mother had not yet learned to speak English very well. When I explained how a basketball scholarship would work, she was confused. He turned to her and said 'It means if I play basketball at Ohio State, I can go to college for free.' Then she started to cry with joy," says Taylor.

Another key to Ohio State's late season surge was Bob Dove, who says he "went from first string forward to third string center" after the Minnesota game. He had worked his way to first string center, and averaged 13 points and nine rebounds in the last five games.

* * * *

"Bob Dove even walks left handed," Jimmy Crum used to say.

"I wasn't quick enough for forward, so center was a better position," Dove feels today. Yet Coach Taylor remembers "He wasn't big enough (6'6, 210 lbs.) to play center — we used him at the high post a lot."

Through it all Dove had become a key player on the team. He would be elected Captain for 1965-66 and finish second on the team in scoring. Quite an achievement, but his greatest accomplishment may have been his senior year in high school when he chose a school other than Notre Dame.

"My father was a football All-American at Notre Dame in 1941 and 1942," says Bob, matter of factly. "He played for the El Toro Bombers, one of the service teams, and in the old All-American Football League and in the NFL. Then he coached in college and pro ball after that.

"We lived in Canfield, a suburb of Youngstown. Dad didn't want to push me to Notre Dame, but I remember one Saturday he said, 'How'd you like to take a drive?' We ended up in South Bend, talking to Moose Krause, Dad's friend and the Athletic Director. He offered me a scholarship.

"When we left his office I met a priest. While we were talking he mentioned that he hoped I would have a chance to attend Notre Dame. When I said I had just been offered a scholarship he said 'Hell, son, what are you waiting for?' But I really liked Fred and Frank Truitt, so I ended up in Columbus."

136

In 1949, Fred Taylor was Ohio State's first baseman. [2]

In 1968, Bill Hosket initiates Fred Taylor into the Junior honorary Bucket and Dipper. His eligibility over, Hosket seemed to enjoy the assignment. [2]

The coaching staff 1958-1965: Jack Graf (left), Fred Taylor, Frank Truitt. [2]

The 1960 NCAA championship team. [2]

Celebration in San Francisco's Cow Palace, 1960. Left to right, Joe Roberts. Dick Furry, Larry Siegfried, Dave Barker, Gary Gearhart, John Havlicek, Fred Taylor, Mel Nowell, Bob Knight, Howie Nourse, Richie Hoyt, Jack Graf. [2]

Larry Siegfried (21) drives against Michigan as John Havlicek (5) and Dick Furry (12) prepare to rebound. OSU won 99-52 in 1960. [2]

John Havlicek rebounds against Detroit as Mel Nowell (3) and Jerry Lucas (11) head up court. OSU won 84-73 in 1961. [1]

Jerry Lucas hooks against Walter Bellamy of Indiana. The 96-95 victory was critical as OSU won the Big Ten before winning the 1960 NCAA championship. [2]

Gary Gearhart hugs Larry Siegfried and Fred Taylor tries to steady them after Ohio State beat California 75-55 for the 1960 NCAA title. [2]

Dick Furry carries the NCAA trophy off the plane, followed by Larry Siegfried and John Havlicek. [2]

U.S. Senator John Bricker addresses a crowd of 10,000 at the Columbus Airport for the NCAA victory celebration. Fred Taylor is behind his left shoulder, Mel Nowell behind his head and Jerry Lucas behind his right shoulder. [2]

Four seniors—Mel Nowell (3), John Havlicek (5), Bob Knight (24) and Jerry Lucas (11)—surround Terry Dischinger (in front of Lucas) as Ohio State beats Purdue 91-65 in 1962. [2]

Gary Bradds grabs a rebound in Ohio State's 78-73 victory over Creighton in 1963. Dick Reasbeck (10), Don DeVoe and Doug Mc-Donald watch Bradds take the ball from Paul Silas (35). [1]

Dick Ricketts hits a dramatic jump shot at the end of regulation to beat St. John's 66-64 December 7, 1963. Tom Bowman looks to rebound, Jim Shaffer sets a screen and Don Flatt is behind "Rick". [1]

UCLA's Lew Alcindor (now Kareem Abdul-Jabbar) towers over Dave Sorenson (15), Ed Smith (24) and Craig Barclay (44). UCLA 84-73. [1]

Bill Hosket (25) scores as OSU defeats East Tennessee State 79-72 to advance in the 1968 NCAA Regional. [1]

Luke Witte (34) scores and Jim Cleamons and Mark Minor look on as Ohio State defeats Alabama 74-58. [1]

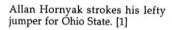

Allan Hornyak strokes his lefty jumper for Ohio State. [1]

* * * *

While Ahijevych and Dove were major contributors, and Sepic had 12 to 18 points every game, the key to OSU's finish was the Captain, No. 4. Ricketts became a dominant force, looking for his shot more often yet hitting 58% in the stretch, grabbing over six rebounds and getting "countless steals and even more assists" in the words of *Citizen-Journal* writer Kaye Kessler. He averaged 27 points per game in the last five as the Bucks beat Michigan State (101-90) and Northwestern (100-87) at home, got outgunned at Indiana by the Van Arsdales and Jon McGlocklin (110-90) then won at Michigan State (97-75).

Reminded of his accomplishments today, Rick says "I probably should have started shooting earlier in the year."

Asked what was on his mind going into the last game of the year against powerful Michigan, the details are clear to Ricketts today. "If we lost our record would have been 11-13. Fred had never been below .500. I didn't want to be on this first losing team."

With that in mind it was only logical for Ricketts to make 14 of 24 field goal attempts, including four straight near the end, score 32 points and lead Ohio State to a 93-85 victory over the 21-2 Wolves, ranked first in the country.

Though he did most of the ball-handling and had twice as many points as any teammate, Rick did not win the game single-handedly. Dove and Ahijevych totaled 26 points and 14 rebounds. Shaffer came off the bench with 15 points and seven rebounds. Sophomore Sepic added 16 points and eight rebounds, while part of a Taylor stratagem. Down 28-18 with 9:11 left in the first half, Taylor put Shaffer in at forward and moved Sepic to guard, a position he had not played all year. At the half it was 39-all.

The second half was a struggle for a while. A Ricketts steal and pass for a Sepic lay-up tied the game at 50-50. Three straight Shaffer hoops got the lead and four straight jumpers by Ricketts opened it up.

When the horn went off fans flooded the floor and Buckeye players carried Ricketts off on their shoulders. For the first time all night he appeared to be losing his confidence; a fall to the floor looked inevitable. But he made it to the locker room.

After the game Taylor sought out Cazzie Russell, who had been on the bench with a 101 degree temperature, and said "I doubt if we could have done it with you in there."

Maybe not, but Bill Buntin (27 points), Oliver Darden (22 points, 15 rebounds), and the rest might still have been the best team in the Big Ten. It was a great finish and, in Fred's words, "won't make the winter so long." The locker room celebration included several high school players who would be part of a very good recruiting class that year.

Dick Ricketts, the best player Ohio State had during the Golden Age who nobody remembers, was only named third team All-Big Ten. He never played in the NBA ("There weren't as many good coaches in the league then as there are today," explains Taylor. "He was good enough to help a team, but not flashy enough to get their attention," says Bill Hosket. "He took good shots, so scouts were unsure of his range. He scored in the team offense, so there was a concern about his one-on-one game."). Ricketts never even played in the NCAA tournament, because "the Rose Bowl Rule" kept two co-championship teams out. He is not a member of 1000 point club because he fed Gary Bradds so well. He ended with 998 points in three years. So fans forget. Yet coaches, players, and broadcasters from the time unanimously cite his coolness under pressure, his competitive fire and his effective, efficient game. His loss would be felt deeply.

On the national level, Michigan blasted Dayton 98-71 and edged Vanderbilt 87-85 before beating Princeton in the semi-finals, 93-76. Michigan lost to UCLA in the finals as Gail Goodrich scored 42 points for the champions.

1965 — 1966

The *Sports Illustrated* jinx visited Columbus, Ohio in 1966. *SI* announced that Ohio State had the No. 8 team in the country, focusing on Ron Sepic: "wavy black hair" ... "leading man" looks ... "high school All-American football end" ... "medical school" ... "playing the saxophone as a youngster" ... but minimizing his conversion from forward to guard. *SI* saw no problems there, especially with sophomore Bill Hosket "frequently and favorably compared to Jerry Lucas" on hand.

To top it all off, *SI* talked about the strong front line returning and forgot to mention that the Buckeyes had been outrebounded by two boards per game by opponents the previous year. Not a great analysis, but it did create a lot of pressure.

"We just had too many guys trying to figure out how they fit in," says Hosket today. "Plus Frank Truitt had gone to Louisiana State University. He had recruited all of us, and it felt strange not to have

138

him there. 'Burky' did a fine job, but it was just one more change during a general time of transition."

* * * *

After playing three sports at Bluffton High School, Bob Burkholder went into the service, serving about 18 months. He enrolled at Ohio State University in the fall of 1946 and went out for football. "I lasted about a day and a half," he recalls. He switched to basketball, playing jayvee as a freshman and starting for the varsity for the next three years. The Buckeyes went 10-10, 14-7 and 22-4, winning the Big Ten his senior year.

"I was just a country kid from a small town. Ohio State was — and is — a great school. It was a very happy experience playing here," remembers Burkholder. "Fred and I were road roomies. We used to lie in bed and say 'Wouldn't it be nice to coach at Ohio State some day?'"

Frank Truitt, who had contributed mightily to the success of the teams during his seven years as freshman coach, accepted the head coaching position at Louisiana State University after the 1965 season. Taylor knew where to look for a replacement.

"Fred called in the spring," remembers Burkholder, "and said 'are you interested in coming back?' I said 'Sure.' My wife and I had dreamed about going back to our alma mater. Fred said 'I need to do some things.' We never talked about it again until August. That's when he offered me the job.

"My responsiblities were recruiting, scouting and coaching the freshman team. I also started a program of team evaluation and team grading. In time we had a career profile of every player in the Big Ten. Players play within a personality, so this career profile was very helpful. We charted different types of fouls: on a drive, on a rebound, contesting a jump shot, offensive. We had data to show the players that shooting percentages were higher on shots taken on a pass back to the weak side than when the shot was taken off a dribble on the strong side. Statistics can really tell a story."

* * * *

Actually *Sports Illustrated* was right to an extent. Ohio State did finish No. 8 — in the conference. But not due to lack of effort.

"I did everything I could think of over the summer to get ready to play guard," recalls Sepic. "I had chairs and boxes scattered around in the alley, and dribbled through them while wearing sunglasses

139

with pieces of cardboard taped to the bottom to prevent my looking down to see the ball. I wore a canvas vest with weights, and ankle spats. I wore gloves with the finger tips cut off, so I couldn't use my whole hand to dribble. I did that all summer and still had trouble dribbling with my left hand. If Fred had switched me today, it might have been okay," Ron considers. "What used to be called carrying the ball is acceptable now. That would have helped."

The season started on the right foot with a 76-74 victory at Missouri. The field goal shooting was dreadful at 35%, but Dove, Ahijevych, Sepic and Hosket (with 20 rebounds) controlled the boards. Al Rowley joined them in the starting line-up and Al Peters and junior Jerry Tischer were first off the bench.

*   *   *   *

"I had been looking forward to that Missouri game so much it seemed like it was over in four minutes," says Hosket today.

Wilmer Hosket, Bill's father, had been first team All-Big Ten while leading Ohio State to the conference championship in 1933. He had starred for Floyd Stahl on three big school state championship teams at Dayton Stivers in 1928 (25-20 over Canton McKinley), 1929 (36-22 over Dover) and 1930 (18-16 over Akron East). Logically it was easy to recruit young Bill.

Not so, according to chief recruiter Frank Truitt. "We really wanted him, I'll tell you that. I saw him play nine times in high school," recalls Truitt. "Kentucky went after him real hard. I was afraid he'd like their offense — he'd have scored like crazy with all those screens they set for their forwards."

"Kentucky did recruit me pretty hard," nods Hosket. "They came 16 times. I remember the number because it impressed me, until I heard that the coach who was recruiting me had a girl friend in Dayton. Was I a priority or an excuse?"

Clearly a priority, based on his other experiences with UK.

"I went down for an informal visit in the fall of my senior year to look around and see a football game. They had a meal for a few of us and my glass at the table had a list of Kentucky All-Americans. They had a great tradition so a lot of the names were familiar to me, especially the current star Cotton Nash. Then I noticed that right below his name was Bill Hosket, 1968, which would be my senior year. That got my attention."

His senior year was near-perfect. Teaming with 6'4 Don May, then 6'6 Hosket led Dayton Belmont to a 26-1 record and a rout of Cleveland East 89-60 in the state final. Hosket was named first team All-Ohio by UPI, May second team. Future Buckeye Mike Swain was also on the second team.

"After the state tournament I received this long telegram from Cotton Nash," remembers Hosket. "He went into considerable detail about our victory and how he hoped I would be enrolling at Kentucky. Then when I took my official visit in the spring I happened to run into him on campus. He asked how our season had turned out, and it was clear one of the coaches had written the telegram and signed Cotton's name. They really had a great atmosphere — they treated their basketball like Ohio State treated football — but they over did some things.

"Other than Kentucky and Ohio State I also visited Duke and Louisville. Several Louisville graduates, including Bud Olsen from their '61 team which almost upset Ohio State, lived in my neighborhood. Plus I had gotten to know Wes Unseld, thought he might end up at Louisville and I liked the idea of playing with him."

So why Ohio State?

"My father died when I was 10, so we had never seriously talked about a college baskeball scholarship. But he had to have an influence. His friends did too, because I was always 'the son of Bill Hosket, the Ohio State basketball player.'

"My mother tried not to influence the decision, but I remember going to the Governor's Mansion during my official visit. Wes (Unseld) and I were there the same weekend. Governor Rhodes saw my mother, shouted 'Ethel' and they embraced. Obviously they had been friends long ago.

"What it came down to was growing up in Ohio and watching those five championship teams. That, and Fred Taylor and Frank Truitt. They really seemed to make a good combination. And they did. Frank was the best teacher of individual skills I've ever been around, and Fred had the best half court offensive scheme I ever saw — Olympics, NBA, 1970's, 80's, 90's, ever. When we'd play Michigan Fred would tell us 'Now we're going to score 90 points tonight. The only question is whether or not we can hold them below that.'

"And Frank would come up with all these creative ideas, so Fred could sift through, consider, and select the ones to blend into the system.

141

"I remember before the first Michigan game in 1965, the freshmen were running the Michigan offense. I was impersonating Cazzie Russell. They even gave me No. 33. Their offense consisted of a series of screens to get the ball to Cazzie — me — for a jump shot. It was one of those nights when everything you throw up goes in. It was fun. I had 20 some points at the half. So Frank goes up to Fred and says 'This stuff (offense) is really good. We need to put this in ourselves.' Here's Fred trying to figure out how to defend against an offense and Frank wants him to put it in the day before a game. Fred just sort of shook his head.

"I think I really knew that Ohio State was the right place when Fred came for his official visit. Just before he was scheduled to arrive things got a little crazy. I had a call from Louisville, and a coach from Illinois rang the doorbell and wanted to talk 'for a couple of minutes.'

"My mother and I are trying to be good hosts, and I'm a little concerned about Fred arriving in the middle of this. I went into the kitchen to get something and there's Fred, talking to my sister. He had come in the back door — I don't know how long he was there.

"Fred said the same thing he told everybody else, 'Two things I guarantee you will happen when you come to Ohio State — you will get a college education and we will work toward winning the Big Ten'. Players later compared notes and it was the same word for word, every time."

After the pressure of recruiting, and before the pressure of being "the next Jerry Lucas" as a sophomore, was the freshman year.

"That was fun. I roomed with Mike Swain, my closest friend to this day. We had met during recruiting — I remember Kentucky telling me Mike was going there, and they told him I was going there, and we both ended up in Columbus.

"The thing about freshman year I remember the most is practicing with the varsity. That was an adjustment. Once I got a couple of blocked shots early in practice, and seemed to get on a roll. I blocked at least one shot by almost everyone of the varsity players. It felt great. I even caught Dick Ricketts by surprise and blocked one of his shots, which was very rare.

"So Fred said 'I don't think he understands you're the *Captain* of this team.' Not two minutes later Rick drove to the basket, I dropped down to defend, he gave a great head fake, I went for it, he jumped into me, knocked me down while making the basket. He gave me a quick glance before running down court.

"As I got up I wasn't mad at Rick but I sure was mad at Fred. But that was life as a freshman, and as a senior too. Fred expected his seniors to step up, even if it was in practice."

Bob Dove remembers Hosket being like Sepic as a freshman. "Lots of publicity, but very unassuming. There was no ego or arrogance to deal with."

"The other thing that stands out from my freshman year," recalls Hosket, "is that at the Appreciation Banquet some of the seniors cried during their farewell remarks because they didn't win the championship. That impressed us as freshmen."

* * * *

In the second game OSU helped dedicate UCLA's new Pauley Pavilion as the newspapers promised the sell-out crowd a chance to see the nation's two best teams. One was the UCLA varsity, two time national champions with several returning veterans and sophomore Mike Warren, who would become an outstanding player and then a well known actor. The other "best" team was the UCLA freshmen of Lew Alcinder, Lucius Allen and Lynn Schackleford, who played before the varsity game. Hosket had 24 points and Ahijevych 17, but the Bruins won 92-66. "I remember being glad we didn't play the freshmen," says Hosket.

Visiting North Carolina shot well from the field, largely due to steals from their pressure defense, and beat OSU 82-72. "We played against the pressure like we were apologizing for having the simple ball," said Taylor after the game. Handling the ball against pressure would continue to be a problem in 1966.

The Bucks won at Butler before exams but shot 19 of 62 to lose 83-58 at St. Louis after tests were completed. Rowley and Peters were both having trouble at guard beside Sepic. Marv Gregory and sophomore Mike Swain got starting assignments and Bob Dove held Iowa State star Don Smith to five points as OSU won 87-70.

Gregory had been honorable mention All-Ohio at Wilmington but came to Ohio State without a scholarship. At the age of four he had lost an eye, but overcame that to captain his high school baseball, golf and track teams. At Ohio State "he was one of our most consistent practice players," recalls Fred Taylor, "even though there were times he just got hammered when he ran into screens which he couldn't see." Gregory had seven points against Iowa State and started the next four games. Kansas came to St. John Arena and won 81-68; OSU victories over Wake Forest and West Texas made the record 5-4.

Ohio State played "probably our best of the season" in the Big Ten opener according to Coach Taylor. However too much Cazzie Russell (32 points) and Oliver Darden (25) meant an 83-78 victory for visiting Michigan.

Michigan State beat the visiting Bucks 80-64, with the only bright spot for the Buckeyes the play of 5'10 junior Warren "Kip" Whitlinger off the bench. The son of Warren W. Whitlinger, Buckeye letterman in 1934-5-6 and captain as a senior, the "legacy" from Neenah, Wisconsin tied Hosket for team high with 14 points. A very quick, up-tempo player, "Kip" had an excellent shooting eye in high school, with a high game of 55 points. Unfortunately, he broke his arm when he was thrown from a convertible in an auto accident in August before he enrolled at Ohio State. It did not heal properly, had to be broken and reset. His only start as a Buckeye came in the next game, a 79-73 win against Northwestern. He saw limited action in a total of eight games as a junior and did not play as a senior. What if he had a) not been injured, or b) recuperated fully, and c) been able to learn to blend his quickness into the Buckeye scheme ...?

At Iowa the Bucks played well using a stack offense which would be a big part of their success in future years, sank 36 of 65 shots (.554) but lost 98-89. One Iowa writer termed the officiating style "No suture, no foul." It was rough. "As referee Russ Kaefer went by the OSU bench, Fred Taylor shouted 'Amazing.' Next trip Fred said 'Absolutely amazing.' Then, just before the technical, Fred said 'All these people and these bright lights and *you've fallen asleep'*," remembers Hosket.

With a 1-3 Big Ten mark the Bucks probably weren't the best team in Columbus. Central Ohio Welding had Gary Bradds, Dick Ricketts, Joe Roberts, Mel Nowell, Tom Bowman, Jim Shaffer and Jim Doughty together in a parks and recreation league.

Al Rowley played well in a starting assignment and Sepic scored 26 as OSU beat Hardin Simmons 72-64, then Rowley had 18 and Al Peters got 20 in his first start in several games in a victory over Wisconsin. The overtime win against the Badgers was the first time all season that five starters had scored in double figures.

* * * *

Junior Al Rowley (dubbed "Rooster" by Jimmy Crum "because he had this crop of red hair and a slim build") had been benched early in the year, before a strong relief appearance against Northwestern earned him a chance to start against Iowa. Today he remembers what he learned on the bench.

"When it happened I was angry, and reacted by pouting. My fianceé told me I was acting like a spoiled brat. She said 'If I were you I'd go talk to Fred.' That was difficult for me, but eventually I did. One day before practice I apologized, said he'd see improvement. If he saw fit, I'd like another chance.

"While we were playing basketball at Ohio State Fred taught us how to compete in the real world. Life is not easy. He taught me not to be self-centered, to look at the bigger picture. He's a great man and he taught me more than just basketball."

Rowley's family had followed the great Buckeye teams in the early '60s from their home in Marion, about an hour north of Columbus. "Rooster" was sixth man on the Marion Harding varsity as a sophomore.

"My junior year (1962) we tied for the conference championship but got upset by Upper Sandusky in the state tournament," recalls Rowley. "I had the flu that game. My senior year I was the only starter back, and Lima Senior killed us in the first game. I remember thinking 'What a year this is going to be.' Then we won 13 straight, lost at the buzzer, and won 13 more before losing to Columbus East in the state finals." Rowley was named tournament MVP.

"My father went to OSU," recalls Rowley, "so they were always in my thinking when recruiting began. I considered Vanderbilt, Michigan and Dayton. I later found out that Cincinnati was interested in me but I never knew it. They would call and my mother would tell them I was out, or not give me the message when I came back. She was still mad at them for the two times they beat Ohio State.

"My only official visit was to Ohio State. I went down and said 'If you want me, I'm coming!' That was that."

At Ohio State, Denny Meadors remembers "the Rooster" much like everyone does — "average ball handler but good defender with good speed and a good jump shot." Rowley started the majority of games played while he was on the varsity and was a solid Big Ten player at 6', 168 lbs.

When his Buckeye teammates remember Al, they always comment on his health — or poor health — or hypochondria. "He had more things wrong with him than most people have things," says one.

"When we went to Houston to play his sophomore year we were on the bus to the game and he said his stomach was upset," recalls

Bob Dove. "I was joking around, handed him his hat — Fred always wanted us to wear hats when we traveled — and said something like 'If you don't feel good, use your hat.' When we got off the bus I noticed he didn't have his hat on. Sure enough, he had filled it up and left it on the bus."

Rowley had more to learn on the road.

"One trip I roomed with Marv Gregory. We all knew he had impaired vision, but I didn't realize he actually had a glass eye. Before he turned out the light he took his eye out, put it in a glass of water by the bed, and said 'Rooster, I'm going to keep an eye on you tonight.' That sort of shook me up."

Another strong memory of Rowley's sophomore year is the leadership of Dick Ricketts. "He was a very strong person, a very savvy individual. He was a great leader for our team, and single-handedly beat Michigan. He did a lot to help me become acclimated to college ball." Andy Ahijevych remembers Rowley as "an instigator, like Ricketts."

Without Ricketts, and with Sepic learning a new position, Rowley struggled in the first half of his junior year. In the second half he locked up the starting guard spot. Between his junior and senior year he spent an interesting summer with another college athlete who would impact the Ohio State program many years later.

"I was majoring in financial planning and insurance," recalls Rowley, "and had worked with Lincoln National. They selected 10 students from throughout the country for a special program, and I was one of them. It was held in Fort Wayne, Indiana and my room-mate was a Maryland basketball player named Gary Williams.

"We went everywhere to play ball, including more than a few places we had no business being. We became good friends, in fact when I found out he was being considered for the Ohio State job, I called everyone I could." Williams was head coach at OSU 1987-89, before leaving for Maryland.

*   *   *   *

A victory at Illinois would have brought the Big Ten record to 3-3 and might have set the stage for a late season rush. But the Bucks lost a 78-77 decision to the Illini (5-1). Captain Bob Dove spent 18 minutes on the bench with fouls, and Bill Hosket missed 12 minutes. Both fouled out, as did Rowley.

146

Visiting Purdue fell 68-54 as the starting five of Peters — Hosket — Dove — Sepic — Rowley played the first 38:45 and generated a 68-49 margin. But the Bucks lost 81-61 at Indiana and to Iowa at home, 86-80. Their record fell to 3-6.

All five starters scored 15 or more, led by Al Peters' 28, and OSU won at Minnesota 102-98. But the stop at Northwestern resulted in a 78-77 loss. Then Michigan State came to St. John and blasted the home team 98-79.

Bill Hosket had 33 points in a victory over Minnesota and 32 in a loss to Purdue, but Ohio State ended its first losing season under Fred Taylor with an 11-13 mark.

Lack of speed, lack of size, lack of consistency and lack of a take charge guy were mentioned by *Citizen-Journal* columnist Tom Keyes in his review of the season.

On other floors, near and far away, Taylor's coaching heritage was becoming apparent. Just a few blocks from St. John Arena, Doug McDonald was developing a power in his first year at Upper Arlington High School. At West Point 24 year old Bob Knight had a fine first year as head coach of the Army team.

On a national level, 1966 would become known as the year UCLA did *not* win the NCAA. Big Ten champion Michigan lost to No. 1 ranked Kentucky 84-77 in the Mideast Regional. Kentucky beat No. 2 Duke 83-79 but lost to Texas Western, later University of Texas at El Paso, 72-65, in the final game.

1966 — 1967

With starters Hosket, Sepic and Rowley back, along with "the most competitive freshman class since I've been here" according to Coach Taylor, plus Michigan, Iowa, Minnesota, Wisconsin and Purdue each losing four starters to graduation, there was cause for cautious optimism as the 1967 season approached.

Then their starting center was lost on the first day of practice.

Fred Taylor had decided to move Bill Hosket, now 6'8, to center and Ron Sepic back to forward. This put the best rebounders closer to the basket and more quickness into the line-up. Hosket had worked hard over the summer, scrimmaging regularly with NBA stars like John Havlicek and Larry Siegfried, and recent alums like Joe Roberts. "I was ready to play," he recalls. About 10 minutes into the first practice he twisted his left knee.

"I sat out nearly three weeks," says Hosket, "while doctors tried to determine if the problem was ligament or cartilage or both. Today it would be scoped and a player could be back in a month. Also today a player could sit out a year, then play an extra year after graduation. Then you couldn't play while in grad school. Besides, I wanted to play."

In addition to the anxiety, pain and frustration of the injury, today Bill Hosket remembers a visit from Coach Taylor. "He came to my apartment to see me after the injury. He was very caring and reassuring. That meant a lot, because while we were in school he was a little distant from the players. Maybe he had to be, since he was in charge. After school, as we all know now, there is no distance — we are just good friends. When I was hurt I got a glance into the future to see that friendship during a difficult time, and I appreciated it."

So Hosket tried playing, tried resting and tried to get the doctors to decide. Nothing seemed to work. He never got to work at his new position and Taylor "took our plans back to the drawing board and prepared as if Hosket wouldn't be available."

That meant working two undersized sophomores, 6'6 Steve Barnard of Columbus West and 6'5 Steve Howell of Columbus Eastmoor, at center. Both had averaged in double figures on the freshman team but Howell, who had 20.1 ppg, was an excellent shooter facing the basket and unproven with his back to it. When word circulated about Hosket, the Big Ten coaches picked Ohio State to finish ninth. Michigan State was the favorite.

Two seniors (Sepic and Rowley) and three sophomores (Jeff Miller, Denny Meadors and Barnard) led the Bucks to a 2-0 start with victories over Butler 74-67 at home and at Iowa State 79-77. The road win bordered on miraculous because: 1. The OSU leading scorer was sub Steve Howell, 2. Sepic and Miller played the last 20 minutes with four fouls each, 3. Senior Rowley had foul trouble also and Sepic played most of the second half with four sophomores, 4. The Bucks didn't lead in the second half until Meadors made a drive at 1:04 to play to make the score 77-76. But 2-0 felt good.

A trip to Kansas brought the Bucks back to earth as the Jayhawks led by 30 before winning 94-70.

The only Buckeye who stood out against Kansas was Lima Shawnee sophomore Jeff Miller, who had 26 points (11 of 17 from the field) and six rebounds.

* * * *

"Jeff Miller was a tough kid," remembers Fred Taylor. "He learned his basketball on the playground, and had a scorer's mentality. His most unique talent was the ability to maneuver in traffic and still create a good shot. Some people go inside and put up a prayer — Jeff was able to get a good shot when it didn't seem like he had enough space to do it."

Miller had been the biggest prize in an excellent recruiting year, the last one in which Frank Truitt was involved. Truitt left to take the head coaching job at Louisiana State University in the spring of 1965, after helping Taylor sign Miller, Steve Howell, Denny Meadors, Larry Hisle, Steve Barnard, Bruce Schnabel and John Halley. Miller was first team All-Ohio and UPI Player of The Year as a 6'4, 205 lbs. forward for Lima Shawnee, undefeated prior to the tournament. Hisle was also first team, Halley was second team, the others honorable mention, except Schnabel, who was All-West Virginia first team.

Miller led the freshman team in scoring and was a starter as soon as he was eligible as a sophomore. Even as a sophomore he was "a decent defender" — high praise for a sophomore from Fred Taylor.

* * * *

OSU beat Washington State and TCU in St. John Arena as Hosket began to play. Then Bob Knight's Army team almost upset the home team, but lost on a Steve Howell rebound basket, 61-59. A 6' guard from Chicago named Mike Krzyzewski, later to become an outstanding coach at Duke, had six points for the Cadets.

The trip to Greensboro, North Carolina for a Friday-Saturday pair with Duke and North Carolina provided a range of emotions from anger to elation to shock, and proved to be both the mountain top experience and the beginning of the end of the season.

Fred Taylor addresses the anger. "Vic Bubas and I had set up the Friday game and Dean Smith called to schedule us for Saturday. I said something like 'No. We aren't going to wear ourselves out Friday, then play you Saturday after your guys spent the night before at home resting. That would be crazy.' He promised to schedule a Big Ten opponent, he mentioned Illinois, or someone comparable for Friday. With that clear understanding we arranged to play Saturday.

"That summer we got their schedule — we always got them in advance to arrange our scouting — and they didn't have a game Friday. Their last game was something like the Tuesday before against a weak opponent. I went in to see Dick Larkins, our Athletic Director, to cancel the game. Obviously I was unhappy. Dick said 'No, the contract has been signed and Ohio State will honor the contract'."

Elation came when Ohio State avenged a one point loss in 1964 and a double overtime loss in 1965 by beating Duke 83-82. Ron Sepic earned the game ball as he hit 14 of 19 shots and scored 32 points. Bill Hosket scored 16; Jeff Miller had 13 points and a team high eight rebounds. But right behind Captain Sepic as star of the game was Denny Meadors, fire in the back court and ice on the foul line. He made a one and one at 0:17 to go, despite two consecutive times out by Duke Coach Bubas, to clinch the victory. For the night he had 10 points on two of two from the field and six of seven at the line. He was clearly the guard the Bucks had needed in 1965-66.

* * * *

"We had a good team at Dayton Stebbins", recalls the 6' Meadors. "Our center was David Bell. He was 6'6 and scored about 19 points per game. Ohio State recruited him but he went to Tennessee. And Bill Long, the future Ohio State quarterback, was a good player. One game Woody Hayes was there to see Bill, Ray Mears of Tennessee to see Dave, and Frank Truitt and Don Donoher (Dayton) were there to see Dave and me. But we lost to Belmont (Hosket and May) and Chaminade (putting together a team which won the state the year after Meadors graduated) in the state tournament.

"Our coach was Jim Morgan, who had played at Louisville with Charlie Tyra in the mid '50's. I remember he was very impressed with Fred. I wanted to play close to home, and had followed the Big Ten, so I went to Ohio State over Louisville, Dayton, Wake Forest and some of the MAC schools.

"In May, 1965, the day I agreed to go to Ohio State but before signing, I was at a shopping center. Some guy I didn't know was picking on a guy I did know a little. When I tried to break it up I was hit in the left eye with a bottle.

"For three days we didn't know whether or not the eye could be saved. There were two different surgeries then, and two more before fall. Glass had cut the eye, causing pressure to build up and therefore glaucoma. The eye still has scar tissue, and is legally blind. To protect the ball from defenders, I developed the habit of dribbling by the left sideline. This exposed the ball to the court, but at least I had good vision in my right eye and no one could sneak up on my left side.

"Anyway, Fred called when he heard and came to the hospital as soon as he could. He said 'If you never put on a uniform, you still have that grant. Don't worry about a thing, just get well.' That gave me a great sense of comfort, and later even more incentive to contribute to the team to repay his kindness," says Meadors.

"After I told him that," recalls Taylor, "I went to Dick Larkins, our Athletic Director, and told him what had happened. If I was in trouble I wanted to know it then. He said 'If you had done anything else I'd have kicked your — — —, you big lug.' I loved working for that man."

Meadors' recuperation was far from smooth. "People told me to rest the eye over the summer but it didn't seem to be improving," he recalls. "One day in July or August I went to the gym and took 20 shots, hit nothing. I cried." Having averaged 22 ppg as a senior, he didn't know if he'd score again in a game.

"My freshman year Bruce Schnabel from West Virginia and John Halley were starting guards, and Joe Sadelfeld (on baseball scholarship as a pitcher) and I were pretty even as the top back-up. About halfway through the year I got into the starting line-up, and a little later my eye seemed to stabilize. Previously I had been a finesse player, but I got more aggressive. The keys to playing time for me were passing and defense.

"I worked very hard the summer before my sophomore year. I wanted to start, and thought I could. Bo Rein (football player) and I stayed in Columbus and built concession stands in the football stadium," Meadors concludes.

He had become an absolute fixture in the line-up, starting every game for the 6-1 Buckeyes, shooting 45% from the field and 69% from the line. He was back from the eye injury.

* * * *

North Carolina, rated No. 3 in the country with Larry Miller, Bob Lewis, Bill Bunting, and Rusty Clark, probably didn't need the extra rest as they rolled over Ohio State 105-82.

Plus Denny Meadors was injured. He would play in bits and pieces for the rest of the year, but did not approach his earlier level of effectiveness until his junior year.

"The doctors had trouble diagnosing it. First they said it was tendinitis. All I know is I couldn't get on my toes, couldn't jump, had no quickness and a lot of pain. When they did exploratory surgery they found that the left Achilles tendon was three-fourths torn. I was fortunate — the technology then might not have been sufficient for me to ever return if it had been fully torn."

With Meadors gone, Sepic battling shin splints, recent starter Schnabel suffering throat trouble and Hosket doing all he could to play himself into shape at the unfamiliar center spot, the Bucks went into Big Ten play a little shaky. But the trip to Minnesota was a success as all five starters hit double figures and the Bucks won 78-65. Joe Sadelfeld got the starting call and scored 16 points as the Bucks overcame a 4 of 16 night from the field by Ron Sepic. ("Sepic had a wrist turn on his shot," recalls assistant Jack Graf. "That kept him from being a consistent shooter.")

Sadelfeld was a 6'2 sophomore from Cincinnati St. Xavier, where his team narrowly missed the 1965 state championship, losing 54-53 to Columbus South in the final game. He earned a spot on the all-tournament team with his play. An excellent southpaw pitcher, he had broken his left arm during the summer of 1965 while playing baseball. That injury caused him to miss his freshman season of basketball; later a broken bone in his hand ended his basketball career as a Buckeye, as he chose to concentrate on baseball.

Sepic's shooting woes (one of 10) against Indiana, combined with only one field goal from the guards, resulted in an 81-80 loss to the visitors. Bill Hosket scored 32 points and had a game high 15 rebounds, despite fouling out on a questionable call with 5:03 to go.

Eighteen first half turnovers caused an 84-73 loss at Georgia Tech. OSU was playing so badly they lost at home to Minnesota, which they had earlier beaten on the road and which had lost four straight.

* * * *

"The guard play hurt us against Georgia Tech," remembers Hosket. "We needed Meadors, but he was hurt. After that game I heard one of the coaches say 'If only Larry Hisle hadn't signed that baseball contract.' It may have been the first time I heard that comment, but not the last."

"Larry Hisle was the best high school defensive guard I ever saw," says Fred Taylor today. Since the 6'2 Hisle scored 23 per game leading Portsmouth High School to the state regionals as a junior and 25.4 ppg as a senior, when he was second to Miller as UPI Player of the year, he had the whole package. He was Scholastic Coach High School All-America as a senior.

What happened?

152

"He was an excellent baseball player at Portsmouth," says Taylor. "In fact as a junior Al Oliver (who also had a productive professional baseball career) was a teammate, in both sports. When Larry came in for Freshman Week you could tell something happened. He signed with the Philadelphia Phillies, and went on to have an outstanding baseball career. I understood his decision then, but I was disappointed. I'd been looking forward to watching him play.

"The other thing was this crazy rule we had at the time. Once a player signed with a school, the school was charged with his scholarship for four years. That was a band-aid solution to the problem of colleges running players off if they weren't good enough to play. After Larry signed to play pro baseball that made him ineligible to play. When "Kip" Whitlinger broke his arm in an auto accident after his freshman year, he couldn't play. Yet we couldn't recruit guards to replace them because their scholarships were taken. It put us in a bind. The next year the rule was changed, at least.

OK, Coach, you have a gun at your head and you *have* to speculate on what kind of player Larry Hisle would have become. What do you think?

"The closest player was probably Jim Cleamons. Larry didn't have Jim's scoring ability in the open court, but he was almost as quick. And Hisle was more physical. He'd have scored 10-14 points a game consistently, been our stopper in the back court and made us a much quicker team."

After a 14 year pro baseball career, Larry Hisle now lives in Milwaukee. His son, Larry Hisle Jr., played guard for the University of Wisconsin.

* * * *

Big games by Hosket (28 points, 18 rebounds) and Sepic (20 points, seven boards), and a quality start by Al Rowley (11 points and six boards) helped the Bucks beat Purdue 82-72. However Sadelfeld re-fractured the wrist which kept him out of action as a freshman and was lost for several games.

Buckeye fans remember the Purdue game for the fight between Roger Blalock and Steve Howell. Newspaper accounts, and Al Rowley's memory, supply more detail.

"Steve fouled Blalock on a lay-up and there was some shoving after that. As Blalock was going to the foul line he came over and knocked me down," recalls Rowley.

It is important to remember that Purdue is an engineering school and Blalock was probably a bright guy. Since Rowley was listed at 165 lbs., and Howell had a program weight of 230 lbs., most likely before he put his second foot on the scale, the Boilermaker made a wise, if not courageous, decision.

Lack of foot speed did not keep Howell from getting to Blalock in record time and pinning him to the floor, before both were ejected from the game.

"Steve had forgiven me for what I did to him on the trip to Duke," confesses Rowley. "I made him a nervous wreck. He had this cough, and I told him to lie down and get some sleep. When he went to sleep, I put blankets on him, turned up the heat in the room and left. When I got back he was taking a cold shower, trying to get his temperature down so he could play." Howell was scoreless with no shot attempts in the Duke game.

Rowley recalls what happened after Howell was ejected against Purdue.

"Jerry Tischer ("he used say 'They call met the Judge because I spend so much time on the bench'," says Taylor) went in for him. I passed the ball in bounds to him, expected to get it back from Tischer and take it up court but he started dribbling. He ran right into Purdue guard Billy Keller for a charge and a turnover. The next day in practice assistant coach Jack Graf said 'There are two people I never want to see dribbling the ball up court against the press. One of them is me, the other is you, Tischer.' "

A 27" snow storm caused numerous travel problems and the Bucks were blasted at Northwestern 100-77. Rowley handled the ball almost exclusively and freed yet another starting guard, Mike Swain, to score 19 points as OSU beat Wisconsin 90-84. Swain and three other Buckeyes were in double figures as Northern Michigan fell 80-74. Despite their injury problems the Bucks were 3-3 in the Big Ten, 10-6 overall.

Iowa edged OSU 73-72 behind 29 points by junior college transfer Sam Williams and Fred Taylor felt snake bitten. "They have won three Big Ten road games in 2 1/2 years, all three against us." Rowley and Swain had each played 40 minutes, and played well. Rebounding was strong (42-29) and shooting, led by Rowley's eight of nine, was nearly 50% for the Bucks. They just couldn't put the game away.

When Purdue overwhelmed them 86-66, the Bucks fell to 3-5.

Victories over Michigan 97-85 and Michigan State 80-64 were encouraging, but three straight losses made a .500 record in the conference impossible.

The season ended on an up note as all five starters — Hosket (24), Miller (20), Sepic (17), Swain (13) and Rowley (12) — hit double figures and OSU beat Illinois 100-79.

The strange year came to an end with Indiana and Michigan State tying for the Big Ten title at 10-4, but no conference team got a single vote in the final UPI rankings. Indiana had jumped from last (4-10) to first in one year.

Bill Hosket won the rebound title at 13.8 per game, finished second in field goal accuracy and fourth in scoring. He made All-Big Ten while recuperating from a knee injury and playing a new position.

"Bill Hosket was a great team player," recalls Bob Burkholder. "I always wanted him to use better block-out techniques and not just rely on his tremendous instinct to read the flight of the ball and know where it was going to be. He'd say 'But I got the rebound' and I'd say 'But you'd get more if you would block out'."

Asked about that today, Hosket remembers without hesitation. "Burky would get on me about my film grades for blocking out even when I was the leading rebounder. I used to say 'But Burky, if everyone blocks out someone still has to go get the ball'."

From the "Iffy Deck" come cards like: Would Hosket have been better without the injury? Could a healthy Meadors have made the difference? If OSU had won those two one point games (Indiana and Iowa), to make them 5-2, would they have finished better? How good would Hisle have been?

In the NCAA Indiana lost to Virginia Tech 79-70 in their first game. Dayton, led by Don May, beat Western Kentucky and Tennessee to go to the Final Four. The Flyers got past North Carolina, but Lew Alcindor and UCLA were much too much in the final.

* * * *

So what happened during these three years of 36-36 basketball? Weren't the players any good?

They were good — there were several good solid Big Ten players on each team. Only two drew all-conference honors — Ricketts in 1965 and Hosket in 1967 — but many could have been contributors on championship teams. In fact they all were, in either 1964 or 1968, except for Ron Sepic and Al Rowley.

It would have helped Sepic tremendously if Taylor could have taken him out for a few minutes during those poor shooting streaks. But there was no one on the bench who could contribute as much as Sepic, even on a one of nine night. And Rowley was a complimentary guard, which he was able to play with Ricketts or Meadors, rather than a primary guard, which he usually had to play as a junior and senior.

One question to ask in closing the three year drought: What about a Buckeye team with Ricketts and Hosket together? Pretty nice pair to open. If only their careers had overlapped.

IX

1968: Third in the NCAA

The 1967-68 season didn't begin in a very promising manner, and declined rapidly after that. The problems of October became bigger before November had ended. But it was to be a magical, maybe even spiritual, season.

The New Testament contains many verses which describe the benefits of ill fortune. For example, "We know that God causes all things to work together for good to those who love God" (Romans 8:28), and "Consider it all joy, my brethren, when you encounter various trials, knowing that the testing of your faith produces endurance" (James 1:2-3). While a book on basketball is not the logical place for a mini-Bible study, a review of the 1968 Ohio State season sends the observer on a search for unseen answers, because the obvious answers are not sufficient.

Around the league, no one considered Ohio State a championship contender. The writers picked Indiana by a narrow margin over Purdue, who featured a highly publicized sophomore shooter named Rick Mount. Iowa, Wisconsin and Northwestern also received first place votes. The coaches had Purdue and Indiana in a first place tie; Michigan State and Northwestern were also well regarded.

Nationally, the evaluation was not good either. *Inside Basketball*, published by *SPORT*, rated OSU ninth — only Illinois was ranked lower. The analysis said "The Buckeyes have two fine players in 6'7 Bill Hosket and 6'3 forward Jeff Miller. ... But unless they get some help, Ohio State is likely to slip below .500 this year." *Sports Illustrated* suggested that a healthy Hosket "might put Ohio State over the .500 mark."

Nor could the press guide be termed overly enthusiastic. "Ohio State should be an improved basketball team this year," was the cautious appraisal of Coach Fred Taylor. "With so many teams being better, we'll have to be stronger just to hold our position in the standings." The Bucks had ended the previous season at 6-8 in the league, tied for seventh/eighth in the standings.

That was the bad news. Then, on Saturday, November 25, it got worse. Outstanding junior forward Jeff Miller suffered a knee injury in practice. It was feared he might be lost for the season opener, possibly several games. In fact he never again played with the same athletic ability which enabled him to start every game, average 14.7 points per game and play 836 of a possible 965 minutes as a sophomore.

"We were *walking* through an emergency scoring play," recalls Taylor. "No one was running. There was no defense. His knee just gave out and he was never able to come back. For a while we thought he could, so we made 'temporary' adjustments for a few weeks. Before the season we had inserted some changes in the offense to take advantage of his ability to drive — he had a quick first step."

What if ...?

"You can't tell how good he could have been, or even if he could have switched to guard when Steve Howell proved himself at forward," says Taylor. "Some people keep getting better, some don't."

"He was better than I was," states Steve Howell frankly. "He might have played guard, or I might have been the sixth man."

"Jeff was our top offensive threat," recalls then senior Mike Swain. "He could penetrate, he was creative, a good passer — he could have been All-Big Ten."

Two days after Miller went down, the varsity had their annual pre-season scrimmage with the freshman team. Howell replaced Miller in the starting line-up, with Hosket, junior guards Denny Meadors and Bruce Schnabel, and sophomore Dave Sorenson. The freshmen only had one player — Jim Cleamons — who would ever become a regular on the varsity, but they won 71-68. With the season opener three days away, the upcoming season looked like it could be disastrous.

Head Coach Joe Carlson, co-captain of Fred Taylor's first Ohio State team in 1958-59, brought his California-Davis team to St. John for the opener and absorbed a 95-52 loss. The Bucks shot 57%, the front line was effective and the guards looked very good. Bruce

158

Schnabel shot well and, after some early nerves, Denny Meadors seemed to be back.

"I had worked very hard during the summer but the ankle didn't seem to be responding," remembers Meadors. "I was concerned. Then one day I must have torn the scar tissue. I was able to run without the limp and 95% of the pain was gone."

"I remember playing defense as a freshman," says Howell, "and having blisters which were very painful. I mentioned it to Denny. His answer was 'Don't think about.' We'll never know how much pain he played through."

Mike Bordner had been a student trainer under Ernie Biggs in 1964, and worked his way up to full-time assistant by this season. He spent time with Meadors and remembers "Denny was an over-achiever, a characteristic of most of Fred's players. Fred's character showed through his teams. Denny did not allow injuries, and he had two which were very serious, to ever be an excuse. And he was always getting something started — he had a great sense of humor."

The Bucks beat Florida State, led by a redhead named Dave Cowens, 76-69 in the next game as Hosket scored 20 points. OSU had a 25 point lead shortly after halftime, but couldn't put the game away. Taylor cited the play of Steve Howell, 19 points and "the best overall defense he's ever played," and Mike Swain, eight points and five rebounds off the bench. Cowens had 15 rebounds and 13 points.

Was Cowens, who would go on to an outstanding NBA career with the Boston Celtics, an obvious future pro?

"He was good, but didn't appear to be that good then," recalls Taylor. "We had looked into recruiting him when he was a high school player in Kentucky but his grades weren't so hot."

Visiting South Dakota provided more good news on the basketball court as OSU won 97-54. Hosket had 26 points and 10 rebounds, to put to rest concern about his knee, bumped in practice earlier in the week. Meadors, one of eight from the field against Florida State, hit five of seven ("But he never really did get his shot back after that ten-dinitis," feels Taylor). Swain "really did a good job," according to Taylor, in a starting assignment at guard. Though Jeff Miller was a constant topic of discussion — "If Jeff doesn't get better, we've got trouble," said Taylor — Steve Howell was hitting 58%. Dave Sorenson, the 6'7, 214 lbs. sophomore from Findlay who some felt would never make it in the Big Ten, held South Dakota's leading scorer Gary

Prink to five points. Sorenson also scored 13 himself, and grabbed a game high 11 rebounds though recovering from a flu bug.

* * * *

"The end of my senior year I was peaking as we got into the tournament," recalls Sorenson. "My high game was 44 points against Wapakoneta, the last game I played. Our next game was Lima Shawnee, but I had developed a severe sore throat and couldn't play. Then I had my tonsils out in June. I hadn't fully recovered from that when I played in the Ohio All-Star game. My performance in that game, with a lot of writers and coaches present, sent me to college with some publicity which was less than flattering," says the Ohio Player of the Year.

"During high school I heard from most of the Big Ten; 80-100-150 colleges, I don't really know. It came down to Michigan, Purdue and Ohio State. I wanted to try for the best. Like any kid, my dream was the NBA. Actually I just wanted to go some place where I'd fit in.

"I remember Purdue really rolled out the red carpet. They had this plan of Rick Mount at guard, me at forward and 7' Chuck Bavis at center. Mount was all they hoped, but Bavis didn't really turn out. They kept telling me 'Don't go to Ohio State, all they ever do is practice.' But I remember thinking they must be doing something right to win all those championships, and my gut feeling was Fred Taylor and Ohio State."

"Dave's high school coach was John Stozich," recalls Bob Burkholder, "and we felt like John was on our side." Stozich served as the State Representative from Findlay before being named Director of the Ohio Department of Industrial Relations by Governor George Voinovich in January, 1991.

"The nickname 'Sunshine'? I guess I was happy to be at Ohio State, because people told me I was smiling all the time. Bill Hosket started calling me that, I think. He sure took me under his wing when I got there, particularly showing me how to play inside. He helped me learn things which I used throughout my pro career. He had this big — how do I want to say this? — frame, that's it, big frame, which he used to get position inside. Defending his moves in practice as a freshman, and passing to him as a sophomore, gave me ideas to blend into my game.

"We both knew how to position ourselves, how to get open and how to pass. There were so many variations off the 'stack'. There was always a way to get open."

* * * *

The "stack" wasn't new at Ohio State — Taylor had used it with Bradds and Shaffer and with Hosket and Dove — but in 1968 it became the focus of Ohio State's offense for many years to come. Never would an offensive concept suit the personnel on hand better than the stack fit the Ohio State front line of Hosket — Sorenson — Howell.

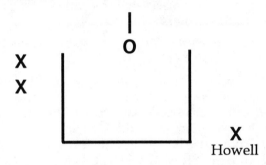

The players would line-up in this arrangement, generally with Meadors handling the ball on the left side of the floor (where the sideline protected his inability to see well from his left eye). Usually Hosket was behind Sorenson, but that was not critical because in this offensive set they were almost the same player. Neither was quick enough to easily get free of a good defensive forward to catch a pass on the wing, or to drive to the basket with the ball after catching it. However, both had good corner jump shots, several inside scoring moves and, after Hosket's tutoring, good basketball minds. "We had to find a way to get them in the line-up together," says Taylor. They had signals, communicated by word or touch, as to when one was going to break inside, outside or to the foul line, or wanted a screen. When playing a team with one defender larger than the other, the Buckeye with the big man would often go outside, leaving a mismatch inside for the Buckeye guarded by the smaller defender. If the defense switched, Hosket and Sorenson reacted.

"We had so many ways to score, the defenses couldn't take them all away," recalls Hosket. "The only real problem was when we played a weak team with two so-so defenders. Then we both wanted to stay inside because we wanted to score," he laughs.

Another key to the success of the "stack" set was the ability of Denny Meadors to "read" which Buckeye was going where, then which should get the ball and at what time.

"My key was eye contact," says Meadors. "I was more used to what they were doing than the defense was, so my advantage increased as the year went on. Usually the low man went to the corner, but when we changed that it was almost always an easy lay-up because the defense over-reacted. Even if the defense knew Hosket was going to the corner he could almost always get the ball, either with Sorenson stepping out to set a screen or by Bill running a circle inside Dave, then going to the corner."

When Steve Howell scored 29 points against New Mexico State, the first of his ten 22+ point games, the offense was complete.

"One way to stop Hosket and Sorenson," recalls Taylor, "was to drop the weak side forward (the one away from the ball) down to help on defense. And teams tried that. Our counter to that was to get the ball to Steve before his man could get back to him. Steve wasn't quick enough to drive but when he got his feet set he was an excellent shooter." Meadors feels Howell was the best pure shooter on the team.

* * * *

"I grew up in Columbus," recalls Howell, a graduate of Eastmoor High School, "and had been a Buckeye basketball fan since the Lucas era. I remember we had people over to watch the Cincinnati championship game and my father ordered pizza. It came after the game ended and I was so upset I couldn't eat any — and I *loved* pizza," says the 6'5 man who played "small forward" at 245-250 lbs.

"Baseball and football were my favorite sports growing up. Though I led the Columbus City League in scoring in basketball as a junior, there were so many calls for football I didn't think about going to college on a basketball scholarship.

"Then you could sign grants with different conferences. I signed with Wake Forest, which wanted me to play both sports. Indiana's football coaches had been recruiting Eastmoor pretty hard so I might have played there."

Howell's Eastmoor basketball team lost six times during the regular season, but the City League was loaded that year. The Warriors got hot in the state tournament. Steve scored 34 as they beat Newark, Central Ohio League champions and 19-1 before the closing loss, 84-72. Future Buckeye teammate Craig Barclay had 14 for the losers. Then Eastmoor beat City League foe Linden (17-2), to win the Central District co-final. Howell scored 35 as the Warriors beat Coshocton but the bubble burst in the regional finals as eventual state champion Columbus South was too quick, winning 76-65. Howell led both teams in scoring (29) and rebounding (13), despite twisting an ankle in the third period.

"I had so much fun in the tournament that when Fred and Frank called, playing at Ohio State in front of my folks sounded great," says Howell.

"Three things come to mind as I think back to my freshman year.

"First, the summer before we used to go to campus for pick-up games. The first game Marv Gregory (going into his senior year, but only about 6'3) guarded me. Several times I went up to shoot and he just jammed the ball down my throat. I thought 'Did I make a mistake? Am I ever going to get a shot off?' After that I went to work to get a quicker release when I shot.

"We had a good freshman team (Miller, Meadors, Steve Barnard, Sadelfeld, Schnabel) and gave the varsity some trouble at times. But what I remember is seeing Fred coach. He was a great technician, always prepared, but he didn't spend much time motivating us. He recruited competitors, planned practice for competitors and thought they'd be ready to play.

"And school was a priority. There was assistance — tutoring — available if you needed it. Still, it was probably Spring quarter before I really adjusted to school."

* * * *

After exams, New Mexico State, 6-0 after beating Purdue at West Lafayette, presented a major challenge for the 3-0 home team. The visitors had six players averaging double figures and the team scored 97.8 points per game. Head Coach Lou Henson, future boss at Illinois, had three players who would establish NBA careers for themselves and there was a story behind the recruitment of each.

When Henson left Hardin Simmons to go to New Mexico State, he hired a former player named Ed Murphy as an assistant. Murphy, later the coach at Mississippi, was playing summer ball at his family's home in Syracuse with a 6'2 flash named Jimmy Collins. At Murphy's urging Henson offered Collins a scholarship without ever seeing him play.

Later that summer Murphy went to Yonkers to visit his aunt, a high school history teacher. She knew little about basketball but had heard one of the students was very good, though only 5'7. The school's coach arranged a game so Murphy could look at the little guy. This led to Charlie Criss, who would play eight years in the NBA, becoming an Aggie.

Then Henson drove from Los Cruces to Indianola, Mississippi, to talk with a tall, skinny black kid not yet in demand in the South. Sam Lacey, who had never been contacted by a white coach, quickly agreed to attend. Lacey became the fifth player taken in the 1970 NBA draft — Collins was eleventh — and Henson had three recruits without seeing any of them play. They would lead the Aggies to three straight NCAA tournaments, all ending in losses to national champion UCLA.

There were many keys to the Bucks' 78-75 win over the athletic Aggies. While Howell scored 29 points on the perimeter, Hosket and Sorenson put together 43 inside. Hosket led all rebounders with 14 and added 10 assists. Sorenson had nine rebounds and shot eight of 13 from the field. Meadors was scoreless but almost single-handedly beat the constant pressure of the Aggies ("That year some of our most aggressive rebounding took place after the ball went through the hoop," recalls Meadors. "Four guys wanted to throw it in to me so they wouldn't have to handle it." Fred Taylor puts it this way: "Some guys couldn't bring it up court, and some wouldn't. That left Denny.").

The other key, to the game and the season, was the use of zone defense.

"Stan Washington at Michigan State was so quick we couldn't seem to keep him from getting the ball. Before him we always played man to man. He started us thinking about other approaches," says Taylor. "Because of the skill level of that New Mexico State team — they were as quick as snakes — we went to a 1-2-2 zone, the first time in 10 years we used a half court zone. When we did, it took New Mexico State 1:35 to get a shot. The crowd got into it, which helped the players, and it was a key to our season."

"We'd scrimmage man to man all week," says Hosket, starting to smile, "then at the end of Thursday's practice Fred would say 'Let's spend five minutes practicing a zone in case we get into foul trouble'. Nearly every game we'd start in man and then spend 35 minutes in zone, because of fouls."

December 20 it was official. It would be necessary to operate on Jeff Miller's left knee and he would be lost for the season.

The Bucks seemed to take the news in stride, as they opened a 42-21 lead at Butler. After all they were 4-0 and Miller's replacement

(Howell) was shooting 63%. When subs went in for the regulars at 3:05 to go in the half, Butler got nine straight points to make things 42-30 at intermission. A nine point Bulldog spurt to begin the second half turned the game into a nail biter, finally won by Ohio State 71-69.

With that the 5-0 Buckeyes, now ranked No. 18 nationally, took off for Hawaii, the Rainbow Classic, and initial opponent Marquette. Coached by Al McGuire, the Warriors were a veteran team with three seniors, two juniors in the starting line-up. They were patient on offense and eighth nationally on defense, with a 5-1 record.

Marquette won the game 64-60, causing Ohio State trouble with full court pressure. Today few people remember much about the game but everyone has a version of what happened when Marquette's muscular All-American candidate George Thompson spat on Steve Howell.

"We had been going at it all game," recalls Howell. "There were comments and he spit on me. The referees didn't see it. The next night we were sitting near Marquette's players, watching some other teams play in the tournament, and I said to Jeff Miller (who Taylor had taken on the trip to Hawaii although Miller couldn't play) 'There's the guy with the funky mouth', referring to Thompson. There were more words, Thompson and I ended up under the stands, squaring off, and Al McGuire came along. He started instigating us ("McGuire said 'Oh come on, if you're going to hit him, hit him' remembers Hosket). Then a priest appeared and Al stepped in as the peacemaker."

When Hosket tells the story it has one added, John Wayne type element. "After Thompson spat on 'Bogie' — we all called him that after Bogie Redmon of Illinois — 'Bogie' said 'After the game we'll meet and settle this.' Thompson said 'If I'm going, my team is going with me.' And 'Bogie' said, 'Bring 'em.' He was a tough guy — lots of football players avoided 'Bogie' when he came along. He probably would have taken on the whole Marquette team by himself."

Well Steve, is that what happened?

"I don't remember saying that exactly, but it does sound like something I might have said at that time in my life," Howell comments.

The loss matched OSU with tough Bradley, 8-2 after a meeting with powerful Houston (11-0). Howell, denied the opportunity to dismantle Thompson and/or Marquette, took it out on the Braves' zone defense, scoring 32. "He was 16 of 21," recalls Taylor, "and they were all jump shots. It was something." OSU 85-62.

That victory sent OSU against host Hawaii, a 25 point loser to Northwestern earlier in the tournament. "Nobody was thinking about basketball — in our minds we were already 8-1," remembers Hosket. In front of about 800 fans the Buckeyes lost 80-76.

"Fred didn't say anything to anyone — he was really upset," remembers Howell. "I didn't even see him for two days after we got back," says Captain Hosket.

Everyone remembers that as the night "Avis" became "Pinto".

"We called Bruce Schnabel 'Avis' because of the 'we try harder' bit," recalls Meadors today. Schnabel had been first team all state at Williamstown, West Virginia, where he led his team to the state finals three years. "He had scored in the 40's several times, but at the Big Ten level he had trouble freeing himself, because he wasn't real quick," remembers Meadors.

"It was almost New Year's Eve and Bruce had some firecrackers," continues Meadors. "He threw one out on the porch, but forgot that his uniform was drying out there. He blew a hole in his white pants. Turns out we're wearing white that night, except Bruce, who has a white jersey and — underneath his warm-up pants — red shorts. Bruce sat on the end of the bench, and didn't look at Fred all night. When Fred called him to send him in, Bruce tried to talk him out of making the substitution. That didn't work, he went in with red shorts and white jersey and became 'Pinto'."

After seemingly enough excitement for an entire season, the Big Ten season was about to *begin*. As Taylor put it "This is a heck of a big, important opener." The opponent was Purdue, ranked in the nations's top ten when the season began. They had Rick Mount (25.5 ppg), Billy Keller (16.0) and Herman Gilliam (13.7), clearly the best perimeter trio in the league.

Firing on all cylinders, the Bucks burst to a 61-46 halftime lead, setting a school scoring record for a half which stood until 1990 when the opponent was Bethune Cookman. Then they extended the lead in the second half to win 108-80. Heroes were everywhere. The team shot 58% and held Purdue to 34%. Hosket dominated (35 points, 17 rebounds) and Sorenson helped (14 points, 11 rebounds). Howell knocked in 24 points and both Meadors and Swain hit double figures. Meadors also had 12 rebounds and, most importantly, chased Mount in a variety of zone-man combinations. Mount made eight of 23 shots and scored 19 points. It was a big victory, in front of the first sell out at St. John since Gary Bradds' junior year, 1963.

"About half an hour after the game I was in the training room, putting ice on my knee. Fred walked in, eating an apple," recalls Hosket. "It had been the best game of my career and I felt good. Apparently so did he, because he sort of patted me on the back and said 'Good effort, #25.' At a time like that you have to make a choice on how to respond. I took the humble route, and said something like 'I guess we owed you that one.' He turned around, took the apple out of his mouth, fired it into a waste basket about 20' away and said 'I guess you're right.' "

Humility was a very good choice. Taylor remembered the Hawaii game.

As Ohio State prepared to travel to Iowa City to meet the veteran Hawkeyes, surgery was completed on Jeff Miller's left knee. Damage was more extensive than first expected, but recovery was predicted to be normal.

OSU had a great start at Iowa, leading 40-29 at the half, and 58-47 with just over nine minutes left. But bad shot selection, too much one-on-one play and foul trouble to Sorenson and Howell resulted in overtime. Even that was only because Denny Meadors made two foul shots at 0:00 in regulation.

In the last minute of overtime sophomore Jim Geddes made a steal, then passed to Meadors who hit Hosket for a driving lay-up and a foul by Chad Calabria. A technical was called on Calabria — OSU had two free throws to take the lead *and* possession of the ball.

"The first one I threw up was a real brick, the second one barely hit the net," recalls Hosket. A Buckeye turnover and a jump shot by Iowa's Ron Norman made the final 74-72 and Ohio State was 1-1.

Despite his foul shots, Hosket had played well, with 26 points and a game high 15 rebounds. For Iowa, Sam Williams netted 32 points, and drew many of the Buckeye fouls.

Another outstanding first half — 58-32 — keyed a 103-70 home victory over Michigan. Sorenson and Hosket combined for 41 points in the stack. Howell punished the Wolves for sagging or playing a zone as 15 Buckeyes played. The negative was foul shooting (19 of 34).

Only "Sunshine" Sorenson (21 points, 12 rebounds and strong defense) drew praise as Ohio State beat Georgia Tech 66-55. Then OSU shot the same from the floor as the line (56%) in winning at Michigan 95-92. Hosket had 26 points and 15 boards, both Geddes and Finney bounced off the bench with double figures. Michigan led

84-76 with about five minutes to play when the front line went to the bench. Taylor "decided to let his big men sit on the bench if they were just going to stand around the court," is the way Kaye Kessler of *The Columbus Citizen-Journal* reported it. Sophomore Ed Smith got five quick points, Craig Barclay had two free throws and a steal, Jody Finney had four points and two rebounds. They teamed with Geddes and Meadors to steal the game. The "rat team" was born.

Non-conference Cornell shocked Ohio State 76-64; more appropriately Ohio State shocked themselves, being out-rebounded 43-34 by the much shorter Big Red, making eight of 18 foul shots and getting only 27 points from their front line. Again the "rat team" came in. Led by Jody Finney's 19 they almost outscored the four starters (Meadors played both platoons). Entering the game with 13:15 to play they took an eight point deficit to a 58-58 tie by 6:28. Then they ran out of fire power, the starters still didn't have any, and the game was over.

Dave Sorenson was smiling after hitting 10 of 14 shots, scoring 23 points and grabbing 18 rebounds in an 86-64 defeat of Wisconsin at sold out St. John. Hosket and Howell added 33, and ten players scored, but free throw woes continued (six of 18).

A 78-77 road win over Indiana, expected to contend for the championship, was a key to the title.

"We were shooting fouls at I.U. like we always did after practice," remembers Craig Barclay. "Fred had said 'make seven straight, then we go eat.' We'd make five or six or four, and someone would miss. It was getting late, and we had dinner reservations. That added to the pressure of our poor shooting in recent games — we just couldn't get to seven.

"After a miss Fred called for the ball we were using and 'threw out' an invisible ball. I don't remember who 'caught it', but Fred said 'Go ahead, shoot it, we have to go.' So the player 'shot it'. Then Fred said 'Did you make it?' Now we understood. We 'made' seven straight and went to dinner, loosened up."

Ohio State also made 20 of 24 free throws in the game, won on 6'3 sophomore Dan Andreas' 10 foot jump shot at the buzzer. Denny Meadors played, in the words of his coach, "The little rascal's finest game ever for us — he was great." He had only one turnover against constant Indiana pressure and scored 15 points. Finney was a big spark off the bench with 12 points and five boards; Howell and Hosket split 36 points.

Michigan State fell 90-62 as OSU continued to dominate St. John Arena against Big Ten opponents. Howell led with 22 points, Meadors and Sorenson had 16 each, "Sunshine" had 16 boards. Hosket had 12 points despite 17 minutes on the bench with fouls and Jody Finney, who had earned a start with four double figure relief jobs in six games, had nine points and 11 boards.

Sports Illustrated said "The Big Ten is beginning to take Ohio State seriously."

Wisconsin proved a poor host and Ohio State lost 86-78; OSU was out-rebounded 36-25. Then the Bucks lost at Minnesota 83-79. Hosket and Sorenson totaled 49, and Meadors had 19 for his fourth straight career high game, but they got little help. "Bogie" Howell's shooting was off again; he hit only four of 13 after a two of seven game against Wisconsin. The rest of the team was zero for 16 from the field. The Bucks had lost their lead. Iowa was 6-2, upcoming Northwestern tied with Ohio State at 6-3. Purdue was 5-3.

Losing that game at Minnesota is fresh in the minds of Buckeye players more than two decades later.

"It was the low point of my career at Ohio State," says Craig Barclay. "The team wasn't playing well, Fred tried various combinations and none of them worked. I think everyone on the traveling team played, except me. I was depressed, even thought about transferring."

"I had lots of relatives in the area," recalls Howell, "and went out with them after the game. I got back 45 minutes late, but we never had bed checks. Well, that night we had a bed check. I got benched, and didn't start for two games."

"Seemed like things happened on that trip," remembers Mike Swain. "For variety, Fred got a train from Minneapolis to Chicago. It was an overnight sleeper, then we flew in from Chicago. Rather than sleeping on the train, we had a card game, and stayed up all night. The next day we got back and found out Fred had been next to us. He hadn't gotten any sleep 'cause we made so much noise." Early the next week Kaye Kessler reported Taylor had "a king-sized headache" and was hinting at two new starters.

Coach Taylor never said anything about his sleepless night. "I always figured you caught more flies with honey than with vinegar," he says today. "Besides, I could always get back at them. When we had a particularly tough practice, they didn't always know the reason. I did tell them, 'If you're going to break the rules, do a good

job. I may have done it better. If not, I may have seen it done better.'
I always tried to avoid ultimatums, because when you do and something happens you are caught in a crack and have to act."

The Bucks continued to click at home as Northwestern fell 87-67. Surprise starter 6'5 Ed Smith had 15 points and 11 rebounds and held talented Wildcat Don Adams to seven points. The other new starter, Bruce Schnabel, held Dale Kelley, a 19 ppg scorer, scoreless in the first half. OSU out-rebounded the best rebounding team in the Big Ten by 12.

When Iowa lost to Purdue 86-73 while Mount scored 38, OSU was back on top with Iowa at 7-3. Purdue was 6-3. No Big Ten teams were ranked in UPI's top 20.

On the trip to Purdue, with first place at stake, Smith and Schnabel started again but both went scoreless as OSU lost 93-72. "Bogie" came off the bench for 16, but Purdue scored too often and too easily. The Boilers made 12 fast break goals caused by Ohio State's poor offensive execution. The only good news was that Jo Lynn Finney was born to Jody and Linda Lee Finney.

In a must win home game the Bucks beat a tough Illinois team 95-75. Howell returned to the starting line-up and hit 12 baskets for 26 points. Sorenson added 21 points and 12 boards, while Hosket had what would later become known as a "triple double" with 14 points, 10 rebounds, 10 assists. Meadors scored 15, and Finney had 14 in a relief role. Things looked better. Michigan beat Purdue (7-4) but Iowa (8-3) knocked off Michigan State. OSU trailed by one half game, with two to play.

In Captain Bill Hosket's last home game OSU got 73 points from the front court starters and overwhelmed Indiana 107-93. A capacity crowd saw "Hos" score 25 points and grab nine rebounds.

Today he remembers a story about "one of our home Big Ten games my senior year, but I don't remember which one." Since all seven were one-sided victories, no wonder they blend together. The Indiana spread of 14 points was the closest but that score was 58-40 at halftime.

"Dave Sorenson," relates the Captain, "had an excellent shooting touch and a nice hook shot. ("I called it the 'Johnson and Johnson' shot," says broadcaster Jimmy Crum, "because it was soft as baby powder.") Toward the end of a game we were going to win, Sorenson made a beautiful right handed hook. The crowd loved it, Fred jumped up — it was something.

"The next trip down I heard my barber, Jimmy Clark, yelling from the crowd. I didn't particularly have rabbit ears but I heard him. Maybe he was close, maybe the voice was familiar ... Anyway, he's saying 'are you going to let that sophomore show you up?' So I moved to get the ball, put in a 12' hook on the right baseline. Felt pretty good.

"Right after that Sorenson got the ball, moved to his left, tossed up a 14-15' left handed hook and swished it. He hung the net — perfect. I said to myself 'This little game of HORSE is over'."

"Dave had a personality similar to Hosket's," says Burkholder today. "Those kids had fun, and it was fun being around them."

As the Bucks prepared for their last game of the season at Illinois, the situation was not hopeless — but close. They had to win a road game, something they had done only twice in six Big Ten games, and hope Iowa lost at Minnesota or to Michigan at home. That would mean a tie for the title. This year, for the first time, a play-off would decide the conference representative to the NCAA in case of a tie.

With the Bucks on their last road trip of the conference season, Hosket has another story about "a road game my senior year."

"We normally watched films the night before a road game," says the Captain, "and I had picked up a reel of film from the 1950 season." Ohio State had won the Big Ten and ultimately lost 56-55 to eventual NCAA champion City College of New York. "Fred was out of the room, and I grabbed the 1950 reel, handed it to Jack Graf who was running the projector. All of a sudden everyone was laughing — the quality of the film was terrible, the uniforms were funny, Burky was out there and Fred was so thin. As we're laughing there's a loose ball on the film. Fred's going through people to get to it, almost throwing them out of the way. He's playing just as hard as he has told us to play. What started out to be a practical joke had turned into a very valuable lesson in intensity and effort."

* * * *

While Hosket isn't certain the story about whether the 1950 film took place on the Illinois trip, he has another story which definitely did.

"Missing those two foul shots at Iowa was still very much on my mind," he recalls. "I had been putting in extra time since then working on foul shooting by myself, and was doing that before our game with Illinois. After shooting at one rim I went down to the other for a while. I thought I heard something — it sounded like 'Iowa' — but

171

couldn't see anyone. Then I saw Meadors, hollering from the top of Assembly Hall. He was shouting 'Iowa' and trying to make me think it was subconscious or something.

"Let me say one thing about those free throws he made at the end of regulation that Iowa game. They look good in the score book but they were ugly — they bounced and rolled all over the rim before they dropped."

Hosket and Meadors had — and have — a relationship which even their Buckeye peers don't understand. "We got on each other a lot, but not like that '68 team," says 1971 super-sub Bob Siekmann.

For example, the two Dayton area players have different theories on the reason for foul problems the inside players always had during the 1968 season. "They couldn't guard anybody," says Meadors. "We always had to sag to help them." Hosket maintains "The guards couldn't guard their men, so we had to pick up drivers and cutters and defend our own men."

That relationship continues today.

"I must have met 30 people over the years who said 'Denny Meadors told me about you. He said he's the primary reason you got to be an All-American.' It happens on the golf course, in business meetings, on telephone calls," says Hosket, shaking his head.

"I've told three times that number," says Meadors confidently. "He's going to be hearing that for the rest of his life."

Hosket's best reply might be one he makes in connection with a question about rebounding. Not noted as a leaper, he ranks second to Jerry Lucas on Ohio State's career rebounding average list. What was the secret? "I played with Denny Meadors," he deadpans, implying that Meadors' poor field goal shooting provided an increased number of rebounding opportunities.

One thing they agree on is the annual mile run at the OSU Golf Course after pre-season conditioning — they hated it. "Fred used it as an indication of who was in shape, we always wondered what running on a golf course had to do with Big Ten basketball," recalls Meadors. "Guys like Geddes, Halley, Barclay, Andreas and Finney were the best. They ran in one group. Hosket, Swain, Howell, Sorenson and I ran in another group. Oh, and Bruce Schnabel too — he had the school record for throwing up four straight years after the run. Our group trailed their group, took a breather before the turn about halfway, then caught up after the turn and trailed them in. It wouldn't have been right to beat them."

* * * *

Returning to the 1968 season, Ohio State beat Illinois on the boards 45-32 and on the scoreboard 67-64. The Illini held Sorenson to his season low of five points but he got 15 rebounds. Howell led all scorers with 25 points, and got 14 rebounds. Hosket had 19 points (making his only free throw) and 11 boards. Meadors and Finney, in relief of Schnabel, had nine points each. However Iowa beat Minnesota 91-72. Both games were played March 4.

The annual OSU Basketball Appreciation Banquet was held March 5 at the Ohio Union. Iowa was a 15 point favorite to beat visiting Michigan (5-8) March 9. Fred Taylor said he was "hopeful of an opportunity to play more games," that he would send Michigan Coach Dave Strack a Varsity O blanket if the Wolverines won Saturday, and that Ohio State would continue light work-outs in hopes of a play-off. Denny Meadors was named Captain for 1969 and Mike Swain stole the show with his comments. And everyone *really* thought the year was 1) successful and 2) over.

March 7 the Big Ten announced the playoff for the conference representative to the NCAA tournament would be held at Purdue March 12 at 9 p.m. EST — if necessary. When Michigan beat Iowa 71-70, it became necessary.

"Denny (Meadors) and I were listening to that game on radio," recalls Howell, "with our Delta Tau Delta fraternity brothers. It was the most excited I've ever been in sports."

Michigan had jumped to an early 27-11 lead, and was ahead 54-38 when sophomore star Rudy Tomjanovich went out with a leg injury. Iowa came storming back in those final 15 minutes, but not far enough.

Iowa coach Ralph Miller had predicted a close race in November, one that "may go down to March 9." Actually it went to March 12.

Dayton writer Jim Ferguson congratulated Meadors for "winning a championship in four short days as Buckeye captain without even playing a game."

While playing Iowa for a trip to the NCAA was a thrill, it was a challenge as well. The Hawks had a strong, very athletic team led by 6'3 All-American Sam Williams, a 25.1 ppg scorer. He had taken 13 foul shots while scoring 32 points in the first game. He led the conference in free throws attempted in 1967 and 1968, and was Big Ten MVP in 1968. Second leading scorer 6'6 sophomore Glenn "The Stick" Vidnovic had been scholastically ineligible for the first game, but had averaged 13.8 ppg since. His back court partner was another sophomore, Chad Calabria, a 13.7 ppg scorer. Houston Breedlove, Ron Norman, Joe Bergman, and Dick Jensen also played heavy minutes.

Bruce Schnabel got the call at the revolving door guard position and joined the four regular starters in double figures as Ohio State beat Iowa 85-81 to earn a chance to face East Tennessee State in the Mid-East regional. "He played an outstanding game," recalls Taylor. "We needed his ball handling against their pressure and he got out quickly for some easy baskets when they attacked the offensive boards."

A snowstorm prevented most OSU fans from traveling to West Lafayette, and resulted in only 4816 fans in the stands. But Hosket and Howell made the game — they played the entire 40 minutes and scored 24 and 22 respectively. Hosket added 11 rebounds and five assists. Meadors converted a clutch one and one foul opportunity with 22 seconds left, to end with 13 points and seven assists. Sorenson was solid. Iowa shot only 36.4% from the floor. But that was not uncommon — OSU opponents were below 40% for the year while Ohio State set a Big Ten record at 51.5%. The reason was defensive rebounding — "NO SECOND SHOTS," as Coach Taylor put it. Blocking out and going after the ball enabled a group of players with below average quickness to perform well at the defensive end all year long.

Decorating the balcony was a banner reading "Miller's victories are Taylor-made," referring to six straight Iowa victories over OSU. The banner, and the memory of Miller's post game comment in January ("I knew we would win with nine minutes to play") may not have been necessary to inspire the Bucks, but they didn't hurt.

* * * *

Throughout the year OSU had received productive play at the guard position beside Meadors, "but you never knew when it was coming or from where," says Taylor.

"Mike Swain gave us good size (6'4, 206 lbs.) and solid defense, if his man wasn't too quick," recaps Taylor. Swain had overcome an operation to his right knee as a freshman and a separated left shoulder as a junior to be a major contributor on the Big Ten champions. In addition he was a starting pitcher on the 1966 NCAA champion baseball team. "Jody Finney (6'3) was our best shooter but less of a defender, particularly as a sophomore," says Taylor. "Bruce Schnabel (6') was our best ball handler against pressure. That's why we played him against Iowa, even though he had to guard guys like Vidnovic and Norman (6'3). And Jim Geddes was the best athlete of all."

Sometimes that type of change undermines the continuity of a team. Partly due to the consistency of Hosket, Sorenson, Howell and Meadors — Howell missed two starts, the others none — and partly because it was an unusual year, the team won the Big Ten despite playing musical chairs at one guard position.

* * * *

The day before OSU met East Tennessee State, two significant events took place. Selection of the All-Big Ten team by conference coaches reflected the past; the NCAA Press Dinner reflected the future.

Mount (conference scoring leader), Williams (second) and Hosket (sixth) were unanimous choices for first team. They were joined by Joe Franklin of Wisconsin (third) and Dave Scholz of Illinois (fifth). Dave Sorenson was named to the second team.

Fred Taylor described the Press Dinner in the April 15, 1979 edition of *Midwest Basketball News*. "Coach Al McGuire of Marquette spoke first. He quickly set the tempo by stating 'Marquette will beat Kentucky tomorrow night because Marquette is mentally tougher than Kentucky and would wear white since they had first choice of uniforms.' Adolph (Rupp) came up out of his chair red faced and sputtering — — —. He eventually left little doubt to those attending how he felt about such effrontery in Lexington and just how ready Kentucky would be to play. Frankly, the other two coaches knew the winner of their game would meet Kentucky in the final game on Saturday night — and that was the case!"

To meet Kentucky the Bucks had to get past the Ohio Valley champions. That was accomplished 79-72 in typical fashion:

- 22 points by Howell, his fifth straight game with that many or more since returning to the starting line-up
- 18 points and 20 rebounds by Hosket
- Seven of nine shots for 14 points by Sorenson despite foul trouble
- 12 points and good ball handling by Meadors, who also held ETS scoring leader Harvey "Skeeter" Swift to seven of 21 shots
- 58.6% from the field by OSU, 39.5% for their opponent

- OSU carelessness after a big (18 point) lead and 61% shooting at the foul-line
- Plus another solid start by Schnabel (nine points) and an excellent relief stint by the hero of the Northwestern game, Ed Smith (four points, five boards)

As Taylor anticipated, Kentucky manhandled Marquette 107-89.

After Friday night no one wondered why Kentucky was ranked No. 3 in the country. Ohio State, on the other hand, had been less than overwhelming against the Ohio Valley Conference Champion. *Sports Illustrated* said "Ohio State doesn't seem capable of beating Kentucky." Sorenson recalls "When I saw Dan Issel two years later at an all star game after our senior year, he said 'When I saw you guys play East Tennessee State I packed my bags for the West Coast.' "

The Wildcats had good reason to be confident — they were good. Sophomore center Issel would become Kentucky's all-time leading scorer with 2138 points in only three seasons; Mike Casey, a guard, is their ninth leading scorer today and forward Mike Pratt is 19th on the list. Plus Thad Jaracz, center on their 1966 NCAA runner-up, played forward.

Against a heavy favorite on their home floor, Ohio State played a memorable game in beating Kentucky 82-81. It was the Wildcat's first home loss of the year.

OSU led 44-40 at the half, against Kentucky's man-to-man defense. The Wildcats switched to a 1-3-1 zone in the second half. "They had done that against most of their opponents during the year, regardless of score," recalls Taylor. "I was glad to see it; we had some kids who could really shoot when they got their feet set. I'm not sure we could have won if they had played man the whole game." Regardless, Kentucky had the lead 81-80 with five seconds to play. But OSU had the ball, under their own basket.

Captain Hosket had the job of getting the ball in bounds, to someone who would make the shot. "There wasn't time for a complete inbounds play, so we just tried to get the ball to Steve or Dave," recalls Taylor.

"Mike Casey was face guarding me. I tried to get loose, and couldn't," Howell told *The Citizen-Journal*. "Then I saw 'Sunny' open and I knew he'd make it." And he did, banking in a jump shot from about five feet to send 'Cinderella' to the ball in Los Angeles.

Sorenson made 11 of 17 shots, scored 24 points and grabbed seven rebounds. Howell scored 18 points and grabbed 11 important rebounds. Like his two teammates, Meadors played all 40 minutes — he scored six points. Hosket had some foul trouble but scored 21 points and grabbed a game high 15 rebounds. Ed Smith chipped in four points and four rebounds. And Jody Finney had one of his best of several excellent relief jobs during the year, scoring nine points and getting seven rebounds. Finney had a three point play at 1:28 to tie the game ("That was absolutely critical," recalls Sorenson), then slipped "a great pass to me through traffic for an easy lay-up," according to Howell.

After the game Hosket said "This is my greatest thrill — I just wanted this for my dad." Bill Sr. had led OSU to victory in 1933 in the first Kentucky — Ohio State game, 46-30.

Hosket and Sorenson were named to the All-Regional team.

Looking back on the 1968 season today, *every* player notes the Kentucky game as the highlight ("I felt confident about Iowa," says Meadors). After all, some were heavily recruited by Adolph Rupp and friends — and some felt they should have been. Plus beating the No. 3 team in the country on their home floor, with the winner playing in the national semi-finals. Not to mention the "fan support" they had at the game.

"The OSU cheerleaders weren't there, but the Marquette band learned our fight song and all their fans supported us," recalls Howell. "Not only that, but before the game George Thompson came up to me and said 'go get 'em'. Then he and Al McGuire were cheering for us the whole game. One of my friends said the Kentucky announcer said it was the only time Kentucky had ever been out-cheered on its home court."

Maybe the Bucks were still excited about the Kentucky game when it was time to play North Carolina. More likely it was just a case of the best team winning. The score was 80-66, Tar Heels. "I thought we could beat North Carolina, but they were too quick," recalls Sorenson. "Their press was just too much for us. It took us out of our offense, because we were too spread out."

After the game Coach Taylor said "We just didn't get good penetration on their defense. Their fast break hurt us much too often. Our movement wasn't good and the front line didn't help out for the guards. And North Carolina seemed to pick up all the loose balls." Other than that Mrs. Lincoln, how did you like the play?

Before UCLA set a record for largest victory margin in the NCAA final in beating North Carolina 78-55, OSU proved it belonged with

Nos. 1, 2, and 4, by beating Houston 89-85. Howell shot well ("His best of the season," remembers Marv Homan) in scoring 26, Hosket and Sorenson had 19 each as the front line totaled 64 against the big Cougars. Elvin Hayes scored 34 points for Houston.

Looking back, Meadors says "It was a great year. One thing people forget, but I know it meant a lot to Fred, is that we led the Big Ten in academic average that year too."

Shortly after the tournament, try-outs for the Olympic basketball team were held. Elvin Hayes had announced that he was signing a pro contract before the Olympics would be played in Tokyo in the fall, and Lew Alcindor did not choose to participate. Then Pete Maravich, Calvin Murphy and Rick Mount were all cut from the team, partly because Coach Henry Iba believed in a more disciplined style of play and partly because the politics of selection still required various groups be represented. "Experts" predicted a poor showing for the United States team.

Bill Hosket was on that Olympic team. "Playing in the NCAA really helped me be mentally and physically ready for the trials," says Hosket today. "It would have been difficult to play well if the season had ended earlier." He joined future Boston Celtic JoJo White and surprise junior college star Spencer Haywood in securing another gold medal in basketball for the United States, keeping the U.S. undefeated in Olympic competition (until 1972). Ernie Biggs served as trainer for the team.

While early comparison to Lucas may have been unfair, Hosket had held up pretty well. Both were true student-athletes. Hosket was All-Conference Academic three years and Academic All-American in 1968. Both won state championships before their college career, and Olympic gold medals. Both won NBA titles at New York, Hosket in 1970 and Lucas in 1973. Today Hosket trails only Lucas in career rebounding average at Ohio State (17.2 to 12.3). When he graduated in 1968, Bill was fourth behind "Luke", Robin Freeman and Gary Bradds in career total points, and trailed only Lucas and Bradds in career field goal percentage. No, he wasn't the next Lucas. But he was "a nice guy who finished first" according to Jimmy Crum, and he would be sorely missed. Actually, the "next Hosket" has not arrived in St. John Arena any more than the "next Lucas" has.

X

1969-1970: Just One More Rebounder

The next two seasons might have been reproduced from the same copying machine: excellent shooting from the field and the foul line, average rebounding, 17-7 records, All-Big Ten and team MVP honors for Dave Sorenson. With limited exceptions, the seasons included the same players. A tie for second at 9-5 in 1969, a tie for third at 8-6 in 1970 — today that would mean slots in the NCAA, then it meant seats in front of the television. Since Fred Taylor's teams had won eight straight in regional play and five of eight in the finals, imagine what could have happened. Good years to be sure, just not championship years.

1968 — 1969

"Almost everybody from the team stayed in Columbus that summer, working out together in the evening," recalls Captain Meadors. "We worked hard, Purdue was just too good. We missed Hosket — his offense, his rebounding but most of all his leadership. He was really an anchor during the tough times."

With nine of 11 major contributors back from the champions, and the league looking stronger, Fred Taylor said "I'll go for 10-4 again." He had seen Finney emerge as a regular at guard with Meadors, sophomore Jim Cleamons of Columbus Linden McKinley take Hosket's place in the line-up at forward beside Howell, and Sorenson add some size and strength inside. Schnabel, Barclay and Smith appeared to be the first subs off the bench. No one knew what to expect as Jeff Miller tried to come back, though Fred called him "very questionable ... a long way from where he was two years ago." However it appeared unlikely that one of the top freshmen from last year would ever play basketball on the Ohio State varsity — Rex Kern was too involved with football.

"As a freshman he was as exciting as anyone," recalls Taylor. "He was not intimidated by the upperclassmen. He had a 'happy warrior' attitude — he'd get blasted, bounce off the floor and go again. Like 'you got me that time, let's see if I can get you this time.' I knew it would never happen, but I really would have liked to have seen him as an upperclassman."

Coach, go to your "Iffy Deck". How good could he have been by concentrating on basketball? All-Big Ten, maybe?

No comment, just a nodding head.

Craig Barclay played against Kern in the Central Ohio League, as a senior at Newark in 1965 when Rex was a junior. "He was best as a junior," recalls Craig. Lancaster had beaten both Columbus Linden and Columbus East in reaching the state semi-finals that year. "His senior year he started to bulk up for football. If he had made the choice for basketball then, he probably would have become a starting guard at Ohio State. He was good."

But Kern wasn't a "loss", more like an "if only". He was busy as quarterback during the Golden Era of Ohio State football, when the Buckeyes lost only two games in three years, finishing No. 1 nationally in 1968.

Returning to thoughts of basketball, conference coaches liked Iowa and Purdue as title contenders. John Johnson, junior college all-American, was expected to step right in for departed Sam Williams at Iowa, which had almost everyone else back. Purdue returned Mount, Keller and Gilliam from the 1968 club.

In the opening game Steve Howell had his jump shot working and scored 20 points as the Bucks beat Ohio University 85-77. Cleamons, Sorenson and Finney joined "Bogie" in double figures, Meadors had nine and the bench chipped in 17.

Mighty UCLA was next, coming to St. John Arena after beating Purdue 94-82. Lew Alcindor was joined by seniors Lynn Shakelford and Ken Heitz, junior John Vallely, and sophomores Curtis Rowe and Sidney Wicks. They were big.

The Bucks prepared for the Bruins by running their offense against a freshman team waving tennis rackets. "We might as well forget about a lay-in drill," figured Taylor. "You never forget something like getting a shot blocked by a tennis racket," says Dan Andreas today.

Sorenson (14 of 23) and Finney (six of 10) hit their jump shots, but the other starters didn't (six of 30). UCLA had too much inside — 42 rebounds to 26 — as the Bucks lost 84-73. Alcindor had 21 points and 19 rebounds.

Today, when John Wooden thinks back to that game, and others with Ohio State during his career, he chooses to focus on Fred Taylor. "Who someone is as a person is more important than what kind of coach he is," says Wooden. "Fred Taylor was a credit to the coaching profession.

"I try to judge coaches by how close they come to getting the most out of their material. That tells more than won-loss percentages," feels Wooden. "He always got the most out of his material."

"One other thing I remember about Fred is the good rapport he had with his players. You have to have that to teach well. When it comes to talent, that 1961 team of Lucas, Siegfried, Nowell and Havlicek was one of the best groups that ever played," according to the man who saw most of the best ever, and coached several of them.

Ohio State bounced back from the UCLA defeat to beat Harvard 89-74. Sorenson and Finney stayed hot, and were joined in double figures by Cleamons, Smith and Barclay.

*   *   *   *

"Jody Finney was a very good one on one player," recalls radio broadcaster Marv Homan.

"He wasn't overly fast or quick, but he had this uncanny savvy of being able to play with the basketball," says Craig Barclay. "Jody was capable of playing in the system, though sometimes he didn't believe in it."

A 1966 graduate of Springfield South High School, Finney played against some of the best in the old Greater Ohio League. "Middletown, Hamilton Taft, Hamilton Garfield, Lima Senior were strong competition," Finney recalls. Other times he sharpened his moves "playing alley ball against older guys on the playground." The end result was a 22.9 ppg average as a senior with a high of 38 in one game and first team All-Ohio honors, along with Player of the Year

181

Dave Sorenson. Future Buckeye teammate Craig Barclay was second team, Ed Smith third.

When it came time to choose a school, Jody considered about 70 offers before narrowing the field to "OSU, Duke, Ohio U., Miami, Cincinnati and Kentucky. Recruiters Bob Burkholder and graduate assistant Wyatt Webb, OSU tradition, state loyalty and the fact that Ohio State always played a good schedule" led him to become a Buckeye.

"The thing I remember most from my freshman year is playing forward against Ron Sepic every day in practice. That was a good match-up," Finney recalls.

As a sophomore converting to the back-court, Finney played first on the "rat team," and by the end of the year was a major contributor off the bench. His growth continued and he was a regular as a junior and senior. He became the best Buckeye career foul shooter at .862 (Ricketts is second, Siegfried third). Finney also finished seventh in career field goal percentage at .526, trailing teammates Sorenson (third — .563) and Cleamons (fifth — .542).

Reflecting on his OSU experience, today Jody thinks about Fred Taylor's "preparation, attention to detail and emphasis on teaching the fundamentals. I hated that — I wanted to have fun — but looking back I see how we needed it. It's like the Apostle Paul writes," says Finney, a Christian, "about having the strength to run a race. College athletics develops character and discipline, which is what our lives should be about. Fred taught us that five guys can succeed as a group by suppressing their individual egos and desires."

*　*　*　*

Their first road game of the year took the Bucks to Pullman, Washington to play the Washington State Cougars. Because of his "cat-like quickness," Jimmy Crum had nicknamed sophomore Jimmy Cleamons "the Cougar" early in his varsity career. In his first road game as a Buck, "the Cougar" beat the Cougars on a rebound tip-in at 0:03 to grab a 75-74 victory.

In a scheduling quirk ("Coach Marv Harshman needed a game while he traveled east, and we had an opening," recalls Taylor) OSU entertained WSU in a re-match five days later, winning 84-69. Sorenson had 24 (in each game), Cleamons 17 (14 the first time), and Howell and Finney were in double figures both times.

Jud Heathcote, Michigan State head coach, was a young assistant on that Washington State staff, and thinks back to the only games he "coached" against Taylor's Buckeyes. "I had tremendous respect for his coaching ability, beginning with those games. He was an 'old time' coach, who concentrated on discipline, teaching and education — not television, shoe contracts and money as we are accused of today. When you talk about the really respected coaches in NCAA history you talk about men like Ray Meyer, Marv Harshman and Fred Taylor, great coaches.

"His teams truly dominated the Big Ten. When you look back at what he did, how he did it and what he still stands for in the game today, you can't help but be impressed," concludes Heathcote.

Sorenson hit a career high 32 points and grabbed 14 boards as Ohio State beat visiting Butler 74-71. Jeff Miller played only his second game in two years and scored four points, including a big basket at 2:42 to give the Bucks the lead at 68-67. In the last minute Cleamons hit a breakaway basket and two foul shots to ice the game.

The trip to Florida State "pointed out to me what a first class operation Ohio State had," recalls Jody Finney. "It was very hot in there, and the gym was small." Assistant coach Jack Graf remembers "They had windows in the ceiling for ventilation, but they wouldn't open them. I was just sitting on the bench and my clothes were soaked clear through."

Despite Dave Cowens' 12 points and 12 rebounds, OSU escaped the oven with a 93-86 win. Jody Finney was "hot" (eight of 13 field goals, 12 of 14 fouls for 28 points), Sorenson "outplayed Cowens for the second time" according to Taylor, with 22 points and nine boards, and Howell had 12 points and nine rebounds. But the key to the game was probably sophomore Jim Cleamons, with his 17 points and excellent defense.

* * * *

"At halftime Fred is going through the Florida State team and he says 'Skip Young had 10 — you've got him in the second half,' nodding at me," recalls Cleamons. "I remember thinking 'I don't want him.' Even while we were playing that game I had been pulling for my partner (Young). My idea for a perfect game would have been for him to do well, and us to win. That way he could feel good, could talk, but we'd have the victory. I had always told him I could stop him, but I never wanted to have to do it. We were too close. Now if I didn't do it, we wouldn't win the game — *and* I'd have to hear him run his mouth.

183

"We had been friends forever, and 'Skipper' had always been 'the man'. When we were sophomores at Columbus Linden McKinley he played varsity more than I did. As seniors he made all state. He liked being 'the man'. It hurt me to have to stop him."

After their 19-3 junior year, when the Panthers lost a "13 point lead in the fourth quarter to Rex Kern's Lancaster team in the regionals," Young and Cleamons dedicated themselves to winning the state championship as seniors.

But Eddie Ratleff and Nick Connor had arrived at Columbus East. As sophomores they led East to an unbeaten City League season, including a 79-75 victory at Linden. "Yet that game was the key for us. They were ahead by 20, but we came back to close it to four. We proved to ourselves we could compete with them," remembers Cleamons, who had 19 of his game high 27 in that second half rally.

The rematch came in the regional finals. In a defensive struggle the Panthers avenged their earlier defeat, winning 43-34. Cleamons had 11 points and 11 rebounds, East had the only loss they would suffer over three seasons (1967, 1968, 1969).

That took Linden's record to 20-2 and a semi-final game with Canton Lincoln, the only other team to defeat them (56-53) during the year. Lincoln fell 54-50, setting up a state final with No. 1 ranked Cleveland East Tech. Linden jumped to a 15-6 lead and ended up winning 83-56.

The UPI All-Ohio team included Rudy Benjamin, Dayton Roosevelt and later Michigan State; Jim Harris, Lorain Admiral King and later junior college and Indiana star; Jeff Stocksdale, Lima Shawnee and later Indiana; and junior John Fraley, as well as Ed "Skip" Young of Linden. Rex Kern averaged 22.7 ppg and made second team. Jim Cleamons didn't even receive honorable mention.

"The biggest reason I went to Ohio State was a long talk I had with Fred," says Cleamons. "I was going out, the phone rang, it was him, and we talked for about an hour. What did I want out of life? How important was playing time? What about fitting into the system? It was a real heart to heart talk.

"Yes, anti-black stories about Fred were part of the heart to heart talk. I had heard things and they weren't all positive. After talking with him I felt good. That night I asked my mother and my aunt if they minded if I went to Ohio State. They were neutral. The next day I talked with 'Chick' (Linden varsity basketball coach and Ohio State assistant baseball coach Vince Chickerella) and we asked each other questions. Then I decided.

"No, I never had any racial problems with Fred or the basketball people, but I do remember one history teacher my freshman year. We had three mid-terms, equally weighted. I got C-D-C; she gave me a "D" in the class. I went to see her and she said 'I know you're an athlete.' That infuriated me, but I later found out those kinds of things happen in all colleges. In your hometown the stories get magnified.

"If not Ohio State, I might have gone Duquesne in Pittsburgh. I loved their tradition but they were in the middle of the city and didn't have a campus — I wanted the aesthetics like Mirror Lake. I really liked Kent State too. Frank Truitt was the coach then, great guy. But my girlfriend was going there and that didn't seem like a good idea.

"My freshman year I remember we got on a roll and beat the varsity in the pre-season scrimmage. Steve (Howell), Denny (Meadors) and (Bill) Hosket didn't like that. We caught hell all year in practice —every day they beat on us. We dreaded going some days. I tried to rally the forces, and the varsity probably saw me as the leader of the team. It was tough."

Craig Barclay offers another view of Cleamons. "He came to school with a chip on his shoulder. He was defiant, like it was a waste of time to be a freshman. When he came back as a sophomore it was like someone had waved a magic wand, a total change. He fit the system and was a natural leader. He was a great teammate."

"When we scrimmaged that year," recalls Taylor, "Jim was quicker than anybody on the varsity. He'd get inside for a lay-up, turn and sneer at his defender, then make the shot. I had to talk with him, and get him to think how he'd feel if someone did that to him."

Even "Cougar" recalls bringing some of the wrath of the upper classman on himself. "When we'd run the opponent's offense I'd say something to my roommate Ed Smith like 'School's in session.' Maybe the other players took it personally. Another saying I had was, 'I'll school you before I fool you!' "

While comments like that leave considerable room for misunderstanding, anyone who has played pick-up basketball remembers a guy (or gal, now) who was easy to hate when he was an opponent, but a valued teammate when the sides changed. When Jim Cleamons was a freshman he didn't settle for being "fed" to the varsity each night. And he wasn't very tactful about it either. When he

185

was eligible for the varsity, he was much more fun to play with than he had been to play against.

But first there were some books to conquer. Jim was ineligible part of his freshman year. "After two quarters I had a 1.625 average. Both my sisters had been valedictorians, so this was not acceptable," Jim recalls. "I put everything I had into academics Spring quarter, didn't even work out in the spring. Fred was wondering why I wasn't playing and I told him I was spending that time studying. He always said school was first, and he meant it, so that was OK. I had a 2.4 for the quarter — that was the turning point." Cleamons later made Academic All-Big Ten.

"Jimmy was quiet when he was in school," remembers Jimmy Crum. "You could ask him a 30 word question and he'd answer it in four."

"He's the quickest player Ohio State ever had," says Marv Homan. "Clever and smart. I'd rank him with Larry Siegfried as the best Buckeye guards I saw."

* * * *

Ohio State outrebounded a much taller Washington team 41 to 36 but were outshot 49% to 36% and lost 64-59. The Bucks only had six baskets in the first half.

With a 6-2 non-conference mark, OSU traveled to Bloomington and led Indiana 54-36 before hanging on to a 90-82 win. Sorenson's 24 led the team in scoring; all starters ended in double figures and Barclay had seven off the bench.

"By my junior year I had become the first sub," recalls Craig Barclay. "That meant I started off the game sitting next to the coach. Nobody wanted to sit next to Fred, for two reasons. First, he used to make comments during the game. Not the kinds of things he said any other time, really candid thoughts off the top of his head. He used to keep his hand in front of his mouth, and usually turned toward his assistant. But sometimes his hand slipped and you heard. Then, when you went in the game, sometimes you wondered what he said about you. Second, he wore these heavy wing-tip shoes. When he got upset he stomped his foot; you had to make sure your feet weren't nearby. Still, I decided it was the best place to be. It was more likely that I'd be first choice to go in."

An 84-69 home victory over Wisconsin left OSU and Purdue the only unbeaten conference teams at 2-0. Sorenson had 21 points and 17 rebounds, Howell scored 20 and Meadors hit 16 points while holding high scoring Clarence Sherrod to four.

A road victory at Michigan, where Wolverine junior Rudy Tomjanovich was averaging 27.4 points, made OSU 3-0. After Ohio State's 98-85 victory first year Michigan Coach Johnny Orr said "Cleamons wasn't just great, he was super great. He drove, shot, rebounded, passed off, did everything." Cleamons had 11 of 16 field goals and nine of 10 fouls for 31 points, and 10 rebounds. Sorenson hit 12 of 15 shots and junior Dan Andreas bounced off the bench for 12 points and 13 rebounds. Tomjanovich scored 18 points.

Today Orr, now at Iowa State, recalls coaching against Fred Taylor. "He was a super guy. You won't find a coach who didn't respect him. I hated to see him get out of coaching; thought he was much too young. He told me you need two offenses in the Big Ten — home and road. At home you can run, on the road the officials won't let you get out and go."

Balanced scoring helped Ohio State survive a six of 17 shooting night by Sorenson and beat Georgia Tech 73-66. "Sunshine" came back with 33 as Cornell fell 96-78. Jeff Miller hit three baskets at the end of the blow-out, but that was the last time he would score more than two points in a Buckeye game.

UPI now had the Bucks ranked #17 in the nation at 11-2, behind #8 Illinois and ahead of #20 Purdue. Undefeated UCLA got all the first place votes.

With only one league loss, Illinois came to Columbus determined to tighten the Big Ten race. The game was 62-61 Ohio State with 4:12 to play when Cleamons took over: jump shot, rebound basket, feed to Sorenson, steal and lay-up and OSU had a 76-67 victory. Sorenson had another 30 point game, and Taylor his 100th Big Ten coaching victory.

With a 4-0 record Ohio State visited 3-0 Purdue. The game was tied at the end of regulation at 83-all but the Boilers put it away in overtime 95-85. Meadors, Barclay and Finney took turns controlling Rick Mount, who hit eight of 22 shots for 20 points, but Gilliam scored 22 and Keller 21. Sorenson had 30 again, this time hitting twelve straight free throws. So close. What if OSU had won that game? How would the season have developed?

Along with the frustration of the close overtime loss to undefeated Purdue was the joy in the emergence of Dave Sorenson as an unqualified star. His 24.5 ppg scoring average ranked 24th nationally, he was shooting .554 from the field and .793 from the line, plus grabbing 11.3 rebounds per game. All this despite being the only Buckeye taller than 6'5. "If we had just had one guy 6'9 to bang with Dave, ...," ponders Jody Finney — and everyone else — today.

Before their rematch with Purdue the Bucks had to travel to Madison, Wisconsin to play the dangerous Badgers. Wisconsin was only 7-10 but had victories over such national powers as Kentucky, Kansas and Marquette. With balanced scoring by their starters and cold nights by Sorenson (four of 16 and the victim of three quick fouls) and Finney (three of 11), Wisconsin added another scalp, 77-73. That made Purdue's (6-0) visit a must game for the 4-2 Buckeyes.

Ohio State outscored Purdue 88-85 in the critical game. Mount's 35 point output was surpassed by balanced excellence by Finney (28), Sorenson (24) and Cleamons (21), plus a total of 13 by Meadors and Howell. As was the case so often during the year OSU won the game at the foul line, hitting 26 of 31 free throws (ten straight by Finney) to overcome an eight basket deficit. Purdue coach George King said "It's just that Ohio State doesn't foul. They're amazing. They play tough defense and don't foul."

First year coach Bill Fitch instructed his Minnesota team to hold the ball even when they trailed, and got a 58-41 loss for his stratagem. Cleamons was high scorer with 15 points on only eight attempts. He was leading the conference in field goal accuracy at 61%.

But Illinois' Randy Crews held Clem to three shots and two points as the host Illini beat OSU 73-57. The game was a team nightmare. State was outrebounded 45-29, called for seven more personal fouls, and shot only .438 from the field. Jeff Miller reinjured his knee and would never play again as a Buckeye. Sorenson's game high 25 points was the only bright spot, except for the impact on Cleamons which would surface several games later.

Pre-season co-favorite Iowa fell to 4-6 in the conference with an 88-81 loss at St. John Arena. The Bucks shot well, outrebounded Iowa and put the game away with a strong finish. "Sunshine" had 32 points and 17 rebounds, both game highs, and Cleamons added 21 points and seven rebounds.

At 15-5 OSU ranked 15th in the country, but trailed No. 7 Purdue (16-4) by two games in the conference. If the Bucks had won that overtime loss at West Lafayette, they would have been tied.

Road losses at Northwestern (86-83) and Michigan State (85-72) ended Buckeye title and NCAA hopes. They were outrebounded and outshot from the floor.

"After the Michigan State game," remembers Cleamons, "Fred showed me an Illinois newspaper quoting Randy Crews after our game with them. He was bragging, saying 'I held him the whole game. When the refs didn't call it, I knew I had him.' And the worst thing was, he had me because I was too busy being angry to play basketball. That was the last time I let anger control me on the court. I decided to use that energy to get the job done.

"After the season I was visiting on the Ohio University campus and saw a sign which said 'If it angers me, it conquers me.' That brought understanding to my game and my existence. I have referred to that game and that sign throughout my life."

Apparently "the Cougar" had a great deal of energy to use in the last two games. He had 37 points in a 108-86 victory over Indiana and 35 points in a 95-86 victory over Michigan. Too bad Illinois was not on the schedule — Cleamons might have scored 50 against Crews.

* * * *

As the season was winding to a close, UPI carried some quotes by a coach who was irate about the way the NCAA was arranging its tournament games. His team's first game was scheduled for 5:05 p.m. His comments follow. "I've been in sports all my life and the last time I played at 5 o'clock at night was on a playground in Harlem. College boys are supposed to be amateurs and all of sudden they're slaves of TV. After playing 26 games to get there, we have to rearrange our whole lives at the demands of someone not even connected with any college." The speaker was Marquette coach and future NBC commentator Al McGuire.

* * * *

Though their late season road losses cost Ohio State a Top 20 finish, assistant coach Jack Graf spoke for everyone at the Appreciation Banquet when he said "In my many years of coaching, this group came closest to reaching its full potential."

Dave Sorenson was selected MVP and Captain for the coming season. "Sunshine" was unanimously selected first team All-Big Ten, and also made the NCAA District Four team.

Undersized 6'2 forward Jim Cleamons, ignored for All-Ohio honors in high school, led the Bucks in assists and minutes played —

189

915 of a possible 965. He trailed only Sorenson in points and rebounds and was second team All-Big Ten.

Today Dave Sorenson reflects on that season, in fact his entire Buckeye career, saying "Fred was able to evaluate players' talents and capabilities, then devise an offense to suit that talent. He wouldn't ask you to do something you couldn't do. That allowed us to do as well as we could as a group, which was true every year I played."

In the NCAA UCLA won again, defeating Purdue 89-76, after the Boilers had beaten Marquette and North Carolina. Coach Taylor had overestimated the balance in the Big Ten — the Boilermakers won 13 of 14, their only loss being in Columbus.

1969 — 1970

"Second verse, same as the first" went a song by Herman's Hermits, popular near the time. The idea fit the 1969-70 Ohio State team. Howell and Meadors had graduated, but Andreas and Barclay had started the last few games of the 1969 season to gain some experience. With Sorenson, Cleamons and Finney, the starting five was set, but only featured one player — "Sunshine" — was over 6'4. In 1969 OSU had been outrebounded by their opponents — this year would be the same.

As Jody Finney looks back on the year he remembers thinking "It was our mind set to win the Big Ten every year. That's what we expected."

Fred Taylor was aware of the rebounding disadvantage which seemed likely, and had a strategy. "We had to pressure the other team with our offense," he says. "We certainly couldn't overpower anyone. We didn't neglect defense, but we *had to score*. We couldn't recover from bad shots. The pressure on our offense turned out to be a good thing — they responded and played better."

Early in the year, much of the basketball talk around town centered on the OSU freshman class. Some "experts" were calling it better than the Lucas-Havlicek-Nowell-Gearhart-Knight group, based on the nearly 170 points per game the six had averaged in high school. Before the season started, the varsity beat the freshmen 54-26 in a 25 minute game. The game was abbreviated either to let the varsity scrimmage the jayvees (which they beat 30-16) or to allow the freshmen to begin to rebuild their confidence. In any event Jim Cleamons, leading scorer with 27, was on the winning side for the third straight year and the varsity had moved back to center stage.

There they stayed as Fred Taylor got his 200th coaching victory with a 96-92 win over Wake Forest. Sorenson (31), Cleamons (26) and Finney (23) handled the scoring, the team hit 32 of 38 from the foul line and sophomore Mark Minor was the only sub. The Bucks won 112-89 at Butler, setting a school road scoring record which still stands. Against Northern Illinois OSU shot 36 of 40 from the foul line in winning 106-99. The "Big 3" of Sorenson (28), Cleamons (28) and Finney (25) had 81 points. Senior Craig Barclay had 19, including 11 straight at the line. He had settled into the guard position well.

* * * *

"It had been a risk to go to Ohio State," recalls Barclay. "I had played forward in high school at 6'3, and they wanted me as a guard. I had to become a much better ball handler.

"My goal as a sophomore was to travel, particularly on that trip to Hawaii. As a junior I wanted to play, and as a senior we were all expected to be team leaders. In my mind, when I started as a senior that vindicated my choice of Ohio State.

"In high school I played for Dick Schenk at Newark. We had some good teams, but never made the state tournament. We lost to Eastmoor (Steve Howell's team) my junior year and Columbus East in double overtime in my last game.

"I had thought about the Ivy League, but wanted to enjoy school and sports and heard it was very difficult to do both there. Vanderbilt called and I thought about William and Mary because Jack Downing, who was one year ahead of me at Newark, was there. When Fred contacted me I was thrilled to be considered; it motivated me to work. I remember he took us to the Jai Lai for dinner, which I later found out was pretty standard. My parents liked him and I was just in awe. I grew up with Lucas and Havlicek and when he offered the scholarship, that was it.

"During the summer before my freshman year there was open gym at St. John Arena and the players who were in town had pick-up games. After going the first time I went into the locker room and heard Bill Hosket and Ron Sepic talking about the new guys. Hosket said 'Barclay will be around for four years.' Compared to their other comments that was very flattering.

"I remember a lot of pressure to start on the freshman team, because we had seven guys on scholarship. Then one of the guys, Eddie Jacobs, a high scorer at Wellston, left school. He was a terrific guy

191

(and made first team All-Ohio averaging 25.6 ppg at 6'1) but he didn't have the necessary athletic skills to compete.

"One thing I learned early as a freshman was not to show up the upperclassmen. Once I stole the ball from Ron Sepic. The next play he drove, placed his elbow on my nose, put me on my back, scored and looked at me. Then he helped me up. He was a nice guy, it was just part of the process. I later found out that if Sepic hadn't responded right away Fred would have said something like 'Does he know you're a senior?' and Ron just decided to avoid that.

"I started out low on the totem pole. I wasn't as good as I thought I was, and I didn't think I was very good. The thing that helped me most at Ohio State was that I was coachable ("He never made the same mistake twice," recalls Taylor). I relied on playing within the system. From watching Fred's teams on television I knew how much emphasis Fred placed on the system, so OSU seemed like a good place for me."

"When I started playing more it was a relief during team introductions, because my teammates were kidding me about being first in my graduating class. They said 'Every time he introduces you, the size of your class gets bigger. You better start playing or he'll run out of exaggerations.' The other thing he'd say is 'I was afraid to recruit Craig. He might ask a question in the huddle I couldn't answer.' Yeah, right."

For the record Barclay was first in his class of 560. While he was certainly intelligent and definitely coachable, he was more than that. Asked what he remembers about Barclay today, Jim Cleamons says "He was a hard worker, and one of the best spot-up jump shooters I ever played with." Meaning, if he had time he could trade shots with guys like Sorenson, Finney and Hornyak, who you played with at Ohio State? And NBA teammates like Jerry West, Gail Goodrich, Dick Snyder, Austin Carr and Bingo Smith? "Yes," Clem nods. That's a shooter.

* * * *

A good Ohio University team out-hustled and out-rebounded the Bucks 82-80, but road wins at Alabama and Tulane were encouraging. The "Big 3" were the only ones in double figures in an 84-77 victory over Fresno State but all starters hit that mark in an 89-80 road victory at TCU.

The Bucks prepared to open the Big Ten season with a 7-1 record, shooting 55% from the field and 84% from the line.

Minnesota, 4-3 in non-conference, fell 78-71 as OSU opened the Big Ten at home. There were no Buckeye substitutions for the five who had started every game. The road was not as kind, OSU losing at Illinois 77-59. The Illini outrebounded the Bucks by seven, caused 23 turnovers, and outshot the visitors.

Ohio State scored often in beating Michigan 103-95 at St. John Arena. Sorenson and Cleamons split 57 points almost evenly, Finney added 22 and Andreas and Barclay the rest. Though he didn't score, Ed Smith contributed effective defense against Rudy Tomjanovich when Sorenson had foul trouble. Tom Keys of *The Citizen-Journal* wrote that many pro basketball scouts were in the audience including Red Auerbach of Boston, Pete Newell of San Diego (which drafted Rudy T.), Freddy Schaus of Los Angeles and Dick Motta of Chicago.

The Bucks blew Northwestern away 93-67 behind 72 points from the "Big 3". Many subs played but not Jim Geddes, out for the fourth time during the year with a shoulder dislocation. An excellent athlete — "He could stand flat footed under the basket and dunk," remembers Barclay — Geddes was troubled with injuries throughout his basketball career and was better known as a baseball pitcher.

Next OSU hosted neighboring West Virginia and, behind Finney's 30 points, won 84-70. Since the Illinois loss Jody was 29 of 45 from the field — 65% —boosting his season mark to over 61%. "When he was on a streak I marveled at him," recalls Cleamons. Jody was now spending an increasing amount of time in "the stack" with Sorenson. This freed the now experienced Cleamons to play more guard, where his open court skills could be more valuable. The change was of benefit to both, but was varied according to opposing match-ups. One more counter for opponents to have to anticipate.

Fred Taylor always said "It's tough to beat someone twice," and that was pointed out again when Ohio State lost at Minnesota, 77-76. The Bucks were outrebounded by four. Only four players scored for Ohio State; the offense did not create enough pressure.

In their final non-conference game of the year, OSU beat Georgia Tech 74-71. Visiting 6'9 star Rich Yunkus, the tenth leading scorer in the nation with a 29 point average, made 11 of 12 shots and five straight free throws for 27 points. However Sorenson almost matched him with 26 and had more help.

A 68-64 victory at Northwestern behind 18 of 21 at the foul line, Captain Sorenson hitting all 11 of his, made the Bucks 4-2. The problem was, both Illinois (5-0) and Iowa (4-0) were undefeated.

Purdue (3-2) came to Columbus in a critical game for both teams — the loser would appear to be out of the race. Three losses would be bad, trailing three teams might be worse. To warm up the Boilers had disposed of Michigan 116-103 as Rick Mount scored 53 points. Yet Fred Taylor remarked "What really worries me is that they're recovering about 56% of all rebounds and we're getting only 46%." The Boilers had 6'10, 6'8, 6'7, 6'7, 6'6, and 6'5 front line players to rotate with Mount and quick Larry Weatherford.

Unfortunately Taylor was right. Purdue got 16 more rebounds than Ohio State, and an 88-85 victory. The Bucks trailed 43-32 at the half, but came roaring back as Cleamons hit 10 of 12 attempts from the field. Just not far enough. Mount was held to 32, after averaging 41.5 points in his previous six games, by Barclay, Cleamons, Andreas and some combination defenses.

* * * *

"I remember we tried almost everyone on Mount," says Dan Andreas. "I had him for a while. Once I had good pressure, went up with him, he landed out of bounds on the side and still made it. The majority of this shots would have been three pointers today.

"I still kid my wife Lois about what she did after that game, because it was so out of character. Fred used to call her 'Miss Goody Two Shoes,' she was so sweet. Well, she didn't like Rick Mount, and was pretty upset after the game. She went to the Purdue locker room, convinced them she was a fan and talked them into giving her a picture of Rick. Then she talked to their coach, George King, and asked him to have Mount come out and sign the picture. Rick came out, signed it, gave it to her, and she tore it up. Right there in front of him. We were only dating at the time but that's when I knew she was a true Buckeye."

Dan had attended Garaway High School in Sugarcreek, Ohio, very close to Berlin Highland where Andy Ahijevych played. Garaway was a small Class A school, and was beaten by Bridgeport in the state tournament his senior year. He remembers his coach "Glen Baver, (as) a strict disciplinarian who worked on the fundamentals and was all business at practice."

Mostly recruited by small schools "like MAC, Ohio Conference, I remember going to North Carolina State for a visit. Press Maravich was the coach then, and I played in a pick-up game with his son." "Pistol Pete" Maravich later led the nation at scoring when he and Press were at LSU.

"But when Ohio State called and "Burky" came to see me, I was overwhelmed. It was everyone's dream to go there. Then I went to dinner with Fred and Andy at the Jai Lai, and was so excited I probably didn't say three words. He said 'Are you interested in coming to Ohio State?' and I just said 'Yes'."

"My counselor in high school had said 'Don't go to a large school, like Ohio State. Go to a small school and be happy.' He still lives here, and I've mentioned a couple of times that he was wrong."

Thinking about his freshman year at OSU, Andreas recalls "It was a helluva lot of hard work. I was petrified the summer before, and did a lot of running so I'd be in shape for the season. Then we had pre-season conditioning and I almost died. It was tougher than I ever imagined. Then in practice we were cannon fodder for the varsity. I always had to guard Ron Sepic, and got the crap beat out of me. He was physical. We'd be pushing, shoving, calling each other names ... then every once in a while he'd pull me aside to let me know he really liked me, that it was nothing personal. (The interesting thing is that Finney recalls playing against Captain Ron Sepic every day in practice too. Sepic really had an impact his senior year.)

"Also I was on academic probation as a freshman. I practiced and played in the informal games with local teams, but couldn't play the games with Michigan and Toledo. That made me improve my study habits and I ended up Academic All-Big Ten and got three degrees from Ohio State.

"The other thing about my freshman year that stands out is my roommates. Everyone on the freshman team was with another basketball player except me. They put me with Jim Stillwagon and Dick Kuhn. Football players are different. It seemed like Jim always had his head in this harness, lifting weights to build up his neck.

"We lived in Parke Hall, on the 11th Floor. I walked in during finals week Spring quarter and there was Jim, letting off steam. He had taken the screen out, and put a piece of carpet by the window. He was hitting golf balls out the window, and bouncing them off the dorm across the street. When he ran out of golf balls he took 45 rpm records and started sailing them. One just missed a guy and stuck in a tree. Woody (Hayes) found out and got mad.

"Back then the basketball and football offices were very close to each other in St. John Arena. My sophomore year I was going to see Fred about something and Woody Hayes came up to me. I was about 6'4, 220 lbs. at that time. He grabbed me, pushed me up against the wall with his forearm in my chest and said 'Would you ever consider playing tight end for me?' I didn't know what to do. I said 'Whatever you say Coach' and he left.

"My sophomore year in basketball I was worried about how I would fit in. I hoped to travel, especially since we were going to Hawaii. It was a good year, because we accomplished so much as a team — Big Ten title, beating Kentucky at Kentucky. And it was good to be a teammate on the varsity instead of scum as a freshman.

"My biggest personal thrill was the Indiana game. It's every player's dream to score the basket at the buzzer to win a game. Fred set up a play for Hosket to take the last shot. Meadors had the ball, looked for Bill (Hosket) but he was double teamed. Nobody was guarding me. Denny threw it to me on the right side of the foul line, it went through and the buzzer went off. John Halley picked me up, screaming 'We won, we won, you did it.'

"I was excited. To get to the locker rooms, you had to go down and underneath the floor. I got mixed up, and went in the Indiana locker room. I shook a few hands, tried to act like I wanted to be there and left. When I went out the door, there was Fred. He said 'You're in the wrong locker room.' He still kids me about that today.

"My junior year I got to play more as the season went along, and my senior year I was a starter. Sorenson, Cleamons and Finney did most of the scoring for us. Dick Otte of *The Columbus Dispatch* called them 'The Three Man Machine'. Craig Barclay and I considered ourselves 'The Oilers' of the 'Machine'."

When teammate Jim Cleamons remembers Dan Andreas today he smiles, nods and says "He really busted it every day in practice." High praise from a coach.

* * * *

Road victories at Michigan State (89-66) and Indiana (100-83) raised a glimmer of hope as OSU shot 65% from the field. *That's* keeping pressure on with your offense.

Though Illinois had lost five straight to drop from the race, Purdue (8-2) kept winning and Iowa never did stop. The Hawkeyes outrebounded Ohio State 47-30 in St. John and won 97-89. Dan Andreas remembers guarding John Johnson — "He had 38 and I thought I did a good job. He could score from anywhere."

OSU won at Wisconsin 98-86, as sixth man Mark Minor chipped in nine points, but lost at home when they looked past Michigan State,

82-80. Outstanding Spartan sophomore Ralph Simpson had 29 points. Iowa, on the way to an undefeated conference season, thumped the Bucks 113-92, doubling them on the boards 44-22.

The season ended on a positive note as OSU beat Wisconsin 96-87 to finish tied for third with Illinois at 8-6. Sorenson had 30 to pass Robin Freeman and become the school's second leading career scorer behind Jerry Lucas. Craig Barclay had 16 points, and remembers deciding to shoot more than usual. Coach Taylor noticed that, called Barclay over and said "I don't care if you shoot it, but at least get your feet set."

Barclay continued to reflect on his time with Fred, saying "He treated us like men. For a kid out of high school, that was a shock. He worked so hard to treat us all equally and fairly that you were never quite sure if he liked you. Late my senior year, Fred asked me to help out the next year as a graduate assistant and was instrumental in helping me obtain two post graduate scholarships. I guess I found out. Needless to say, I owe him a lot."

Dan Andreas has a fond memory of his coach and the Wisconsin game as well. "Against Indiana I had hit my elbow on the floor. Didn't think much about it, just kept playing. The next day at practice it was the size of an orange. Dr. Murphy had to lance it — you wouldn't believe the stuff that came out. I played the next four games, but it hurt like crazy. Before the Wisconsin game I couldn't lift my arm over my shoulder. I told Fred I couldn't play, that he should start Mark (Minor), and thought that was the end of it. Just before the line-ups were introduced Fred came up to me and said 'You're starting.' I was surprised, but didn't say anything. Then the first time the ball went out of bounds to stop the clock, Mark came in for me. Fred said 'I wanted you to remember that you started every game your senior year.' And I do remember that."

For a team with a 17-7 record, it was a remarkable year. They shot .544 from the field to tie the NCAA record set by Davidson in 1964. They shot .808 from the foul line, the first NCAA team to top .800. Oh, for one more rebounder.

Again Sorenson was named MVP, first team All-Big Ten, All-NCAA District Four and honorable mention All-America. Again Cleamons led the team in playing time and was second team All-Big Ten. Finney was honorable mention All-Big Ten. Jim Cleamons was elected Captain for the coming season.

Nationally, Iowa was eliminated from the NCAA, 104-103, by Jacksonville in the Mideast Regional played at St. John Arena. Despite the graduation of Lew Alcindor, UCLA defeated Jacksonville 80-69 to win their fourth straight championship.

XI

1971:
Clem Leads the Kids

Rebuilding for the 1970-71 season was even more extensive than after the Lucas-Havlicek-Nowell class graduated in 1962. Then starters Doug McDonald and Dick Reasbeck returned for their senior year, and Gary Bradds and Jim Doughty had spent a year as important reserves. Now only one starter returned, and Jim Cleamons was being moved from a combination guard/forward to the team leader in the back court. Now only one substitute with significant experience was back; Mark Minor had accumulated 63 points and 48 rebounds while playing 22 games.

The graduating seniors had taken with them 71% of the points scored during their third straight 17-7 regular season and 69% of the rebounds. Also, Captain Cleamons figured to be less of a rebounder as a guard than his junior year, when he had grabbed eight a game.

The Scarlet and Gray would be green, no question about that. Except for Cleamons the Bucks would be very short on experience, but exaggerations of the talent on hand were a bigger concern than lack of ability. Fred Taylor and Bob Burkholder had assembled a tremendous group of high school players.

Three members of the class had been first team All-Ohio Class AA on UPI's five man team, something even the Lucas-Havlicek-Nowell class could not claim. But then the fact that Hondo was selected second team speaks to the lack of reliability of all state teams as much as anything else.

- Allan Hornyak, 6'1 lefty from Bellaire St. John in the Ohio Valley, had led the nation in scoring with 41.9 ppg. His average had *tailed off* after the first ten games, which included consecutive nights of 86 and 61, when he had an average of 48.6. By shooting 60% from the floor and 80% from the line he took his team to a 20-2 record. For his career he totaled 2385 points in 78 games, 75 points less than the mark set by Jerry Lucas. Additionally he had an 89% academic average, led the St. John's football team to a 9-1 record as quarterback, and, in two years of baseball, threw three no-hitters and two one-hitters when he wasn't playing first base.

- Dave Merchant, 6'1 guard from Marion Harding, signed with Ohio State two weeks after Hornyak. Merchant had averaged 27.5 ppg as a senior, finishing second on his team in assists. He shot 48% from the floor, 75% from the line and jumped center. He was also a standout baseball player, good enough as a shortstop and catcher to be heavily pursued by the Philadelphia Phillies.

- Luke Witte, 7' center from Marlington with a 32.5 ppg average, turned down North Carolina after narrowing the long list of schools to "the only two who didn't hint there might be something extra for me". The tallest player to sign with the Buckeyes already had developed a variety of scoring moves; considering the history of All-Big Ten centers under Taylor, news that the tall kid with the blonde curly locks would become a Buckeye must have been bad news around the conference.

While not first team Class AA All-Ohio, the other three members of that class had outstanding credentials as well. Bob Siekmann of Cincinnati Oak Hills, a 6'3 forward, had a 23.7 point average and a third team All-Ohio selection to his credit. Another baseball player, he had been an outstanding pitcher in high school. Mark Wagar, 6'8 from Avon, had been the first Buckeye recruit in the class. A second team class A selection, Wagar scored 25.6 ppg at center but was recruited to play forward. The final recruit was 6'2 Gregg Testerman from Lebanon, where he played guard and forward, averaging 20.5 ppg for his 17-5 team.

Other than having difficulty with the varsity in practice — "We were poor," recalls Bob Siekmann. "Fred was upset because we couldn't make the varsity sweat." — the new players adjusted well to college life. All received at least a 2.6 grade average in their first quarter, so none loomed as an academic risk. As expected, Hornyak and Witte were the leading scorers and seemed to be the two most likely to figure quickly as sophomores. The freshman team went 11-1, losing only to Michigan when five Buckeyes fouled out at Ann Arbor. Mark Wagar remembers that game as "our introduction to life above the rim."

The basketball team was able to escape public scrutiny early in the year due to the overwhelming interest in the 9-0 football team. The senior class of Kern-Tatum-Stillwagon-Hayden-Brockington-Sensibaugh-White-Jankowski et. al. had beaten Michigan, had a date with Stanford in the Rose Bowl, and was contending with Texas and Notre Dame for No. 1 ranking nationally. This allowed the young basketball players to make their individual adjustments to the role of members of a college team in relative anonymity.

"What we tried to communicate to players every year," recalls Taylor, "was 'If you don't score and the team wins, that's good — but you have to figure out why you didn't score. On the other hand, if you scored a lot and the team lost, maybe there is something more or something else the team needed from you. Team success is most important, but it still can't cover individual responsibility. That's not an easy idea — some people never get it."

How quickly would the young Buckeyes of 1970-71 get it? Would they ever get it?

The Utah State Aggies of LaDell Anderson were a major challenge for any team that year, much less a club with only one senior on the traveling team. They returned three regulars from a team that posted a 22-7 record and went to the NCAA. In contrast, OSU opened with Cleamons, Minor, sophomores Witte and Hornyak, and 6'9 junior forward Mike Macknin of Mayfield Heights, who had played 41 minutes the year before.

OSU fought back from a 52-39 halftime deficit to make the score 82-81 Utah State with just over four minutes to go, but lost 95-89. As expected Captain Cleamons played well, scoring 28 and directing the action. As hoped, Hornyak (23 points) and Witte (20) came through.

OSU won the next two games at home, beating East Tennessee State 71-63 and Alabama 74-58. Then No. 7 ranked Pennsylvania, returning Corky Calhoun, Bob Morse and Dave Wohl from a 25-1 team the year before, came to Columbus and won 71-64. The Ivy League power would take a 26-0 record to the NCAA tournament. While the Bucks were 2-2, their losses had been to outstanding teams. The competition was accelerating their development, though it was not easy. Today Luke Witte remembers "The Pennsylvania game was the low point of the season for me. I threw the ball away three times, felt frustrated and over my head."

* * * *

"I remember Luke having great habits," recalls Jim Cleamons today. "I can see Don DeVoe working with him, and Luke taking 150 hook shots before every practice." Don DeVoe, at OSU for a year as a graduate assistant, remembers "Luke had a great attitude, working with Mark Wagar and me before practice every day. He really wanted to prove himself. Had a nice shooting touch and ran the floor well."

"Luke was a very personable guy," remembers Allan Hornyak. "In Fred's offense a guard and a center must work well together, and I thought we did."

"He was more like Bradds than Lucas. He wasn't smooth, but he was effective," says Dr. Bob Murphy. "And unselfish," adds Marv Homan.

"For a seven footer he was athletic, though an average jumper," recalls Siekmann. "Good hand eye coordination — I remember him juggling to improve that."

"He was one of the most talented people I ever ran into," says Mark Wagar. "A big 7' kid, he had some ups and downs. He wasn't as emotionally mature as some at that age, but he often rose to the occasion."

One way to describe Luke Witte might be through recalling a scene in the classic Frank Capra movie "It's A Wonderful Life". George Bailey, played by Jimmy Stewart, and his father are talking. George is ready to leave for college, having worked at the Bailey Building and Loan for several years to save money. His younger brother Harry is graduating from high school and will take George's place, but Mr. Bailey is concerned about Harry's youth. "He's the same age I was when I started," says George. "Yes, but you were born older," says Mr. Bailey.

Some college kids are "born older," mature beyond their years. Jerry Lucas was, Bill Hosket was, recently Jim Jackson was. They were able to accept the pressure which comes with tremendous athletic talent almost immediately. Gary Bradds might have been, but he wasn't in the spotlight as a sophomore. Dave Sorenson might have been, but he had Hosket to help him.

Most college students aren't "born older". Luke Witte wasn't. For most, college is a time of transition, of maturation. And they do these things without the pressure of being a 7' center required to provide the inside scoring so necessary for their team to be successful.

Some people are "born older", some "age gracefully," some "develop early." Over the course of a lifetime, it all balances out. However basketball players aren't under the microscope of public scrutiny for a lifetime, only as long as they are athletes. Luke Witte, as much as any high profile player at Ohio State during the Golden Age, was still maturing while he was under the microscope.

* * * *

Teammate Allan Hornyak, "Mr. Outside" to Witte's "Mr. Inside", was not the normal 19 year old going away to college to grow into being a man, trying to figure out life on the way.

"How many freshman in college," asks Witte today, "know exactly what they want to do in life and have a back-up plan in case that doesn't work out? Allan did. He came to college with the idea of playing in the NBA. If that didn't work out, he was going home to live where he felt secure and work in the mines."

"Even though we played together for four years," continues Witte, "I didn't really get to know him well at Ohio State. He spent most of his time with his friends at the dorm and his girlfriend, who he later married. I spent most of my time at the fraternity. When we were both drafted by the Cleveland Cavaliers we spent a month together in training camp. That's when I found out he is much deeper than people realized."

"He was directed," recalls Wagar. "He said exactly what he was going to do and he was true to his word. He said 'I came to play ball and I'll do what I have to do to stay eligible. If I can't play ball I'll go back to the Valley.'

"He also had a sense of humor," continued Wagar. "I was known as not having the best hands in the world. When a game was wrapped up, and constantly in practice, he'd put spin on his passes to make me look bad."

"He went to the right school," feels Marv Homan. "He was not a one-on-one player — the system and the screens helped him. He was a gifted shooter." Mike Bordner, trainer, remembers "a quick release like Dennis Hopson, or maybe Kelvin Ransey in later years."

"He didn't elevate much on his shot," says Merchant, "but he had an explosive first step and that quick release. He was faster than people realized too. When we ran dashes, only Cleamons could beat him."

"Allan was competitive," says Captain Cleamons today. "Confident, too. He knew he was good. He was clever rather than quick; street-wise. He had a shooter's mentality — shoot to get hot, shoot to stay hot."

"I've been streaky all my life," comments Hornyak today, "and I loved to shoot. I remember shoveling the snow off driveways to shoot in the middle of winter. We'd play at night too. We didn't have any lights, but we had fluorescent nets. We couldn't see the rim, but we could shoot just over the net, so that's what we did.

"When I played in high school as a freshman — in the starting line-up after the sixth game — and sophomore I had mostly a set shot. Man-to-man defense could stop me. The summer before my junior year I worked on a jump shot. I started at 2', then 3' and out. Bellaire St. John was 14-6 my junior year. Senior year we lost our first game to Bridgeport, Havlicek's old school. They were about our size, but were Class A and we were Class AA. They went to the small school finals that year. Then we won 20 straight before losing to Zanesville, a much bigger school, in the tournament.

"One of the reasons I went to Ohio State was I thought I could play right away. And it was close to home. Dean Smith came to my house but he was playing that platoon stuff at North Carolina and I didn't think I'd like that. UCLA had so many players, and seemed so far away, that I decided not to go there. Kentucky was very interested for a while but in the end they thought I was too small."

Allan had decided on Ohio State several weeks before his announcement. But it almost didn't work out as he expected.

"I went to Columbus for the state tournament with some friends, to relax and get away from the recruiters even more than to see the basketball. Fred had given me tournament tickets, and I agreed to go to a dinner he was hosting for the high school recruits who were in town.

"My friends and I were walking to the dinner and we went past an outdoor court. We decided to challenge the winner. So we played a full court game in dress pants and street shoes. Then we were sweaty and decided to skip the dinner. We sold our tournament tickets and did something else.

"The thing is, Fred missed us at the dinner. Mark Minor told me later Fred sent him to our seats at the game to see what had happened, and introduce himself as a possible future teammate. Mark went to where we were supposed to be, saw the men we sold the seats to and went back to Fred. Fred said 'Mark, is anything wrong?' and Mark said 'I don't know, Coach, these guys are pretty old.' He thought Fred was recruiting some 30 or 40 year old guy."

That was the funny part, but not to Taylor. "I called Allan and told him 'Ohio State is withdrawing the scholarship offer,'" he says. "'If we can't count on you to fulfill your obligations to attend a simple thing like a dinner, why could we count on you to do what's necessary to attend college and play basketball?' We were finished with him."

This wasn't a bluff, it was a final decision. A player being heavily recruited by UCLA and North Carolina and everyone else was told to go elsewhere because he missed a dinner and scalped some tickets. Fred Taylor lived in a world of right and wrong. Hornyak's action was clearly wrong; if it indicated that more such actions were to follow, best to stop the process immediately and look for a reliable person with *almost* as good a jump shot.

After being courted, coaxed and pampered for months, this was completely unexpected. However Hornyak recovered, apologized and convinced his coach-to-be that the incident was more a matter of misunderstanding than an indication of character. The scholarship offer was extended again. A few days later Allan Hornyak committed to Ohio State.

"My freshman year was a learning period," recalls Hornyak, known as "The Bellaire Bomber." "I had played football primarily to build up my strength, and had become pretty good at posting up high school players. Trouble is, they were 5'8, 5'9 and now the college guys are 6'3, 6'4. When Jim Cleamons guarded me he shut me down. He held me to five points in one game. I had to learn to move without the ball, use screens and stay patient. I'd have liked to bring the ball down court and let it fly, but that wasn't the way things were done at Ohio State. I was becoming a believer in Fred's offensive system. I learned the defense couldn't stop the offense if the players didn't hurry it."

* * * *

Hornyak had 25 points and Witte 24 as Ohio State beat Butler 96-77. Cleamons only took 11 shots, concentrating on running the offense, but still added 17 points. Mark Wagar joined Mark Minor in the starting line-up and the Buckeyes left for the Far West Classic in Portland, Oregon.

When Ohio State lost to Stanford 78-74 in overtime, the result was not a surprise. In four games, all four Far West teams advanced in the winners bracket. No outsider would win in 1970; only one had in the 16 previous tournaments. What was surprising was the play at the end of overtime when Hornyak made a clutch basket to tie the game and was hit in the nose for a likely trip to the foul line. Instead the basket was waved off and he was called for an offensive foul. When the call was later shown on television on a sports report, the announcer said "This is the first time anyone has committed an offensive foul with his face." Cleamons had 30 points on 12 of 16 from the field and Hornyak and Witte had 16 points each. Oh well, it didn't hurt as much as the loss by the football team to Jim Plunkett's Stanford team four days later. What hurt the most was the bruise to his heel which Clem sustained in the first half. He played the remainder of the game, but Dr. Luther Keith advised holding him out until the Iowa game January 9, the start of the Big Ten season.

Hornyak had 28 points and Witte 22 as OSU beat Harvard 103-87. Merchant took Clem's place in the starting line-up and scored 14 points. Wagar, Minor and Siekmann hit double figures and 11 players saw action. Everyone on the trip played except the Captain.

The final game matched the Bucks with Big Ten rival Indiana, selected alongside Purdue and Illinois to be the elite of the conference. Joby Wright, Rick Ford and James "Bubbles" Harris from Lorain Admiral King (who "scored 50 against Marion Harding when I was a sophomore," recalls Merchant) returned as starters from 1970. But they were overshadowed by sophomores John Ritter, Steve Downing and particularly George McGinnis. As Fred Taylor put it, "If he (McGinnis) is 19 then he was 18 when he was born because that guy is all man". Before his first collegiate game, Big George, 6'8 and body sculpted by an NFL coach creating a tight end, had led the U.S.A. team in scoring and rebounding in the World University Games in Italy. The Hoosiers were 6-2, the losses being in overtime against Kentucky and a three point defeat by Washington State when visiting teams lost in the first round of the tournament. They were a Top Ten team, and Jim Cleamons couldn't miss a challenge like that.

"McGinnis had been talking stuff all summer at the World University Games. I wanted that game," says Cleamons today. So he got permission to test the heel in warm-ups, said he could start and played all 40 minutes.

All five Buck starters scored in double figures, the team shot 55% but a 48-30 rebound deficit was too much. Dave Merchant remembers a play "when Bob Siekmann went after a ball, accidentally hit McGinnis square in the jaw with his elbow and McGinnis didn't notice it. That's when I knew we were in trouble." The score was 85-77, despite Mark Minor's team high 18 points and a superb defensive effort to hold McGinnis to 19.

* * * *

"I had a great coach at Solon," recalls Minor. "Harold Andreas was the head coach at Cuyahoga Falls High School when Bob Knight was assistant there right out of Ohio State. He was later assistant to Knight at Indiana. He was an excellent teacher, and sheltered me from recruiting my senior year. When the season was over he helped me select the schools to visit.

"My final choices were North Carolina State, Florida and some Ohio schools. When I visited North Carolina State they had 300 recruits in the same weekend. We all stayed at the same hotel. They took a group of us to this house for a party, and put out a keg of beer which had North Carolina State Athletic Department stamped on it. That wasn't for me. The truth is, from the eighth grade on I had gone to the state tournament in Columbus. The idea of playing, shooting, even practicing on that floor — what a thrill."

Taylor's respect for Minor accelerated when Mark visited campus and they went to the Jai Lai for dinner. "He ordered a meat loaf sandwich and I told him to order a good meal. He said 'Coach, you don't have to do anything special for me. I'm coming here to school'."

"I really liked playing basketball", says Minor. "Scheduled games, pick-up games, even practice. I remember being a little concerned at my first practice as a freshman at Ohio State. We spent the first 25 minutes learning the proper turns — front turns, rear turns, inside turns, outside turns, 'Hondo' turns. I thought 'what a waste of time'."

'Hondo' turns?

"That's an inside turn where you lead with your elbow. Hold the ball close to your face and extend the elbows. It creates room in a hurry, when the defender gets his chin out of the way. It is called a 'Hondo' turn because John Havlicek did it so well.

"The other thing about my freshman year was the rule 'There's no such thing as fouling a freshman.' That helped make the practices rough.

207

"Sophomore year I played a little and got my nickname — 'Rook' — because I was new to the varsity. Did it last until my senior year? They called me that on the fishing trip we took last fall. The other highlight is I put my feet up on Bear Bryant's desk when we toured the athletic facility at Alabama."

"'Rook' was real quiet and unassuming," recalls Captain Cleamons. "He would play all day if you let him. He really put his heart and soul into it."

"Mark and I used to play on the courts over on Eleventh Avenue," says Hornyak, "against the guys from the city. He was a great teacher of defensive principles. People will tell you I didn't learn any, but he helped me."

"He had the quickest hands I ever saw," says Witte. "He used to juggle. And he was very disciplined in his play."

"When we recruited him," says Taylor, "the thing we noticed was he always had his hands on the ball. He wasn't a shooter, but he knew when and how to deliver the ball. And he was a classic help-side defender, too."

"Fred always told us on defense: 'Your man can't hurt you without the ball. If your man goes to the refreshment stand to get a drink, are you going with him?' I coach a sixth grade team now and I still tell them the same thing," smiles Minor.

One other thing about Mark Minor. Like Cleamons and Hornyak, he was left-handed. "That year we ran our fast break down the left side," recalls Taylor. "I think it confused some people who were used to playing against right handed teams."

* * * *

As Minor was establishing himself as a quality starter, Cleamons was re-evaluating his role on the team. "It was an honor to be selected captain after Denny (Meadors) and David (Sorenson). I had tried to stay in the background as a sophomore and a junior because the leaders were already there. Now I was captain of all these kids.

"I was scoring a lot but we were 4-4. That hurt me. I didn't want that kind of a season. That's when I made the conscious decision to stop shooting as much.

"Fred's offense was always focused on the inside game. I had paid my dues, as a senior it was my time to score. But Allan didn't believe in the rites of passage, he saw himself as a scorer. If Allan and I were both shooting, Luke wouldn't get the shots and the offense wouldn't work as well as it could. I could give up the ball to set Allan up, and in that way help him learn to do that for the rest of us."

"Jim Cleamons was our leader," states Hornyak today. "He taught, he sacrificed, he took the pressure. He was an All-American."

"How do I describe Jim? Pure winner. He did whatever needed to be done to win. I have tremendous respect for him," says Siekmann.

"Not only did he have talent and discipline," says Wagar, "he is the best leader I've ever been associated with, athletics or business. He could have scored 37 ppg, but he chose to take a bunch of young kids to a title. He was the key to our year. I can still hear him saying 'Take that guy and lock him up' on defense, or 'Wags, is that your shot?' on offense."

"We were a little scared of him," recalls Merchant, "and we did whatever he told us to do. We didn't know what was happening, but he not only knew exactly what was necessary to win, he could do it and did do it and helped us do it."

Mike Bordner, co-head trainer at Ohio State and involved with Ohio State athletic teams since 1964, puts Clem's leadership ability this way: "Cleamons was the greatest captain of any Ohio State (athletic) team I ever saw. Only Rex Kern in football was even close."

And the president of the Jim Cleamons Fan Club, Fred Taylor. "When the coaches talked about recruits or players in the program, we measured them against Jerry Lucas, John Havlicek and Jim Cleamons. These comments were never made outside the coaching staff, but you need a standard of excellence and, for us, they represented the best we could hope to find," says Taylor.

"When a play broke down in practice he would call for the ball out front, tuck it under his right arm, and point with his left hand exactly what had to happen for the play to work. Between the respect they had for him and a little fear, which was OK too, they listened. And before practice they'd be asking him about The World University Games in Italy, listening like little children at grandpa's knee."

"We had quite a team in Italy," recalls Cleamons. "Six first round draft choices. Dana Lewis of Tulsa, Jim McDaniels of Western Kentucky, Cliff Meely of Colorado, John Mengelt of Auburn (actually Mengelt was the fourth player taken in the second round, but as the 21st pick he would be a first rounder today), George McGinnis and I. Also Fred Brown (Iowa), Dean Meminger (Marquette), Austin Carr (Notre Dame) and John Roche (South Carolina) had been at the tryouts.

* * * *

As Yale came to town January 2 for OSU's final tune-up before Big Ten action started, the city was depressed. The football team had lost in the Rose Bowl. The basketball team had a "so what?" 4-4 record. Nobody noticed that three of the losses were against Top Ten teams. The kids deserved more credit than they received, but they didn't need the pressure it would have caused.

Hornyak hit 13 of 19 shots and 32 points, Witte made 10 of 14 to total 26 as OSU beat Yale 95-75. The Captain only took 12 shots but ran the offense and still scored 18 points.

Speaking of offense, it was based on the time tested "stack" concept, but altered to fit the personnel. The stack was moved from the left side to the right side of the free throw lane. Wagar played behind Witte, usually moving to the corner to take the guard/forward pass. Because Wagar was not the threat to score which Hosket, Cleamons and Finney had been, it was relatively easy for the defense to deny his pass to Witte inside. The series took longer to develop; a pass back to Cleamons outside usually followed. If Jim had a scoring opportunity he took it, on the shot or the drive. However usually he looked for Mark Minor on the left side of the foul line. Whereas Steve Howell had been an excellent jump shooter when he caught the ball, that was not Minor's forté. Since his strength was passing, he looked for Hornyak, moving without the ball. Allan frequently broke to the basket for a backdoor lay-up, or faked that and had a jump shot. Another option was a 2-on-2 for Minor and Hornyak with the entire side of the floor open. Anytime during this sequence Witte might be free inside, coming around for that hook shot he had been practicing. The "stack" had been remodeled and found to be completely serviceable.

"Hosket and Sorenson told me, 'That used to be a big man's offense'," remembers Hornyak. "Maybe it was designed to dump the ball inside, but we got some good jump shots from it too."

"We ran plays to get shots for Allan and Luke," says Taylor. "Jimmy got points in transition, when plays broke down — heck, he could get a good shot about any time he wanted to." Yet after his injury in the Stanford game, Cleamons did not lead the team in scoring for 17 straight games. He didn't have to, either for the team or for his own ego.

Going into Big Ten play the team was getting almost five rebounds per game more than their opponents, a pleasant change from recent years. Witte averaged 12, and somehow Cleamons was getting over seven. The Bucks were shooting 48% from the field. Taylor said "The

210

schedule says we're ready," but he was seeing things come together for his youngsters. He felt Indiana, Illinois and Purdue remained the favorites in the conference.

"By far our best effort of the season," Taylor said of the 97-76 win at Iowa. The Bucks hadn't won there since Gary Bradds was a senior. Witte rebounded like the 1964 Player of the Year used to, leading both teams with 14, and Minor had 11. Each had 14 points, to trail Cleamons with 23 and the "Bellaire Bomber" (Hornyak), who had 30.

OSU grabbed a road victory in their last scheduled non-conference game of the year at West Virginia, winning 83-74. Hornyak spent so much time inside scoring a game high 28 points that he got a game high 11 rebounds as well. Siekmann and Merchant played well off the bench.

Mark Minor remembers the West Virginia game for a rather personal reason. "I liked to handle the ball, but I wasn't flashy. At Butler the year before I had passed behind my back to Jim Geddes for a lay-up. Not planned, it just happened. All the seniors said 'You're lucky'. Fred said, 'I'll forget about that because you're a sophomore.' Then at West Virginia I tried another one, and it didn't work. Fred said 'Have a seat.' I hadn't planned either one, but I guess the point is I didn't throw any more, planned or not."

The Badgers, averaging 89 points for the season, went down 83-69. Only Minor (seven of eight) shot well for OSU but Wisconsin was held to 36% from the field and outrebounded for only the second time all year. Visiting coach John Powless said "Ohio State is the most impressive Big Ten team of the three we've faced." He was talking about Illinois (3-0) and Michigan (2-0).

A trip to Minnesota was next for the young Bucks. The Gophers of first year Coach George Hanson got their scoring from Eric Hill and Ollie Shannon, and their physical play inside from sophomores Jim Brewer and Corky Taylor. But Ohio State matched them on the boards, led by Wagar's 12 rebounds and Witte's 10. Witte was the leading scorer with 22 points and, in general, "went after the ball with a great deal of authority," according to Taylor.

Today Mark Wagar feels that "our comeback at Minnesota was the key to our team jelling." The Bucks finished with a 17-4 flurry in the last six minutes to win 68-66.

Instead of keeping pace with Michigan, Purdue and Illinois, all undefeated in the conference, the Bucks lost at home to Michigan State in their next outing. In a strange game, MSU outshot, outrebounded (by

211

51-34) and generally outplayed their hosts. "We should all have our rear ends kicked," summarized Jim Cleamons afterwards.

Contributing to the bizarre atmosphere was the fact that OSU played against their own road jerseys, because Michigan State's green uniforms had been stolen after their workout Saturday morning. "When we came out in their uniforms, it relaxed us and maybe they thought it was just an intra-squad game," winning coach Gus Ganakas told Kaye Kessler of *The Columbus Citizen-Journal*. Senior Rudy Benjamin, who graduated from Dayton Roosevelt and chose the Spartans four years prior, seemed to like the Ohio State uniforms. He scored 19 points. MSU 82-70.

One week later OSU got a rematch in East Lansing. The team had paid for its indiscretions during the week as practices were hard. Star fullback John Brockington stopped in, watched the action and said "Man, football's not that rough." Then the Spartans paid, 87-76, as Hornyak had a game high 25, Cleamons scored 21 and matched Witte's ten rebounds. Wagar and Siekmann scored in double figures as well. Ohio State, now leading the conference in fewest points allowed, was tied for second at 4-1 with Purdue and Illinois. Michigan, leading the league in scoring, was 6-0.

* * * *

Mark Wagar had become "the perfect example of a role player on a successful team," says Fred Taylor. "He played decent defense, passed well, scored some — just did exactly what we needed. He was an integral part of that team."

"We called him 'Hands' because he had a hard time catching the ball," says old buddy Hornyak, getting off one last long distance spinner. "But Fred and the other coaches taught the basics and Mark learned them ... post up, little hook, solid defense. And he had a good 15' jumper."

Witte remembers "going to St. John Arena with Mark the first day we were on campus as freshmen. We played one-on-one — that was my first Ohio State University basketball thrill."

Merchant recalls "Mark's 'no look hook', but he could make it". In his second decade as head basketball coach at Lebanon (O.) High School, he "appreciates Mark's role as a coach." Finally he recalls rooming with Mark. "He had an 8' bed, mine was regular. We couldn't stack them, and didn't have space to fit both in the room. So we propped his up and I slept in the dust underneath." Life in the big time world of college athletics. "On top of that, Luke was right across the hall. He kept his room real neat, but came over into ours and messed things up."

"My senior year in high school," remembers Wagar, "I visited Duke, Davidson, Dayton, Ohio University and Ohio State. I thought I was going to Dayton but when Ohio State asked, that was it. I was the beneficiary of the early days of basketball on television, like Lucas shooting his hook from the baseline. All Fred promised was a good education and a chance to play. He also made it clear that a scholarship was renewed each year, unless you got thrown out of school. That was a time when other schools were running kids off."

"His mother wanted him to go to Dayton," recalls assistant coach Bob Burkholder. "She was disappointed when he became a Buckeye. But after he graduated she gave me a peace offering, because he had enjoyed his four years at Ohio State so much. See that buckeye tree? She gave us that about 15 years ago and it's been planted in our back yard ever since."

"My freshman year it was 'welcome to the Big Ten'; we were fodder for the varsity," recalls Wagar. "We got kicked by their strength and their experience, but you learn a lot from that. Practice was so hard, and so new to me, I had lost 10-15 lbs. by Christmas. But we had a long break, I got fattened up and came back ready to compete."

Since Nick Weatherspoon of Canton McKinley, big school Player of the Year by Associated Press, was starring at Illinois, some fans were grumbling that OSU should have signed him instead of Wagar. In fact Wagar was the *first* player signed by Fred Taylor and Bob Burkholder in the spring of 1969. The coaches felt Wagar could play on a championship team, and he would prove them to be correct.

* * * *

A sold-out Purdue crowd watched the young Bucks win a tough test 69-67. The game was tied at the half, 35-all. Ohio State hit a hot streak against a 3-2 zone to go ahead 55-46 with 8:48 to go, but Purdue made the score 65-all at 1:35. Witte dunked a rebound, Minor hit a foul shot at 0:39 and Merchant made one at 0:17. When Witte grabbed the defensive rebound at the end of the game, the Bucks had pulled off the victory, their first at Purdue since 1963.

Witte had 17 points, and a game high 16 rebounds, in leading OSU to a 52-35 advantage on the boards. Jim Cleamons played "probably his best game of the year" according to his coach. Cleamons scored 12 points, directed the offense, switched to forward when Mark Wagar had foul trouble, and got nine rebounds. When Purdue had the ball

213

he "locked up" Larry Weatherford, who scored ten points, 12 below his average.

That leaves the sophomore with nerves of steel. Allan Hornyak had a great career as a Buckeye, but it probably would have been better if he had played only road games. In his first Big Ten game outside St. John Arena he had scored 30 points against defending champion Iowa. His game high 27 points against Purdue were only fair for him — he would average 26.5 ppg on the road in the Big Ten for the season. That doesn't count 23 in his first varsity game at Utah State, 28 against Harvard in Oregon, or 28 at West Virginia. He loved a challenge.

"Bill Snypp, our Sports Information Director before Marv Homan, had Allan pegged pretty well," recalls Taylor. "He used to say 'Allan is so confident that if he were in the middle of the Sahara Desert and got in a fight, he could reach behind his back for a brick — and there would be one in his hand'. He had no fear of failure, or pressure of any kind.

"I remember after the next year he was asked to try-out for the 1972 Olympics. He said if he made the team he would leave school and go to the NBA. It came out in the papers. I said 'Why did you put so much pressure on yourself? I don't have any problem with your turning pro, but why not just do it? This way you have so much pressure added on top.' He said, 'That's what I thought, and I said it.' Simple as that."

"Purdue never beat us in their gym," remembers Hornyak fondly. In fact Ohio State beat Purdue in every game, registering three road victories and five in all while Hornyak and his class were eligible. During this time Purdue was 25-17 in the conference, so OSU accounted for almost one third of their losses.

"You couldn't hear anything there," he says about Mackey Arena, where you still can't. The Purdue press guide claimed the arena was voted loudest, most enthusiastic and toughest for opponents in the Big Ten in 1990. "They had bench seats put in to keep the fans on their toes, and maybe a little angry," says Hornyak, delighting in the memory of the challenge.

The difficult assignment at Purdue was followed by a very emotional confrontation at home with Illinois. People had been looking forward to this game for almost two years.

* * * *

When Ohio State landed the outstanding recruiting class of 1969, there was a great deal of talk about the players who were *not* signed. Most of the talk, then and later, was about four players who had been in the big school state final game, won 71-56 by Columbus East over Canton McKinley.

Eddie Ratleff was the best of the group. He set the Columbus East career scoring record, led East to an incredible 70-1 record in three years, and was chosen UPI Player of the Year. He would play for the 1972 Olympic team and star for Houston in the NBA.

Coach Jerry Tarkanian says "Ratleff was a major reason why Long Beach became a legitimate power" and that a key to signing the star was when "I went to Columbus and spent six days there." A *Newsweek* article on Jerry Tarkanian mentioned that Ratleff's father had taken a job with the city government when the Ratleff family moved to Long Beach to follow their son's career. The National Collegiate Athletic Association investigated recruitment practices at Long Beach State, and put the school on three years probation. The press release announcing the probation described the violations as "among the most serious which it has ever considered."

Dwight Lamar was All-City at Columbus North as a junior, had discipline problems and was forced to leave school. He went to East for his senior year, scored 17.5 ppg and was a feeder for his teammates. He enrolled at the University of Southwest Louisiana. In 1972 Lamar led the nation in scoring, averaging 36.3 points. The school was later found guilty of over 200 violations by the NCAA. The resultant probation was for four years, during the first two of which "The University of Southwestern Louisiana shall not permit its intercollegiate basketball team to participate against outside competition." Lamar played three years in the ABA and one in the NBA after his eligibility expired. Like Ratleff, Ohio State could not recruit Lamar — his grades were inadequate.

Former Buckeye assistant Frank Truitt was head coach at Kent State University at this time. "We all got bad raps on recruiting then," he recalls. "I got it at Kent State. People saw a great athlete and asked why we didn't sign him. Well, the kid didn't have the grades. What do you say?"

Nick Conner was a 6'6 leaper who teamed with Ratleff throughout that 70-1 record. A fair scorer at 14 points per game, his quickness and strength inside made him an excellent rebounder and shot blocker. He was in the upper half of his class, but had a low test score. He was rumored to be going to Marshall University, then in the Mid-American Conference. When he scored better on the national standardized test late in the year, Ohio State offered a scholarship but Conner chose to go to Illinois.

Canton McKinley star Nick Weatherspoon had battled those three East stars in the championship game, after being selected Associated Press Player of the Year. His Bulldogs had also waged two memorable battles with Luke Witte's Marlington team, both won by McKinley. Luke had scored 65 points in those games, Weatherspoon 63. 'Spoon' went on to play for four teams in the NBA, but chose to turn down a scholarship from Ohio State and play for Illinois first.

"I hosted Weatherspoon and Conner when they visited," recalls Cleamons. "It hurt me when they didn't come here."

Only Weatherspoon and Conner could have been recruited by Ohio State. Both were. Both had the right to attend any school they and the adults who were advising them thought best. Illinois would be placed on two years probation in 1974. However in 1969 Illinois recruited two good Ohio forwards. With them Illinois would finish 5-9, 5-9 and 8-6 in the Big Ten. Whether Weatherspoon and Conner could have made the adjustments necessary to contribute to the success of the team if they had selected Ohio State will never be known. They did have the physical ability.

* * * *

Going into the Ohio State game Weatherspoon had burned Minnesota's Jim Brewer, an excellent defender, for 27 points. 'Spoon' led giant teammate Greg Jackson in rebounding. With Conner having recently joined the starting line-up, the Illini front line was impressive.

However the young Bucks were not intimidated. Led by Luke Witte's game high 13, OSU outrebounded the visitors 40-38 and defeated them 92-72. Though Illinois had a good start, Ohio State led 83-58 with 5:04 to play. Witte "sure was aggressive" according to Illinois Coach Harv Schmidt. Luke led the charge with a career high 27 points and blocked several shots. When he went out with four personals at 10:12 "the rest of the kids wanted to prove themselves and did," according to Taylor. *Citizen-Journal* writer Kaye Kessler said "Judging from Saturday's performance, Conner and Weatherspoon may have made wise decisions spurning OSU offers because they couldn't measure up to the Buckeye sophs." Conner had 15 points and 11 boards, Weatherspoon 11 and eight.

"We put in a new offensive set just for that game," recalls Taylor. "Illinois played a 3-2 or 1-2-2 zone. That gave the offense shots on the wings. Normally we would have Jim on top, passing to Mark (Minor) or Allan. Mark was a good shooter, but hesitant to put it up at times. Neither Jimmy nor Allan had a problem with that," Taylor chuckles. "Since Mark was such a good passer, and 6'5 and able to see the floor, we put him on top, to distribute the ball to Allan and Jim on the sides. Then we had Mark Wagar and Luke rotating high to low inside." Allan hit nine of 19 shots, Clem nine of 16 and Luke 12 of 18. And Minor was playing a position in 1971 which Don Nelson of the Milwaukee Bucks would get credit for creating for Paul Pressey in the mid-1980's — "point forward."

Another key to the game was the play of super sub Bob Siekmann. "He was ready to go, full speed, when he got off the bench," recalls Minor. "Against Illinois, guarded by Conner, who had a big rep as a shot blocker, Bob made a basket off a spin move that would make any highlight film." Siekmann had 16 points and six big rebounds in that game.

* * * *

"We roomed together as freshmen," recalls Luke Witte, "and Bob Siekmann was a down-to-earth guy. But he couldn't match his socks up to save his life." Told that the girl friend of one Buckeye fan in that era was a special fan of Bob's, Luke replied "Everybody's girl friend had a crush on Bob. He looked like Robert Redford. But he had to have his notes out to call a girl for a date."

Minor remembers Siekmann being well prepared on the trip to the Far West Classic. "We went to Disneyland, and got together for a team picture. Bob got a pie — it was lemon — and threw it in my face just as the picture was taken. It made the paper the next day." (Trainer Mike Bordner would caution against giving Minor too much sympathy. "Mark was a real prankster," says Bordner. "He'd hide your basketball shoe, let you think you left it behind, then give it to you at the last minute.")

"Siekmann had a lot of success with baseball before his arm went bad," recalls Taylor. "I think that success developed confidence which carried over. I always said if you play more than seven or eight players, your team is either very good or very bad. He always worked with the first seven. He was mentally into every practice, always picked up the tempo when he went in a game. He definitely had a feel for the game."

"He was a great sixth man," says Hornyak. "He could have started, but it was tougher to come off the bench and he could do it. Very valuable."

Siekmann made one mistake in a game which his friends will never let him forget. "I don't know who we were playing," says Merchant, "but the first half was coming to an end ... 5 ... 4 ... long pass ... 3 ... 2 ... 1 out of bounds. Bob thought the half was over and kept running to the locker room. He sat down and waited for the team. There was 0:01 on the clock, and we were waiting on him to finish the half. When he stuck his head out the door the whole arena erupted."

After acknowledging the memory of that incident, Siekmann recalls his high school career. "At Cincinnati Oak Hills we were good enough to win 18-19 games a year, but we always got knocked out of the tournament early.

"I wanted to leave town, but wanted to be close enough for my parents to see my play. I considered Miami (O.) and William and Mary, for their business school. Joe Sadelfeld was a friend from baseball in Cincinnati; he was an influence for Ohio State.

"At Ohio State, my job was to come in when someone had foul trouble. My role was to hit the open shot, make the pass, keep things moving. Fred had a great concept of offense, and Jim Cleamons and Mark Minor were especially good at getting you the ball when you were open and ready to use it."

* * * *

With three straight well-played games boosting their record to 6-1, good for second behind Michigan's 7-0 and ahead of Illinois and Indiana at 4-2, OSU was still not ranked nationally. Michigan was #8.

Next was a trip to Wisconsin for another hazardous road game. "When we got there Fred took us to this gourmet restaurant," recalls Bob Siekmann. "Dave Merchant ordered steak something or other. They cooked it right at the table, and put all sorts of stuff on it. When the waiter had it prepared just right he put it in front of Dave. Dave scraped the stuff off and said 'Do you have any ketchup?' When the waiter's jaw dropped, Dave said 'No offense intended'."

At the shootaround before the game Hornyak couldn't wait to get a look at the rims. While the trainers were getting ready to tape his ankles, he warmed up without shoes. That may have had something to do with his two of seven shooting in the first half, when the Bucks trailed 41-38. He hit six of ten shots in the second half, and ten straight foul shots in the game, to total 26 and lead all scorers. After all, it was a road game. Witte led all rebounders with 13 and joined Cleamons in double figure scoring in the 79-71 victory.

The 84-72 victory over Northwestern featured 20 points from Siekmann and double figure scoring from Hornyak, Witte and Wagar, but came with a heavy price — Jim Cleamons had either a badly sprained left wrist or a broken one. He would definitely miss the Iowa game at home and might be lost for the season. His place in the line-up would be taken by Dave Merchant but, as Taylor said, "In the last four games Cleamons has really been something special." Fred also mentioned that when Big Ten coaches voted in pre-season for MVP, the Cougar had been a 9-1 choice, unanimous since each coach was prohibited from voting for his own player.

With four sophomores and one junior starting, and the only sub a sophomore, the Bucks beat Iowa 80-71. Witte grabbed 19 rebounds and Minor 11. Witte and Hornyak nearly split 45 points, Minor and Wagar each had nine points, Siekmann had 11 off the bench and Merchant ran the show. This despite the announcement earlier in the day that the Captain had a hairline fracture of a small bone in his left wrist, and would be lost for the season. "We'll take more x-rays Friday. If the pictures are the same, Jimmy will be in a cast for 12 weeks," Dr. Luther Keith, the Bucks team physician told *The Citizen-Journal*. There was no more than a 10 percent chance that the team's only senior starter would play again as a collegian. The burden of running the team was squarely on the shoulders of sophomore Dave Merchant.

* * * *

"I grew up watching Jimmy Crum and the Buckeyes on television," recalls Merchant. "I visited Minnesota, Florida, Houston and Miami (O.). Ultimately I didn't want to leave home. I felt Ohio State was the pinnacle. If you were good enough to play there, you were a success. Plus I had a great visit — Craig Barclay, Dan Andreas, Dave Sorenson, Jim Cleamons were nice guys. That is until we started to scrimmage them as freshmen."

After Merchant wrapped up his career at Marion Harding, playing for Dan Baker just as Al 'Rooster' Rowley did when he was co-captain with Merchant's brother, deciding on Ohio State was the easy part. Then came baseball. "For most guys when recruiting is over you relax. For me, after I signed with Ohio State I was drafted by the Phillies. Tony Lucadello, the same scout who signed Larry Hisle (and 48 other major leaguers), was calling me. They offered $30,000 in cash (three times the annual salary for an engineer at the time, about five times the salary for a grade school teacher) plus a four year scholarship to one of the Arizona schools. It was intimidating to get phone calls every night; you didn't want to go home because you didn't want to face that. The baseball decision was tougher than Ohio State. By the time I got to OSU I was mentally exhausted," continues Merchant.

"We had a lot of pressure as freshmen, for all the notoriety we had. Plus we got beat up every night. We just couldn't stop Sorenson. I remember walking across that cold campus together in the dead of winter, licking our wounds. It really pulled us together.

"I knew early that I needed four other people to help me score. I found a niche to fit into. Looking back maybe I over compensated, didn't look to score enough."

Fred Taylor thinks so. "He went through culture shock at college when he got his shots crammed at first," recalls Taylor. "He had to make adjustments — mentally and in the mechanics of his delivery — and probably lost confidence in his shot."

"We called him 'Rat' because he was all over the place," says Hornyak. "He hustled, just never gave up." Mark Minor remembers "He was intelligent and scrappy, with the textbook attitude for a coach. Plus he had the biggest feet I ever saw on a small man. With all that running around he'd wear out a pair of shoes in three weeks."

* * * *

Merchant had a big responsibility to run the offense smoothly at Michigan, and without Captain Cleamons, who had scored 94 points in three victories over the Maize and Blue earlier in his career. "We knew we had to score a lot to beat them in Ann Arbor. Henry Wilmore and Ken Brady, they would get some points out of their triple stack set," recalls Taylor. "We put in some extra things for Allan — we needed a big game from him."

And did Hornyak deliver! He hit 16 of 28 shots and scored 37 points as OSU took over first place, beating Michigan 91-85. Allan scored 17 points in the first 5:20 of the game; OSU led at one point 39-19. But Michigan battled back to 52-42 at the half. Though Jim Cleamons was able to play some, with a wrist now diagnosed as severely sprained, he was still below par. Since Wagar and Minor had three fouls at the half, the game was far from over. In fact the game was tied once at 74-all. Then Hornyak hit a jumper and teamed with Merchant outside while Cleamons played forward down the stretch.

Witte came up very large, scoring 24 points and grabbing 18 off the boards while fouling out Ken Brady with one point. Minor, Merchant and Siekmann each had eight points. It took a team effort to withstand Wilmore's 42 points and 13 rebounds.

That Michigan game is recalled even today when Hornyak's name is mentioned. "He got an incredible roll," says Minor. "He must have made eight or nine baskets in a row. Years later I met some friends of his from 'The Valley' and they said he did that kind of thing all the time in high school."

"I remember," says Taylor, "he made a shot against Michigan, then stole the in-bounds pass out of a guy's hands and made another basket so fast the clock might not have moved. He was competitive. When a quicker player would take the ball away from him, he almost always just took it right back."

Of course Allan remembers too. "That was our most important game that year. Jimmy was out and we were playing Michigan for first place and there was always a special challenge playing on the road. I felt like there were three levels of appreciation you could get from a crowd on the road. First, if they boo you, that meant you had their attention. If they threw stuff, that was better. But the best was when you had to be escorted out after the game. When I was a senior I got a standing ovation at Michigan." (The Bucks won that game too, 102-87, in 1973).

Finally, Merchant had responded very well to his big challenge, running an offense that shot 55%, holding Michigan Captain Dan Fife to four of 12 from the field, scoring eight and playing the full 40 minutes.

Minnesota was next. The Gophers came to St. John after blasting Illinois 80-64, having won four of their last five games. But Luke Witte played even better than he had the first game against the Gophers, leading both teams in scoring (26 points on 13 field goal attempts — he made 12 of 15 free throws) and rebounding. His 20 boards gave him a total of 57 in the last three games. Clem didn't start, but got 14 points off the bench. OSU 84-70.

The same day Indiana lost at Wisconsin and Michigan barely escaped defeat at Illinois. OSU (11-1) was one victory away from a co-title with two games to play. Michigan had two losses, Indiana and Purdue three each, and they all had three games left.

As Ohio State prepared to play at Northwestern, UPI carried a story that Howard Porter of Villanova, Jim McDaniels of Western

Kentucky and five unnamed college players had signed affidavits that they had not signed professional contracts. Thus they were eligible to continue to compete in college basketball as amateurs. Walter Byers, executive secretary of the National Collegiate Athletic Association, was quoted as saying "We accept the testimony of the students involved." Time would prove that decision to be a mistake.

With Cleamons back in the starting line-up, Witte leading both clubs in rebounds and Hornyak leading both teams in scoring (it was a road game!), OSU beat Northwestern 68-67. The Bucks led 64-52 but a Wildcat rush made Merchant's free throw with 11 seconds left the game winner. OSU (12-1) had a title tie clinched, even if they lost their last game and Michigan (10-2) won at Iowa and at home against Wisconsin.

But the Buckeyes had climbed to No. 11 in the country and had no intention of backing into the championship. Besides, Indiana was coming to town. OSU had been able to avenge its only conference loss to Michigan State, and wanted to even things up with the Hoosiers for the non-conference game in December.

In a season filled with excitement, emotion and brilliant Buckeye basketball, the 91-75 victory over Indiana ranks with any game all year.

"That game was a dream come true," recalls Wagar. "St. John was filled, the crowd was going crazy. They (Indiana) were clearly better than we were physically, but we jelled after the first game. I had to guard Joby Wright, and remember thinking 'How quickly can I get a hip on him (to block out for the rebound)?'. " Wright shot 21 times to score 22 points, but only had six rebounds. In the other corner McGinnis, guarded by Minor, shot 26 times to score 25 points.

"We blocked out so well that year," recalls Witte, "that the rebound often hit the floor." Or else Luke got it — he led the game with 14. Or maybe a guard got it — Hornyak had 12 and Cleamons 10 against Indiana, outrebounded by Ohio State 53-35.

"Biggest reason we outrebounded Indiana?" says the Captain today. "Fred Taylor. He understands the game. He taught the fundamentals of rebounding," continues Cleamons. "There was not a better coached team in the Big Ten — Fred outcoached people". And Jim Cleamons outplayed people. He held high-scoring "Bubbles" Harris to five points, ran the offense to help Hornyak score 24 and Witte 19, and led all players with 30 himself. He only took 17 shots from the field, and made 10. The Bucks shot 60%, Indiana 38%.

222

Dave Merchant remembers a side of the Captain which didn't show up in the box score, but had a lot to do with the success of the team. "I had played when he was out, and now he was back. But when I went into the game, he immediately called a play for me, and set a screen to free me to shoot. When my bank shot went in it was a confidence builder, but the real thrill was that he called my play. That's the kind of leader he was for us."

The Buckeyes shot 65% in the first half, and led 42-30. They stretched it to 52-33 with 16:38 to play. In two minutes Indiana made 13 points; by 7:11 the score was 66-64 Ohio State. Then Witte, Merchant and Cleamons made baskets and it was 72-64. The game was never in doubt after that.

After the game Fred Taylor talked about the shooting, the rebounding, the character and the Captain. If the voting for the Big Ten's Most Valuable Player "is even close, there ought to be an investigation," he said. "After the game I told Jimmy he can't realize what a superb captain he's been."

Clem was elected Big Ten MVP. He had recovered from two injuries, the bruised heel and the left wrist. In hind sight, however, he had one health concern which was never mentioned. At a time when cool was cool, he was so cool that when he drank water there was a major risk that ice cubes would form in his throat. Now that bad is bad, Clem was definitely the baddest of the Buckeyes. One thing he was not, anymore, was angry.

* * * *

The day before the Big Ten season was over, two coaches resigned. Lou Watson left at Indiana "for the best interest of the team, the University and my family." UPI said "his resignation followed widespread rumors the last two weeks of dissatisfaction of alumni, students and players." Though they lost their last game, Indiana finished 9-5 in the conference, 17-7 overall. They had three sophomore starters in George McGinnis, Steve Downing and John Ritter, but McGinnis would turn pro and never play for Indiana again.

John Wooden of UCLA was the first choice to succeed Watson. Wooden said he didn't take the job due to his grandchildren living in California and the benefit of the warm weather to his health. Buckeye graduate Bob Knight, who had compiled a 102-50 record in six years at Army, would take the job, go on to win three NCAA championships and set new records for Big Ten coaching victories.

First year coach George Hanson at Minnesota, with a 5-9 Big Ten record and 11-13 overall, announced his resignation, saying the record was unsatisfactory. He would be missing the chance to work with multi-talented defensive star Jim Brewer and physical Corky Taylor, excellent sophomores, so it is reasonable to assume he was forced out. Minnesota officials had their fourth different coach in five years, a man they were certain would be able to provide immediate success on the basketball court, Bill Musselman of Ashland College.

* * * *

Coaching had been an important part of Ohio State's success. The Captain related his thoughts on Coach Taylor, and nobody worked harder than Bob Burkholder, but Jack Graf was gone. When his father died Graf had left coaching to work with the family business full time. He had been replaced by Ben Waterman, who had coached Dayton Dunbar. Also three former players filled important roles.

Dan Andreas was finishing his undergraduate degree in education, and preparing for the Masters which he would receive in 1973. "We went from cannon fodder to players to graduate cannon fodder" is the way he remembers helping out at practice, when he regularly banged heads with Mark Wagar, his fraternity brother. He also scouted opponents and high school players. "I went to see eight players and recommended two. One was Dan Weston, and the best player was my brother Bill." Both played for the Buckeyes 1973-5. Bill joined the exclusive 1000 point club, averaging 14.4 points in only 71 games. Bill's class was the last before freshmen became eligible.

Craig Barclay was in law school, and spent three years with the team as a graduate assistant. "Since Craig had just been a player, the kids could relate to him," says Taylor. "And they could go to him with problems, sort of like a big brother. They liked him and respected him, he was disciplined and he had an excellent mind for the game — or anything else, for that matter."

Because of his experience as a college coach, Don DeVoe was even more valuable.

When Bob Knight was promoted at Army he called Fred Taylor to find assistants. "Fred recommended me," recalls DeVoe. "I was there for five years. I came back to Ohio State in 1970-71 to get my Masters in Higher Education, and had so much fun working with that team. Then in the spring of 1971 I was hired as head coach at Virginia Tech."

Fred Taylor recalls DeVoe's role as a grad assistant in 1971. "He was so energetic and enthusiastic. The kids liked him because he was vocal and animated. He worked a lot on defense for us that year."

* * * *

The team would need all the coaching they could get in the Mid-East Regional in Athens, Georgia. The field included #2 Marquette, #7 Western Kentucky, #8 Kentucky and #10 Ohio State. After Marquette beat Miami (O.) 62-47, the Bucks were faced with their biggest challenge yet of a very challenging season.

"Marquette loved to press, and they were very good at it," recalls Taylor. "To simulate game conditions the best we could, we had seven freshmen playing defense while we worked on our half court offense. We were practicing at Whetstone High School because St. John was being set-up for graduation ceremonies, and the floor was crowded with 12 players. But Marquette was so quick it seemed like they had extra people, and the offensive players had to use sound skills — like two hands on the ball — to run our plays."

Marquette had the nation's longest winning streak, with 27-0 in 1971 and 12 straight from 1970 when they won the National Invitational Tournament. George Thompson was gone, but Al McGuire was still quick with the comment. After beating Miami to advance to play the Buckeyes, "Chairman Al" said: "We don't get to play Ohio State, they get to play us."

Their senior star was Dean "The Dream" Meminger, a 6'1 guard from New York City who would be a late first round draft choice by the New York Knicks. He had made first team UPI All-America while scoring 21.3 ppg, but had not made the World University Games team the summer before. Having played against him at those try-outs at the Naval Academy, Jim Cleamons "knew I could play with Dean and wouldn't let him outplay me."

Already emerging from the shadow of "The Dream" was 6'11 sophomore center Jim Chones, a shot blocker with averages of 17.5 points and 11.5 rebounds per game. "Fred described him as 6'13," remembers Minor. Chones would only play one more year at Marquette, signing early with the ABA. After two years in the ABA he played eight years in the NBA, including three as a teammate of Jim Cleamons with the Cleveland Cavaliers.

Bob Lackey, nicknamed "The Black Swan", was a 6'6, 210 lbs. forward averaging over 13 points. He would go on to play briefly with

New York in the ABA. Gary Brell was the other forward. He averaged 14 points and was at times a devastating defender.

The other guard for the Warriors was sophomore Allie McGuire, 6'3 son of the coach. An underrated player in his own right, Allie later played for the New York Knicks.

The Warriors were a legitimate threat to win the NCAA and elevate Coach Al from rebel to television idol. But that change wouldn't take place until later, 1977 to be exact. This year Allan Hornyak's two free throws with six seconds to play gave the Bucks a 60-57 lead. An uncontested basket made the final 60-59 and OSU advanced.

Jim Cleamons led both teams in scoring with 21 points and held Dean "The Dream" to 11, ten below his average. Luke Witte hit a key hoop down the stretch to close with 13 points; he led both teams with 11 rebounds. Hornyak had foul trouble, missing about 10 minutes of the second half, and a poor shooting night but still had 11 points. Siekmann provided his spark off the bench, scoring 10 points and grabbing four rebounds. Wagar and Minor held Brell and Lackey below their season's scoring averages. Another team victory, in which Merchant was an unsung hero. He only scored two points but defended Meminger when Cleamons played forward, and had other heavy minutes when Hornyak was out with fouls. His ball-handling was critical.

After the game Fred Taylor referred to the comeback from five points down with less than three minutes to play by saying "These kids have done it before — nothing surprises me." To sum it up he said "The big thing was we handled their press and Meminger." Ohio State only had 11 turnovers in the game.

Thinking back to that game today, the man who produced so many outstanding centers remembers "watching Witte and Chones banging in there. Almost turned me into a spectator, watching those two young studs go at it. I had to be careful not to think about Luke doing that for two more years in the Big Ten."

Thinking back to that game today, Mark Wagar remembers the preparation of the coaches and the youth of the players. "Marquette used a wheel around their center. They'd sort of lull you to sleep, then get a quick score. As soon as they went to that, Allan or Jim called a command and we went to a zone. When they adjusted, we went back to man-to-man. It really bothered them. But we were just kids, national limelight or not. Our hotel was across the street from a golf driving range. The day before our game we all went across the street to hit golf balls."

Witte remembers his sinus problems. "At the Mid-East Regional I was all plugged up, felt like I was in a bell from the ringing in my ears," recalls Luke.

"Even when Luke didn't have his touch," says Minor today, "he still got other teams in foul trouble because with our offense they had to concentrate on him." And Witte was a good rebounder, especially when the Buck forwards blocked their men off the board. "We emphasized blocking out all season," says Minor. "Some people got upset by it. I remember Lackey complaining to the referees like it was illegal."

Next was Western Kentucky, which had beaten an outstanding Kentucky team 107-83 on Thursday to reach Saturday's Mid-East Regional Final. The Hilltoppers were led by 7' Jim McDaniels, another teammate of Cleamons at the World University Games and the fifth highest scorer in the country. Today Wagar refers to him as "a 7' Joby Wright with range out to 25 feet." McDaniels had scored 35 against Kentucky and would play seven years of pro ball after college. The other starters were 6'8 Clarence Glover, who had 18 points and 17 rebounds in the regional semi-finals; 6'5 Jerry Dunn; 6'3 Jim Rose, who scored 25; and 6'2 Rex Bailey.

The game was nip and tuck early. At 19-19 OSU hit a 14-2 spurt in less than five minutes, to lead 33-21. Five McDaniels baskets narrowed the score to 40-34 at the half. OSU shot 51.7% in the first 20 minutes, Western Kentucky 42.8%.

Neither team shot well in the second half, making Western's 14 rebound margin for the game even more significant. Luke Witte grabbed 17 and Cleamons had seven, but no other Buckeye finished with more than three. Meanwhile Glover had 22 rebounds and 6'5 Dunn had 15. Since turnovers were even at 17 each, the rebound margin gave Western 15 extra shots.

Still, Witte's hoop gave the Bucks a 69-67 lead. When McDaniels traveled, the Bucks had the ball at 0:47. But a turnover — some say a foul of Hornyak which was not called — gave the Hilltoppers another chance and Rex Bailey made a short jumper to tie the game at 0:11. It was his sixth basket in seven attempts in the second half, and made him seven of nine for the game. For the year Bailey shot 37%. Yet OSU had one last chance. After beating pressure Hornyak pulled up for a

227

12' jumper, which he hit about 70% of the time. Not this time. Overtime.

Jim Cleamons, who today explains the defeat with few words — "I got into foul trouble" — had missed much of the second half with fouls. He scored three baskets in the overtime, but the Bucks lost the five minute period 12-9 and the game 81-78.

Hornyak, the only OSU starter who wasn't in foul trouble by the end, led the team with 26 points. Witte had 23 points and Clem had 12; no one else had more than seven. Wagar did a particularly good job on McDaniels, who scored 31 points but had to launch the ball 35 times to get them.

Wagar "experienced my boyhood dream, being introduced by Curt Gowdy" and remembers "thousands of people greeting us at Don Scott Field when we got back — that was a thrill."

Disappointing at the end, it had still been a great Ohio State season. They finished No. 10 in the country, AP and UPI. Cleamons, Big Ten MVP, made All-Conference with Hornyak, Witte, Henry Wilmore of Michigan, George McGinnis of Indiana and Fred Brown of Iowa. The Bucks had done something only one other OSU team did during the Golden Age, going undefeated on the road in the Big Ten. Only the 27-1 1961 team matched that achievement. Amazingly the sophomore dominated Buckeyes led the Big Ten in defense. They allowed 72.7 points per game, second best Purdue averaged 78.3 points allowed, and no one else could hold their opponents below 80.

The national championship was held in the Houston Astrodome. Western Kentucky played Villanova, whose star forward Howard Porter, like Western's McDaniels, had been denying all year that he had signed a professional contract. Current Boston Celtic coach Chris Ford was a junior on that Villanova team. Western lost 92-89 in double overtime. After UCLA beat Kansas 68-60, the Bruins beat Villanova 68-62 for their fifth consecutive title.

Eventually both Villanova and Western Kentucky were stripped of their tournament medals because Porter and McDaniels had signed professional contracts. Neither team appears in official NCAA records for the 1971 tournament. In a perfect world Ohio State would have had a chance to advance, because Western was ineligible. They would have played Pennsylvania, 28-0 before losing to Villanova 90-47. Penn could have looked past the team they had defeated in December. Another way to look at it is, if OSU had gotten past Western *they* would have beaten Villanova.

By dealing cards from the "Iffy Deck", OSU could have reached the final game against UCLA either of two ways. But would they have won, against John Wooden's crew of Sidney Wicks, Curtis Rowe, Steve Patterson and Henry Bibby? They would appear to have been overmatched, like they were against Michigan, Indiana and Marquette. Could they have? As Fred Taylor said after the Marquette game "These kids have done it before — nothing surprises me."

* * * *

In the 12 year period from 1960 through 1971, Ohio State won seven Big Ten championships. Six of those years — 1960, 1961, 1962, 1964, 1968 and 1971 — they had the best field goad percentage in the conference. In 1963 the Buckeyes won the Big Ten title and finished 1.5% behind Illinois, the field goal percentage leader — and conference co-champion. In 1970 OSU set a conference shooting record but lacked the rebounding necessary to win the conference. Still, a high correlation between team shooting effciency and championship seasons.

On the other hand, only twice — 1963 and 1964 — did Ohio State have a conference scoring leader. As discussed, Gary Bradds scored because the team needed him to play that role, not because he was concerned about his personal statistics. Normally scoring leaders and championship teams do not go together. Purdue had seven scoring leaders (Terry Dischinger 1960-1-2, Dave Schellhase 1965, Rick Mount 1968-9-70) and only one championship team (1969) during The Golden Age of Ohio State Basketball.

But Ohio State produced more than basketball championships during this time— it educated men who would become productive members of society. The final chapter of this book will deal with what these men, in their 40's and early 50's, are doing today.

XII
Fred's Formers Today

The purpose of this book is to tell the story of the championship era or Golden Age of Ohio State basketball from the point of view of the players and coaches who achieved the victories. The book is written in the third person, in order to let them tell their story their way.

From the standpoint of a fan it has been a joy to hear the stories, some for the first time, others which have been repeated so often they were long ago committed to memory. Rereading 20-30 year old clippings and articles, seeing game tapes and researching the records — that was as much fun as I had hoped.

This chapter, though, represents something different than anything I expected.

In talking with these men, every now and then I was surprised to realize that they were no longer 20 or 21 years old, running around a basketball court in canvas Converse shoes. In my memory they were frozen in time, but in actual fact they had matured, raised families, changed careers ... some had even retired.

When I remembered Richie Hoyt I was immediately back in high school. Then I met with Rich Hoyt ("I knew you wanted to talk about Ohio State basketball when you asked for Richie Hoyt, because no one calls me that unless they know me from that time," he said.). We were overlooking the city of Columbus, in an office which did not exist 30 years ago. When I remembered Andy Ahijevych I was home from college attending the double overtime loss to Duke at St. John Arena. Then I met Andy for lunch and we both had gray hair.

The purpose of this chapter is to update the reader on the lives today of the men who provided the championships. To do this I sometimes change from third person detachment to first person involvement. Hopefully this will not be as confusing for the reader as it was for me.

* * * *

"Fred's Formers" is an informal group of men who played for Fred Taylor at Ohio State. They get together for a golf outing every fall because they like the memories, they liked each other as young men and they like each other today.

The men first became friends with others in their recruiting classes, then their teammates. Through "Fred's Formers" the players from the late '50's and those from the mid 70's have gotten to know each other as well. The circle, based on the common bond they had with Fred Taylor and Ohio State, has continued to widen with time.

Such stability of relationships is rare today. There are many examples of basketball players who play for two or three coaches during their career at one college, or who transfer once or twice and play for several at different schools. How many "annual reunions" do they attend? Even in the case of a player at one school with one coach, unless the coach stays at the school for a long time and needs the help of a former player, or the player needs the help of the coach, how likely are they to stay in touch? Fred Taylor hasn't coached at Ohio State since 1976 and he is still involved in the lives of many of his former players, individually as well as through "Fred's Formers". Maybe that is the difference between investing your time in someone else's life and using someone else's life to advance your own.

I followed Fred Taylor as a fan from the time he became coach in 1958, but had my first personal contact with him in 1974. Like so many people, I asked him for a favor.

My grandmother had become an Ohio State fan while sending me newspaper clippings when I was in college. By the 1974-5 season it occurred to me that she might like to see a Buckeye game. She was in her early 80's, and had developed the habit of saying "No" to everything. Some of us do that much earlier in life. She said she couldn't go. Since she had not said she didn't want to go I persisted, and began to realize she would enjoy it.

The problem was, she was not able to climb steps. I needed to get seats which were *very* accessible, and had no contacts. So I wrote a letter to Coach Taylor just as if I knew him, outlined the problem, and sent a check made out to the University. Back came the tickets, Mezzanine, about five steps up, right by the door.

My grandmother wore a red dress to the Butler game December 2, 1974 and saw Ohio State win 96-69. When she saw Fred Taylor she said "Oh my, there he is."

After I took her home, my mother called to see how everything had gone. My grandmother said "If I die tonight, I will be perfectly happy. It was such a joy."

In working on this book I have come to realize that Fred Taylor has probably done hundreds, maybe thousands of "little things" like that which have pleased or inspired or challenged or helped people.

Years later I got to know him a little bit when we worked on *Midwest Basketball News*. I remember driving to Indianapolis together for the Mid-East Regional. We saw Magic Johnson lead Michigan State over Louisiana State on their way to the NCAA championship. When we went to the Big Ten pre-season media day I saw the love and respect the coaches had for him. Then he helped me with a pre-season article on the Big Ten race for *Street and Smith's Basketball Yearbook*, emphasizing the importance of seniors to championship teams.

When we stopped working on the magazine we did not have any contact for a long time, except through his oldest daughter Janna. She and I worked together for a while at E.F. Hutton. Then I called him in September, 1990 with the idea for this book. Could I come out to The Golf Club and meet with him to discuss it?

He was interested in the idea, and told me Denny Meadors had the list of "Fred's Formers". He thought they would be willing to help. I told him that I would need to spend quite a bit of time talking with him for the book to work. The players had to comment on a limited perspective of three years, he had to comment on a total perspective of 12.

He said he would help, but he didn't say it quite that way. "I'll do what I can this fall," said Taylor, "but I'm a lot easier to get along with in the winter," is what he said. What he meant was, "The golf course will be open for a while, and I have responsibilities there when it is. I'll do all I can all the time, but I can do more in the winter."

Throughout the writing of the book he was extremely helpful, whether introducing me to Jerry Lucas, helping me get a meeting with someone who initially misunderstood the purpose of the book, answering numerous questions or reviewing the chapters so I did not miss the focus of something he or someone else said. His recall was impressive; he even corrected something Jerry Lucas had forgotten!

233

He did say "No" to one request. The answer was a bit disappointing but the way he handled it encouraged me that he would be "easy to get along with."

When he said "Fred's Formers" had an outing coming up soon, I asked if I could go. He said "No." Not "I'll think about," "I'll check," "I'll get back to you" — just "No." He explained that he wanted to respect the privacy of the players and coaches who would be there, which I understood. I appreciated the clear answer, having worked with too many people who say things they don't mean and cause problems because they are unable to face an issue. I like "Yes" and I can live with "No." On the other hand, "Maybe" and "Later" are tough. We would get along.

Actually, things could not have worked out better. He made an announcement about the book at their dinner, and apparently endorsed it in some way. When I called the players they were anxious to talk.

*   *   *   *

Fred Taylor resigned as Head Basketball Coach at Ohio State in 1976.

Today he is Manager of The Golf Club in New Albany, a community east of Columbus. He and Eileen live in the same house in Upper Arlington they bought in 1960. I recommend stopping by when he is playing Mr. Fix-it. He describes himself as "about as handy as a bear cub wearing boxing gloves."

I got a chance to witness the regard the community continues to have for him on a night in February, 1991. We went with Jim Shaffer and Tom Bowman to see Dick Ricketts' South High School team play against OSU recruit Antonio Watson's Eastmoor team for the City League South title. I was able to crash a mini-reunion of the 1963-1964 championship teams. There must have been a dozen strangers who walked up to Fred just to say hello, that they enjoyed his teams and that they wished him well. Then *The Columbus Dispatch* mentioned that he had been in attendance. It seemed that some people are in the public eye because of what they are, others never leave the public eye because of who they are. Columbus refuses to forget Fred Taylor.

Asked to reflect on basketball today, with all the differences since he coached, he says "With all the changes in basketball, the worst thing they ever did was make freshmen eligible.

"You take a player who spent his entire high school career being set up by teammates who sacrificed to make him a star. He has gotten used to that over three-four years. Then you put him on a team with

12-15 other stars who received the same treatment. And take away his freshman year out of the spotlight, where players used to be able to learn about sacrificing for their teams and to make their mistakes in private.

"It's been 40 years, but I still remember Ohio State fans booing when I missed a shot against Wisconsin. And I was a senior. What impact does that have on a freshman? Sure it depends on the freshman, but it will be damaging to some.

"So what do you have now? A person who may be crushed from an athletic experience, a team of players who never had a chance to learn to sacrifice and, most importantly, a student whose academic achievement is at risk. Not to mention a coach who has to deal with all the problems this creates."

Taylor enjoyed the accomplishments of the 1991 Buckeyes and was a true fan of the team. "With about six weeks to go in the season I got out the 1971 championship ring and began wearing it," he says. "Figured it couldn't hurt." Superstitious fans — and that is redundant — might say it helped.

Jack Graf balanced helping out with the family business with being an Ohio State assistant from 1945 to 1970, but when his father died he had to take over full time responsibility for Graf & Sons, Inc. He has now retired from the business of making doors and windows. Looking back he says the secret to all those championships was "Fred Taylor. He was a natural leader, and he was so well prepared. He was the key."

Frank Truitt spent one season at Louisiana State University as head coach in 1965-66, but quickly realized it was a mistake for four reasons. "When I went there they said that we could have a new arena in two years, that I could carry over my 17 years retirement from Ohio and that I would be tenured on the faculty, like I was at Ohio State. None of that happened. The fourth reason was I just assumed I could recruit blacks and didn't think to ask before I took the job. The Athletic Director asked to see my recruiting list and said 'You can't recruit these guys. We aren't ready for this'. I was just a coach, and it never occurred to me that could be a problem. I really liked the people and the players, but the weather was so hot. In March my grade school daughters were crying over the heat."

So Truitt looked home to Ohio, found out Kent State was considering applicants for their head job, and got that position. He inherited a team which had been 42-91 in the last five years, made them competitive in the Mid-American Conference but never got the championship he sought.

From 1973-78 Truitt served as golf coach. He resigned as basketball coach after the 1974 season. In 1977 his golf team finished first and he was chosen MAC Coach of the Year.

Today Frank Truitt and his wife Kay work with King Thompson Holzer-Wollam Realtors. "I always planned to coach 30 years, then go back to real estate. I got my real estate license in 1952, and kept it in escrow."

The Truitts live in Upper Arlington, about a mile away from Fred and Eileen Taylor and less than two miles away from the Grafs.

"Ernie Biggs died on August 17, 1971. Some dates just stick in your mind," according to Mike Bordner, then Ernie's assistant. "In 1969 he was diagnosed as having leukemia, and was really sick during the 1971 season. He had the leukemia under control but his resistance was down, he got pneumonia and died."

Mike Bordner has been head trainer for men's basketball since 1972, and co-head trainer since 1974. Today he recalls the day Fred Taylor resigned by saying "In athletics, it was the saddest day of my life. The tears ran down my cheeks when he showed me his resignation. He was ahead of his time as a coach."

* * * *

Many of the players spent time in the National Basketball Association, or other professional leagues, after college. The entire starting five of the 1960 NCAA champions — Joe Roberts, John Havlicek, Jerry Lucas, Larry Siegfried and Mel Nowell — played in the NBA. That would be impressive today — then it was remarkable. At that time there were nine NBA teams with 11 players each. Today 27 teams carry 12 players each.

Joe Roberts was the first Buckeye from The Golden Age to play in the NBA. After his senior year he was drafted in the third round by the Syracuse Nationals, forerunner to today's Philadelphia 76ers franchise. As the 21st player taken, he would have been a first round choice today. A reserve forward for three years, his best year was his second. In 1962 he averaged 7.7 points and 8.0 rebounds.

In 1966-67 Roberts was the player — coach of the Columbus Comets in the North American Basketball League. That led to a year in the American Basketball Association with Kentucky in 1968, his last season as a player.

Roberts worked for the State of Ohio for several years, then became an assistant coach at Western Michigan University. Among the players he recruited was Frank Ayers of Springfield, Ohio, brother of Randy Ayers, now OSU head coach. Roberts then moved to the University of Iowa as an assistant, before serving five years with the Golden State Warriors. "I liked coaching in the NBA," he recalls. "The referees were fair on your road games and there was no illegal recruiting." He has taught school and sold real estate since then, except for a stint of 1 1/2 years as an assistant with the Los Angeles Clippers. He lives in northern California.

Dick Furry was one of four consecutive Buckeye basketball players to win the Western Conference Scholar Athlete Award (Larry Huston was first, Furry, Richie Hoyt and Jerry Lucas). His major was accounting and he worked for Ernst & Ernst in public accounting for eight years after graduation. Today he is President of Day-Glo Color Corporation in Cleveland, Ohio.

Furry remembers Taylor's "clear ideas of how the game should be played, and ability to incorporate star players into a team concept" as the reasons for Ohio State's success.

Howard Nourse is Vice President of Milligan College in Tennessee.

David Barker now owns the David Barker Art Gallery in Columbus, which he enjoys because "it combines an artistic outlet with the opportunity to deal with people." He remembers Fred Taylor stressing "what this school can do for you" during recruiting. Barker says "What I got from Ohio State more than anything else is a level of self-confidence."

Rich Hoyt married Woody Hayes' niece, and their daughter Mary Beth attends Indiana University where Bob Knight keeps track of her grades. Dr. Bob Murphy, who worked with the team so long, is still the Hoyt family physician. Rich is President of Varsity "O" Alumni.

Hoyt is Vice President of Operations at Gates McDonald, which has 40 offices to provide self insurance and self administration services to large and small companies and municipalities. He is responsible for delivery of services to the customer.

After his senior year Larry Siegfried was the third player taken in the NBA draft. A big, strong shooter, who could handle the ball and defend, he had everything a pro team could want in a guard. The Cincinnati Royals selected him to play beside Oscar Robertson, who had come within 20 assists of averaging a triple double (points —

30.5, rebounds — 10.0, assists — 9.72) as a rookie. Plus they already held the rights to Jerry Lucas for the 1962-63 season.

Siegfried refused to sign with the Royals.

"It was an emotional time," he says today. "There was a lot of animosity between Cincinnati and Ohio State. I took that animosity personally, a decision that reflected my background. If any other team had drafted me I'd have gone to the NBA. I just couldn't shift my loyalties that fast."

Instead he signed with the Cleveland Pipers in the newly formed American Basketball League. "It was a new franchise in a new league that was going to fold before the next season," recalls Siegfried. "Our coach, Bill Sharman, had never coached before and there was no structure, no organization, no planning. Fred had broken me of my selfishness and I needed a system." Larry played significant minutes early in the year but his playing time dwindled. He was a forgotten man when the Pipers won the only ABL championship.

Cincinnati still wanted him, but he refused to sign. The St. Louis Hawks obtained permission to bring him to their camp.

"I thought I had the Hawks made," Siegfried said then. "I was playing well, I was beating other guys one-on-one and the ball was dropping for me. Both Bob Pettit and Cliff Hagen (Hawk All-Pros) gave me a lot of encouragement. "Then one night after playing an intrasquad game, we were getting off a bus when Coach Harry Gallatin yelled at me. 'Hey, Siegfried,' he said, 'it was nice knowin' ya'. That's how I got cut, that's how I learned that St. Louis didn't want me."

Larry spent the 1962-63 season teaching health and physical education at Hamilton Township High School near Columbus, playing for several semi-pro teams in Ohio, and watching John Havlicek have an outstanding rookie year with the Celtics.

After Boston beat Los Angeles in the NBA Finals, Hondo called Sieg and said "Red Auerbach wants to know if you are interested in playing ball next year." He did not mention that much of the reason Red was interested was that Havlicek had spent the winter telling Red that Larry could help the Celtics.

Siegfried couldn't accept the opportunity because his rights belonged to the Hawks. "I had to go to their camp in the fall. I gave it my best shot, but I was cut again. My confidence was shot through this experience," he says today.

But Auerbach brought him to Boston, and, based on one work out, offered him a job. Sort of. For the 1963-64 season Siegfried would be

238

the 12th man on the Celtic roster. At that time teams traveled with only 11 players. Siegfried dressed only for home games.

In his first season Larry played 31 games and averaged 3.3 points per game. But "with time the power started to come back," he says today. "It was a slow process but I began to gain the confidence of my senior year at Ohio State."

Before the 1965 season, Siegfried beat out Ray Flynn of Syracuse for the last roster spot. Flynn was later elected mayor of Boston. From 1966 to 1970, Sieg was the best foul shooter in the NBA. He led the league in 1966 (88.1%) and 1969 (86.4%), and was second in 1968. He scored 12-14 points per game every year, and helped the Celtics win championships in 1966, 1968 and 1969. Celtic announcer Johnny Most described his defense nightly by saying "Siggy's in his (opponent's) shirt". Bill Russell, the coach in 1967-69, said Larry "used to say you can't play no ball sitting around. So I fixed that. I played him 40 minutes in four straight games. Then he went around saying you can't play no ball when you're tired." Something was always wrong, still, but Larry Siegfried was a valuable Celtic.

In the 1968 championship over Los Angeles, Siegfried scored 10 straight points, 22 in all, to help Boston win the deciding sixth game 124-109. After the game Laker Jerry West said "Siegfried did it. If it hadn't been for him we would have beaten them."

Someone suggested that Siegfried could do just about everything. "He sure can," said West to *SPORT* magazine. "He's learned it all. But nobody could ever have taught him to go after the ball the way he does. That" — West pointed to his chest — "you have to have here."

Siegfried's best year was in 1969. In addition to leading the league in foul shooting he had career highs in minutes, points, shot attempts, rebounds, assists and scoring average (14.2 ppg). He was third on the team, behind Russell and Havlicek, in minutes played. The team finished 48-34, but fourth in the Eastern Division. Russell and Sam Jones were in their last season and the Celtics were on the decline. Yet Boston beat Philadelphia 4-1 and New York 4-2 to advance to the Finals to play the Lakers. Again.

This would be the seventh time Boston played the Lakers in the Finals from 1959 through 1969. Despite the addition of Wilt Chamberlain to all time greats Jerry West and Elgin Baylor, despite losing the first two games of the series and despite the home court advantage

L.A. had due to their superior regular season record, it was the seventh straight time Boston won.

West scored 53 points as the Lakers won the first game 120-118, and they won the second 118-112. Back in Boston the Celtics won 111-105 as Havlicek scored 34 and Siegfried 28, but they trailed in the fourth game by one point with six seconds to go.

Boston called the emergency scoring play which Ohio State had used to defeat Indiana in 1960, when Siegfried made the shot, and Louisville in 1961, when Havlicek sank it. Hondo had put the play in one day when Russell was late to practice. Called "Ohio", it required Sam Jones to come off a triple screen, and Havlicek to pass him the ball. Sam's shot rolled around ... and around the rim before falling in. Boston 89 Los Angeles 88.

"All I wanted to do was shoot the ball high, with some backspin on it, so Russell could have a chance at the rebound," said Sam Jones, the hero. Fact is, Coach Russell had taken himself out of the game to get the five best shooters on the court. Russ said "Sam, I know I've got long arms but that would have been one helluva rebound."

The Lakers won game five 117-104 but Boston won game six 99-90. Los Angeles hosted game seven.

Laker owner Jack Kent Cooke had broken the bank to win this game. He had sent three players and cash to Philadelphia for Chamberlain, then signed Wilt to an unheard of contract (something like $250,000 for four years). But he may have gone too far when he bought the thousands of balloons suspended in plastic sacks from the ceiling of the Fabulous Forum. As John Havlicek wrote, "This gave us additional incentive at a crucial time."

With the score 103-102 Boston, former Iowa star Don Nelson, now a Celtic, took a shot which hit the back of the rim, bounced higher than the backboard, and went in with 1:17 to go. The Lakers rushed up court but Siegfried stole the ball, got fouled and made both shots. The final score was 108-106.

As Havlicek was being interviewed by ABC after the game, Red Auerbach interrupted and said, "I just want to know one thing. What the hell are they gonna do with those balloons up there?"

It was the first time a team had won the NBA Finals after trailing 0-2. Only Portland, in 1977, has done it since. It made 12 consecutive times the Celtics had won the seventh game of a series.

With Russell gone, Boston went 34-48 under first year coach Tom Heinsohn. Siegfried scored well, and would have finished second in the league in free throw shooting if he had enough attempts, but things were not the same. He had become an outsider with management by being the Celtics' first contract hold-out and by frequently disagreeing with Heinsohn. Larry had worked well with Russell, who had said of Siegfried, "He's a brilliant guy. He can diagnose and solve problems faster than anyone I've ever known, except maybe Red." Siegfried felt Boston should slow the ball down without an excellent rebounder, Heinsohn favored pushing the ball up court at every opportunity to get easy shots. In the power struggle Larry lost and was placed in the expansion pool. He retired after the 1972 season.

After his nine year NBA career Larry Siegfried came back to Ohio State for a year to assist Fred Taylor, then was an assistant with the Houston Rockets for three years. "The tough thing about the NBA," he reflects today, "is knowing 'How do I plug into society when my career is over?' "

"Today I take my experience in life, the successes and the failures, the ups and the downs, and use them to influence others. That way they can enjoy the benefits of their championships," says Siegfried. "Winning, or making money, that's no big deal. The important thing is developing a value system, which is based on understanding, which comes only after awareness. If all you want to do is make money, sell drugs." Siegfried will use shock to make his point. His business card reads Larry Siegfried "Winning Attitude — Consultant — Workshop — Speaker."

"At Ohio State we learned that a group of people pulling together is much stronger than five superior athletes going their own way. Bob Knight is still proving that today, and so is Randy Ayers," says Sieg.

Gary Gearhart is in Lima, Ohio where he has been a manufacturers representative for Josten's Company since shortly after graduation from Ohio State. He works with high schools in supplying class rings and graduation announcements.

John Havlicek was not the best forward in the history of the NBA, nor the best guard. He never played center. However he might have been better at more phases of the game than any player in league history, and he is on the short list of the best *players* ever.

His rookie year he was designated the player to carry on the Celtic tradition of making the last two shots before introductions. He kept the job for 16 years, making All-NBA eleven times. That first year he played more minutes off the bench than teammate Frank Ramsey, then regarded the premier sixth man in basketball.

241

When he became sixth man, John was so good that he was starting for the Eastern Division in the NBA All-Star game while serving as the Celtic's first replacement.

Hondo was selected to the NBA All-Defensive team eight consecutive years. Since the team was not selected until 1969, he had played in the league seven years and was 29 years old when the string *started*.

When Havlicek retired he had played more NBA games than any player in history, and trailed only Wilt Chamberlain in minutes played and field goals made.

He averaged over 34 minutes per game in his final season, 1978, when he played all 82 games, averaged 16.1 points and shot 85.5% at the foul line. He scored 29 points in his final game, a victory over Buffalo. He was 38 years old.

John Havlicek played on eight championship teams, the first in 1963, the last in 1976. His particular favorites were the 1968, 1969, and 1974 clubs which, in his words, "combined talent with brains and finesse ... (they) surprised people." They were overachievers, like he was.

In a sport of massive egos, one of the greatest stars of all time saw himself as "an Ohio State player". He explains what that description meant to him. "When I called myself an 'Ohio State player'," says Havlicek today, "it referred to a standard of excellence we had under Fred Taylor, as people, players and teammates."

But this "Ohio State player" almost never played professional basketball after college.

Hondo considered three offers to play professional sports. The Celtics offered $15,000 in 1962 ("but they started with $9,500," points out Fred Taylor); the Cleveland Pipers $25,000, an apartment, a car ("but I was basically skeptical about the league," Havlicek reflects) and the Cleveland Browns $15,000 and a car. "I figured that if I could play for the Browns, who had drafted me, I could stay in Ohio, and I like Ohio," says Havlicek. "And the football season is short, the pay was the same as basketball, and football was not as demanding as basketball. Plus the NBA didn't have the glamor of the NFL back in 1962. And I knew that if I didn't make the Browns, I could go back to basketball."

When Hondo signed with the Browns the Celtics were less than pleased. In the last four drafts, the only first round choice to help the team had been Tom Sanders in 1960. Still, Havlicek had not played football in four years and they signed him for a position — wide receiver — this former quarterback had never played. He couldn't possibly make an NFL contender. Could he?

He didn't, but he came sooo close. He ran the third fastest 40 yard dash in Browns history (after Jim Brown and Bobby Mitchell) and showed outstanding hands. Then he forgot about football before football forgot about him. After he was cut, Denver and Houston offered him try-outs. The Colts and the Redskins contacted him later. For five straight years the Browns invited him back to camp to try out again. But John was not to be a football player. He headed for the Celtics camp.

John had been a great college basketball player, but Lucas' shadow was so long that many people did not realize it. At 6'5, playing with the best rebounder in the country, Hondo averaged more rebounds than recent center Perry Carter did at Ohio State. Havlicek was a defender with the well-earned reputation of a Billy King of Duke, or Stacey Augmon of UNLV. He made over 50% of his field goal attempts and nearly 75% of his foul shots. He never missed a game and averaged just under 15 points on a team which did not need him to score. He could — and would — pass the ball.

Red Auerbach, then Celtic coach, told *SPORT* magazine why he took John in the first round, with the ninth choice. "That was one of the best years for college talent I can remember. I had a choice of Terry Dischinger, Chet Walker or Havlicek. John was not a great shooter or ballhandler because he didn't get the ball that much. But I thought he would play defense. And I thought he might be a swing player (between guard and forward).

"He came to my summer camp about a week after he was cut by the Browns," continued Auerbach. "He worked out against the other rookies. After about 35 seconds I said 'Holy smoke, this Havlicek is better than we thought'." Seventeen years later a rookie made a similar impression on Auerbach at his first practice. It was the first time, but not the last, that Larry Bird would be compared to John Havlicek.

Because it would take a book much larger than this one to do justice to John Havlicek's NBA career, the interested reader may want to read his autobiography *HONDO — Celtic Man in Motion* or any history of the Boston Celtics to further digest his greatness. Or possibly the NBA record book. However one story and some comments from his contemporaries are helpful.

In 1973, tied 1-1 with the New York Knicks and Jerry Lucas in the Eastern Conference Finals, Havlicek ran into a blind pick and felt a pain in his right arm. He missed his next shot badly and did not play well in the remainder of a 98-91 loss. After the game his arm hurt too much to get dressed by himself.

The next day the pain increased and he went to the hospital. He had a partial shoulder separation and tearing of the joint capsule. It would heal with time, but he missed the fourth game. Boston played well but lost 117-110 in double overtime.

For two days Havlicek practiced shooting left-handed. He scored 18 points as Boston won game five 98-97. New York won the series in seven games, but how many basketball players could accomplish what Hondo did? Or would even try to?

Current NBA television analyst and Hall of Fame player Rick Barry looks back on Hondo's NBA career and says "He was not great in any one area, but he was exceptionally good in all. I see him more than I did when we were playing, and he agrees with that assessment.

"Well," continues Barry, "you'd have to say he had great stamina. And great versatility. And he was a great competitor. And he is a great guy. I would have loved to have had him as my teammate."

"In high school he scored around the basket," says Bob Knight, "but in college he developed into a good shooter from 15'. In the NBA he made himself a good shooter from 20'. He made use of his own abilities."

Matt Guokas, now Orlando Magic Coach, then Philadelphia 76er player, once said, "I'd give my right arm to have the stamina of John Havlicek." For a basketball player, a right arm is a pretty high price to pay for something as nebulous as stamina. But Guokas had to guard the guy, who reportedly had a heartbeat of 40 beats per minute (72 is normal).

Bob Ryan, a newspaperman who covered the Celtics, once wrote "To see Havlicek 1969-71 was to see nightly miracles." In 1971 Hondo was the second leading scorer in the NBA, and fifth in assists. At 6'5 he was second on the Celtics in rebounding at over nine per game. He averaged over 45 minutes per game.

One final attempt to portray John Havlicek the NBA player to fans who do not remember him. Start with more endurance than anyone in the game today, add the defensive ability of Dennis Rodman or Dan Majerle, the pride of Larry Bird, 20 points and five assists per game (more if the team needed it), an ego which did not require constant attention, no fear of failure, condense that into one 6'5 man and you have a glimpse of the Buckeye from Bridgeport High.

John Havlicek continues to show up on televised basketball games, as a spectator. He is often seen at the Boston Gardens for Celtic games or wherever the University of Virginia and his son Chris are playing. (Chris' teammate at U. Va., Bryant Stith, is no relation to the Tom Stith who played for St. Bonaventure.)

Hondo owns three Wendy's restaurants, works in promotions for several companies including RJR Nabisco, but is about as retired as he wants to be.

Fred Taylor and John Havlicek are close today. Fred says when they last went to dinner it was obvious that "people in Boston act like he's still playing. They wave, stop and say hello. They have a great deal of respect and love for him."

Much like the people of Columbus feel about Fred Taylor.

Thinking back 30 plus years to when his friend was his coach, Havlicek remembers Fred as "very astute and fundamental. He charted everything. He figured out that on foul shots more are missed to the shooter's right than left, so he always had the third rebounder play on that side. Throughout my Celtic career I remembered him teaching us to block out on rebounds for two seconds, then look for the ball. When Boston pressed, Larry (Siegfried) and I told them how Ohio State did it and that's what the Celtics did. He (Fred) was so well prepared."

Mel Nowell did not have his best year at Ohio State as a senior, but was drafted by the Chicago Packers. He averaged 5.9 points in 39 games, but did not go to Baltimore when the franchise moved.

Like Roberts he played well with the Columbus Comets of the North American Basketball League in 1967. When the ABA was formed he signed with the New Jersey Americans. Nowell played one year, averaged 9.6 points and was fifth in the league in foul shooting. Today he is a businessman in Columbus.

At Ohio State Jerry Lucas was the subject of enormous national press. In addition to his basketball ability, two themes dominated the articles.

Early in his college career he was unique because he chose an academic scholarship rather than athletic aid. He was in school for an education and wanted athletics to be a matter of choice. As a true student — athlete he dominated his sport, but he established his highest priority as education.

After a few college games he had proven himself as a player, and writers began to inquire about the future. Lucas tried to explain that his priorities were in developing his mind and establishing a business career, not playing professional basketball. Writers jumped on the theme of "he won't play for pay" and wrote about that constantly while he was at Ohio State.

When his college career was over Lucas met with representatives of the two teams which held his rights, the Cincinnati Royals of the NBA and the Cleveland Pipers of the American Basketball League. Cincinnati treated him as just another outstanding player and tried to buy him with a check. A very big check for the time, to be sure, but, in Jerry's words, "Just that lump of money, which would not last too long, especially when you consider taxes."

George Steinbrenner, president of the Pipers, approached the challenge of signing Lucas the same way he would baseball players in the free agent market for the New York Yankees years later. He read Jerry's concerns and addressed them. For example, the ABL schedule was shortened and delayed, so Luke could finish his work at Ohio State. The salary offer was supplemented by a portfolio of stocks and investments which would provide growth and income for the future. A two year contract was offered rather than three. Businessmen who would have a potential interest in working with Lucas were included in the discussion. Lucas was listened to and given choices. He signed with Cleveland.

His national visibility was so high that he announced his decision by writing an article for *Sports Illustrated*. He was paid $500 for the article. The money was returned to provide subscriptions for orphans and crippled children.

Then the ABL folded.

Lucas had a personal services contract with two Cleveland businessmen, was involved in seeking an NBA franchise for Cleveland where he would have been part owner, finished his education and helped out a little with the Buckeye team. Mostly the time away from basketball helped him decide that he missed it.

Through it all Lucas was roundly criticized. *The Columbus Dispatch* wrote that he should have announced his decision to play with Cleveland locally, not nationally. *SPORT* magazine carried an article titled "The Curious Comedown of Jerry Lucas." The Cincinnati

Royals felt betrayed — in their minds they owned Lucas when they exercised their territorial rights to a high school senior. George Steinbrenner defaulted on payments to the NBA, and Lucas was part of that group. People who couldn't understand how he could refuse to play professionally were incredulous that he changed his mind.

The next year he went on to a Rookie-of-the-Year season with the Cincinnati Royals. He was the fourth Rookie-of-the-Year in the NBA from the 1960 Olympic team (Robertson in 1961, Bellamy 1962 and Dischinger 1963 before Lucas).

As a rookie Lucas was second team All-NBA. He was first team the next two years, then second team, and first team again in 1968. Three of those five years he was in the top three in the league in field goal shooting percentage. Every year he was in the top three in rebounding, never trailing anyone other than centers Wilt Chamberlain or Bill Russell. In 1968 he outrebounded Russell.

In 1965 Lucas averaged 21.4 points and 20.0 rebounds per game. In 1966 he had 21.5 points and 21.1 rebounds. Other than Lucas, only Wilt Chamberlain had more than one "20-20" in a pro season.

Additionally Lucas played in six All Star games, five as a starter. Every time he started his team won; in 1965 he scored 25 points and grabbed 10 rebounds to be named Most Valuable Player.

Despite the individual accomplishments, Lucas' early years in the NBA were not satisfying. Cincinnati had some good teams, but could not compete with the Celtics. The Royals had two great offensive players — Oscar Robertson and Jerry Lucas — and surrounded them with more offensive players. In the play-offs the premium was always on defense, and the Celtics did it better.

Also when Lucas joined the Royals, Wayne Embry was the center. At 255 lbs., the current Cleveland Cavalier General Manager had to play inside so Lucas played forward. Lucas says today "I loved the center position. I could have played there, and would have enjoyed it more. It just didn't work out with Embry and (later Nate) Thurmond."

On the positive side, he was one of the first athletes to use ice and found that therapy to be very helpful to his knees.

Cincinnati was 41-41 in 1969, Jerry's last full season there. He averaged 18.3 points and 18.4 rebounds but was not selected to the All-Star team. Still, in a mid-season rating of players in *SPORT* by NBA coaches, Luke was rated the second best forward in the league, behind only Elgin Baylor.

Interestingly, *SPORT* magazine had polled NBA players, coaches and owners and asked "Who is the best of basketball's superstars?" in 1962 when Luke was a senior at Ohio State. The answer was Bill Russell, Oscar Robertson, Elgin Baylor, Wilt Chamberlain and Jerry Lucas. Lucas was the fifth player ranked, though he had yet to play a pro game.

After five years as an All-Star he had lived up to that incredible forecast. He was the second best forward in the league, playing out of position at that. Yet it wasn't good enough.

Cincinnati traded Lucas to San Francisco in 1970 for two journeyman players. He played forward beside Nate Thurmond, a graduate of Akron Central High School who attended Bowling Green rather than risk sitting behind Jerry Lucas at Ohio State. Though San Francisco improved their record by 11 games, they traded Lucas to New York for Cazzie Russell in May, 1971.

Red Holtzman, coach of the New York Knicks, remembered Lucas as a center at Ohio State. He had that role in mind in making the trade. Luke filled the bill, and added excellent outside shooting as well, when Willis Reed was injured and played only 11 games in 1972. Lucas led the Knicks to a 48-34 record, with 16.7 points and 13.1 rebounds per game. An excellent passer, he was second on the squad in assists and frequently called plays for the Knicks. His defense of Dave Cowens was largely responsible for the elimination of the Boston Celtics in the Eastern Conference Finals (4-1), but Los Angeles won the championship.

In 1973 Reed and Lucas split time at center, Walt Frazier was All-NBA, Earl Monroe was there for the full year, DeBusschere and Bradley manned the forwards and the Knicks finished 57-25. They beat Baltimore 4-1 in the playoffs and edged Boston 4-3 in the Conference Finals. After losing the first game of the NBA Finals to Los Angeles 115-112, New York held the Lakers to an average of 92 points and won four straight to win the title.

Luke's career was on the decline. He averaged 9.9 points and 7.2 rebounds per game. But after ten years in the NBA he had a championship. The title which had come so quickly in college was finally his in the NBA.

"Even though it was late in my career," he says today, "playing with the Knicks was the most enjoyable time. They were smart players and we had a complete team concept. And I liked the center position."

New York finished 49-33 in 1974, despite a season full of injuries to key players. Lucas had back trouble, and spent several days in traction. The Knicks lost to Boston in the Conference Finals 4-1. After the season he retired.

Jerry Lucas says his biggest basketball thrill was "Winning a championship at every level — high school, college, Olympic and professional. I loved being a part of a cohesive unit, which should be the goal of any player." To the best of Jerry's knowledge only he and Quinn Buckner of Bob Knight's 1976 Indiana NCAA champions have played on championship teams at all four levels.

Luke moved from suburban Atlanta to Middletown, Ohio in 1991. His literacy course, based on 10 years of study, had just been published. "Our system of education teaches people what to learn, but we need to do a better job of teaching people how to learn," he says. He is author of several other books as well.

Jerry Ray Lucas II — "JJ" — will graduate from Middletown H.S. in 1993, having two years of varsity ball to try to break a couple of his father's records. Luke says "JJ" is "just getting interested, but has a great touch. He will be much bigger than I am, has a great reach —7' wing span — but is not a raw athlete."

When Jerry thinks back to playing for Fred Taylor he recalls his coach as being "thorough, well prepared and concerned. We certainly worked hard. He had what you might call an 'old fashioned approach,' which I view as very positive."

Bob Knight, entered The Basketball Hall of Fame as a coach in 1991, joining Taylor, Lucas and Havlicek.

When Bob Knight graduated from Ohio State he and Fred Taylor were not close, because Knight was convinced he should have played more as a Buckeye. Even today his frequent line-up changes reflect a belief that the player doing the job at the present moment should play regardless of past accomplishments of other players. When Hoosier star Calbert Cheaney is on the bench at a key time, for example, the reason may have more to do with Knight playing at Ohio State than what the Hoosiers are doing.

Knight's first job was assistant coach at Cuyahoga Falls High School under Harold Andreas. Andreas encouraged Knight to mend the relationship.

Knight attended a clinic Fred was conducting in Cleveland. When Taylor noticed his former player, he asked him to help demonstrate a drill. Later Knight wrote a letter saying, among other things, "I think every player should have to be a coach before he is allowed to play."

With Taylor's help Knight became assistant to George Hunter at Army. The bad news was he had to join the armed service. That was the good news too; otherwise Knight might have been drafted and sent to Vietnam.

Hunter was fired almost immediately after Knight enlisted. The new coach, Tates Locke, honored Hunter's commitment to Knight, who was Locke's assistant for two years. When Locke went to Miami of Ohio, Bob Knight was named head coach at Army at the age of 24. Later Locke moved to Clemson and was cited for NCAA violations. Knight hired him as an assistant at Indiana and Locke is now head coach at Indiana State.

During his six seasons at Army Knight took the team to the National Invitational Tournament four times. The Cadets were 102-50 (.671) and twice won 20 or more games. He was a coach with a future.

In 1968 he was offered the position at Wisconsin and tentatively accepted it. The day he was to fly to Madison to finalize the deal he called Bo Schembechler, then Michigan football coach. Schembechler had interviewed at Wisconsin before becoming the Wolverine coach and told him not to take the job. Knight didn't. Since then all three Wisconsin coaches have had losing records. Knight might have been more successful, but coaching basketball at Wisconsin is a tough challenge.

Knight became coach at Indiana in the 1971-72 season, the year Ohio State's Golden Age ended. Since then the Hoosiers have gone to a post-season tournament every year but one, never had a losing season, won almost 75% of their games and three NCAA championships. They have reason to hope for a fourth in the near future.

After three years of matching wits on the Big Ten sidelines, Taylor had a 3-2 edge over Knight. Each had won every home game.

The last two years Fred Taylor coached at Ohio State, 1975 and 1976, Indiana went undefeated in the Big Ten — 36-0. Still, their closest victory of 1976 was in Columbus, 66-64, when the Buckeyes played a gimmick defense with 6' Larry Bolden guarding 6'11 Indiana center Kent Benson.

"Nobody was more affected by Fred Taylor than I was," says Knight, "because this will be my 30th year in coaching. He taught me that the approach to play is more important than offense or defense. As a head coach Fred Taylor did more to determine how basketball would be played in the Big Ten than any coach in any conference. Coaches changed their approach to defense and their thinking on shot selection because they couldn't beat Ohio State if they didn't.

"At Indiana our defense is very similar or identical to the way we played in college. At Ohio State we used a lot of sets on offense, at Indiana we use motion. Ohio State ran a sideline fast break. I never liked that as a player, but we do run the fast break down the side of the middle," says the most successful coach in Big Ten history.

Asked to compare the player of 1958-62 with the coach of today, Fred Taylor says "Bob Knight would have a tough time playing for Bob Knight." Concerning coaching against Knight, at Army and Indiana, and Don DeVoe at Virginia Tech, Taylor says "You can't enjoy the win as much as you should, and you never enjoy a loss."

Dick Reasbeck was signed by a California Angels scout who saw him in an Ohio Valley baseball league. Dick had played at OSU, but only after the basketball season. He was in the Angels farm system for two years, and supplies this scouting report on himself: "Good speed, good arm, good fastball hitter, couldn't hit the curve ball."

After baseball he returned to Ohio State in 1965-66 and helped out with the Buckeyes while completing his student teaching. He taught and coached for seven years before joining Consolidated Coal in the Valley. He has been there for 18 years as a consultant for the safety program.

Doug McDonald went from OSU captain to head coach of Marysville High School, something he feels was only possible because of Fred Taylor's recommendation. He also coached at Upper Arlington, Ashland and Tiffin Columbian. He was principal at Tiffin for four years before retiring in 1991.

Jim Doughty returned to Ohio State and graduated in 1970. He works for the United States Security and Exchange Commission in Washington D.C., and is an independent distributor for a perfume company. He says "I compare Fred Taylor to Joe Gibbs of the Washington Redskins football team for their tremendous game plans and ability to make key adjustments at halftime."

Gary Bradds was the fifth player taken in the NBA draft in 1964, by the Baltimore Bullets. It was a bad fit.

Bradds had been an enormous beneficiary of, and contributor to, the system at Ohio State. At Baltimore he was with a team which was developing a new system which didn't require what he could do —

shoot after a pass. They needed experience; regardless of his desire it was his first year.

He played in half the Baltimore games as a rookie and three in the 1965-1966 season. He returned to Columbus. When the North American Basketball League began, Bradds was a leading scorer in the league. One game he scored 34 points while shooting only 14 times from the field, another he got 39 on 15 shots.

"Gary had one leg longer than the other," says his father Donald Bradds today. "The doctor told him to stop playing or the knee would fail. He kept playing but the traveling and all the games caused problems."

When the ABA formed, Gary signed with the Oakland Oaks. The 1968 season was rough at 22-56, but Bradds was playing steadily. In 1969 Rick Barry joined the team, having sat out the previous year for changing leagues. Future NBA coaches Larry Brown and Doug Moe came in a trade, Barry led the league in scoring and Oakland ran away with the league. They finished 60-18, 14 games ahead, then swept the Finals 4-1 over Indiana. Bradds averaged 18.7 ppg and was fourth on the team in scoring. The team averaged 131.6 ppg in the Finals.

The team was sold and moved to Washington for the 1970 season. Bradds scored 13.4 ppg. He played parts of the next season with Carolina and Texas, then retired.

"Gary never intended to play ball after the kids started school. That was 1970 and that's about how it worked out," says his father. "Gary was a homebody, he never liked to travel," recalls his wife Eileen. "When our oldest daughter was in three kindergartens, that was too much. The cut in pay was a problem, but our priorities were clear."

Rick Barry recalls his days as a teammate of Gary Bradds. "He was a terrific guy. Not the most gifted athlete but he was wiry, a good mid-range shooter and he worked hard," says the Hall-of-Famer now pro basketball analyst. "I always appreciated the fact that he didn't try out for the Olympics in 1964. When he didn't, I was invited to take his place."

"He was finishing school then," says Donald Bradds, "and he didn't want to fly over to Tokyo either."

Barry feels Bradds "got all he could out of his ability."

After Gary Bradds finished playing pro ball he and his family settled in the Jamestown area. He taught and coached at two local schools, and taught and served as Athletic Director at Greeneview High School where he played. Greeneview's gym is now called the Gary Bradds Memorial Gymnasium.

Gary Bradds died of cancer July 15, 1983, 11 days before his 41st birthday. His father Donald recalls "He had a mole on his back. It had been removed about two years prior but the cancer had spread."

After he died there were several fund raising efforts to provide money for his children to attend college. Mr. Donald Bradds puts it this way — "Fred Taylor was a fine coach, but after Gary died he has proven to be one of the finest men I've ever known. Bobby Knight too. He's a mighty fine fellow, and has a heart as big as a house. He said if they didn't raise enough with what they had planned to just let him know. 'I'll go out speaking and raise some more,' he said. And Dick Ricketts, Larry Siegfried, Don DeVoe and Jim Cleamons all came down here with Fred Taylor to speak at a banquet to honor Gary."

Mr. Bradds has one more memory to share.

"One day John Havlicek was signing autographs for a promotion in Dayton and Gary's nephew Griffin asked him 'Did you know my uncle?' John took time right in the middle of what he was doing to talk with him. Griffin was amazed that such a famous, and busy, man would take time right then for a little boy (who was a junior in high school by 1991). Havlicek, Knight, Taylor, Ricketts, Siegfried, DeVoe, Cleamons — that's the way they all are."

In 1991 Gary Bradds' son David won the University of Dayton Scholar-Athlete Award, given to the basketball team member with the highest grade average after at least five semesters.

Bradds' buddy Don DeVoe got his degree from Ohio State in December, 1964. In the spring Army coach Bob Knight called Fred Taylor looking for an assistant. Fred recommended DeVoe and Don was hired. "At that time you had to enlist in the Army, which I did for two years," says DeVoe. "I was there five years, the last three as a civilian."

DeVoe returned to OSU in 1970-71 to get his Masters in Higher Education and provided valuable assistance to the Buckeye champions that year. In the spring he was hired as head coach at Virginia Tech, where he stayed five years. They won the National Invitation Tournament in 1973. He later coached at Wyoming, Tennessee and Florida. After 19 years as a Division I head coach he would like to get back into coaching, hopefully at a state school.

253

After his Ohio State career the Dallas Cowboys asked Tom Bowman to try-out. He did, "but after two days I knew football wasn't for me," he says.

Basketball continued to be. He is a player-coach in the top amateur league in Columbus, and said 1991 would be his last year with the American Old-Timers League. His Columbus team included Larry Jones (Columbus East and Toledo) and Fred Saunders (Columbus Mohawks and Southwestern Louisiana); they played against Bingo Smith and Campy Russell of the Cleveland Cavaliers, Buckeye nemesis Tom Thacker from Cincinnati and, until recently, Jim Doughty.

Though approaching 50, Bowman could pass for 30. Always a leaper, he says the problem is "They still play me at forward. It was bad enough rebounding against those guys when they weighed 240 lbs. Now they weigh 290 and there is just no room."

Tom, known to his Buckeye teammates as "Bullwinkle", has his own insurance agency on the north side of Columbus. (If he doesn't stop the basketball he may become his own best client.) His son completed a fine high school career at Gahanna and is a point guard at New York University.

Jim Shaffer operates Personal Retirement Advisors in Pataskala, east of Columbus, "helping people see the importance of investing to preserve their purchasing power." He is pleased that Randy Ayers is "running a clean, class program which the kids and the alums could respect."

After college the Dallas Cowboys contacted Dick Ricketts, but no one in the NBA did. He taught at Crestview Junior High for one year, then was named head basketball coach at Columbus South High School at the age of 23. He took the Bulldogs to the state semi-finals in 1973, then worked with Fred Taylor at Ohio State scouting and evaluating high school players for two years. He returned to South, where he still coaches. In 1986 the Bulldogs finished second in the state. At the end of the 1991 season he had 274 victories, one of the highest totals in central Ohio.

Fred Taylor tells about the *second* time he recruited Ricketts. "Upper Arlington High School was looking for a basketball coach and they asked me to be on the search committee. Dick was doing very well at South, so I asked what it would take for him to consider a change of school systems. When he told me it seemed like a lot. I said 'Dick, when I got the Ohio State job they paid me $8,000.' Dick said 'But Fred, when you got the Ohio State job bread was $.05 a loaf.' I gave him a forearm shot to the chest for that one."

In reflecting on his coaching career,Ricketts says "One thing I first saw at Ohio State has been proven over and over at South, that having people who like each other and want to play together is more important than talent."

Dick's wife Katherine is vice-principal at Briggs High School. When a *Columbus Dispatch* writer asked her if she had mixed allegiance at a South-Briggs game she said "I have no conflict of interest at all. I don't have to go home with Paul Pennell (Briggs coach) tonight."

Jim Brown is the very successful Golf Coach of Ohio State University.

Bob Dove is employed by Bankers Insurance in Houston, Texas, working with independent agents throughout the state, "selling them on the fact that they should represent us." He still plays ball in YMCA leagues with "some guys just out of high school." Did he ever develop a right hand? "No, no."

Andy Ahijevych got a Masters in Business Administration at Ohio State "because Fred helped me get a graduate assistantship." Today Andy is the Assistant Controller in Management Accounting at Battelle in Columbus, where he appreciates the opportunity to serve mankind in innovative and creative ways. He says "I wouldn't be where I am today if not for Fred Taylor and Ohio State. I learned how to cope with adversity and developed discipline, plus received a great deal of visibility."

Al Peters coached jayvees at Lima Bath for one year before joining Frank Truitt at Kent State. "That was the first year Bob Knight was at Army," recalls Al. "It seemed like he called every morning at 9 a.m. to talk with Frank about practice, players, teams or something."

After one year at Kent State Peters went to Texas Wesleyan for five years to teach and coach before "deciding I didn't want recruiting any more." He received his doctorate in Education from the University of North Texas and still teaches at Texas Wesleyan.

Marv Gregory teaches mathematics at Grandview High School in suburban Columbus.

Bob Burkholder, who became assistant coach when Frank Truitt went to LSU, and his wife live in northern Columbus. They still enjoy their buckeye tree, a gift of Mark Wagar's mother. Bob is in real estate sales.

Ron Sepic is an orthodontist, with offices in Uniontown and Pittsburgh.

Al Rowley got a promotion at General Motors while this book was being written. He is now Director of Sales and Engineering in World Wide Planning and Market Development for Delco Remy. "Imagine, me supervising engineers," he says.

After his Olympic success Bill Hosket was the tenth player selected in the 1968 NBA draft. He remembers breaking in as a Knick. "The first night I played in the Garden I looked up at the scoreboard and it flashed a message that said 'Welcome Bob Hosket, Number 20.' They couldn't even get my name right. I knew then that all that All-America and Olympic stuff didn't mean a thing."

Today Mark Minor remembers a discussion with Hosket after Bill became a professional. "When he was at Ohio State," recalls Minor, "one of the weaker parts of his game was in making driving lay-ups. He said 'I still have trouble with the shot, but now I slap my leg when I shoot. That way even when I miss I usually get the foul shots'."

Playing behind Willis Reed and Dave DeBusschere would be detrimental to anyone's playing time, but "Bob" was a part of two excellent teams with New York. In 1969 the Knicks were 54-28. In 1970 they were 60-22, and beat Los Angeles in the memorable game when Willis Read hobbled onto the court for the seventh and deciding game.

After the championship the new Buffalo team took Hosket in the expansion draft. Knee problems kept him from taking advantage of the opportunity for playing time. He retired after two years in Buffalo with an NBA, Olympic, Big Ten and high school state championship to his credit.

Today Bill Hosket is General Manager of Millcraft Paper, just north of Columbus, and is visible to Ohio State and Big Ten fans as a color announcer for the RAY-COM network.

Hosket is a good story teller and loves to share his Ohio State experiences. At the Fred Taylor Roast in 1988 he said "Fred used to talk about Luke and John a lot. We thought it was Biblical." Bill offers one last story which is "post-OSU".

"Denny Meadors organized a benefit game for the Dublin Youth Athletics, and got several Ohio State players to play and Fred to coach," recalls Hosket. Meadors remembers that the group included Dave Sorenson, Dick Ricketts, Craig Barclay, Craig Taylor,

Steve Barnard, Chris Reinhart, Hosket and himself. They were playing Dublin coaches.

"At halftime we were ahead," remembers Hosket. "Fred said 'We're going to beat these guys, the only question is will we look good doing it?' He diagrammed a play which started on one side of the court, then had a pass to the top of the circle and a pass to the other side for an open 12' shot. He assigned the players a position for the play.

"When we ran the play the guy at the top of the circle was the only one who had not been at Ohio State. He was a friend of one of the guys and wanted to play with us, so he was added to the team. Instead of making the pass for the shot, he must have thought he was open so he made a move. He lost the ball.

"Fred turned to Meadors, sitting beside him," continued Hosket. "He said 'Denny, do you suppose we'll do this again next year?' We had a good turnout and Denny said 'Sure, I guess so Fred, why?' Fred said 'Don't invite him back'." Hosket laughed at the memory. It was vintage Fred Taylor. There is a right way to try to do things and a wrong way.

Mike Swain works in Northeast Ohio for Josten's. Gary Gearhart arranged an interview for him shortly after college and now they work for the same company.

Steve Howell lives in Lakeland Shores, Minnesota, outside St. Paul, and is the manager of the Corporate Security Department at Minnesota Mining and Manufacturing (3M). He spent two years in the Army and three with the FBI, and now has a staff of 35 in supervising about 100 offices. He feels strongly about lessons learned while at Ohio State.

"I learned to focus on a team effort. You can have all the stars in the world and not do well, but when you do well as a team you get recognition. Team success is the point," he says.

"Sports helped me work with people. Whether I was benched, upset or out-played it helped me learn to deal with problems. It helped me discipline the desire to succeed, whether in the family, at the job or at church."

At age 43 he still loves playing basketball. "I play in three leagues, but stopped playing in the best ones a few years ago.

"I tried to treat the guards right at Ohio State, so they'd pass me the ball," says Howell. "I would wash and wax Denny Meadors' car."

His fraternity brother now takes care of that himself. Meadors works in Dublin, just northwest of Columbus, in the investment banking business as a government bond trader for Raymond James & Associates.

Jeff Miller is supposed to be in the coal business in Lexington, Kentucky but I was unable to reach him.

Bruce Schnabel went into the mortgage banking business after graduation. After meeting and marrying his wife Jennifer, he became interested in coal mining and moved to Lexington, Kentucky. Through mutual friends they met Joe B. Hall, who had succeeded Adolph Rupp as University of Kentucky head coach, and became devoted U.K. supporters.

"In December, 1988 Bruce had a severe case of the flu," recalls Jennifer. "On the way to the doctor his heart stopped and he died."

When Jennifer decided to sell their house, the Rick Pitinos almost bought it. "They loved it but decided to build their own. They hired me to design the interior for them," says Jennifer, who owns and operates Ashland Interiors. "We have become dear friends," she says of the present Kentucky coach and his wife.

Dave Sorenson was the 26th player taken in the 1970 NBA draft, which included players like Bob Lanier, Rudy Tomjanovich, Pete Maravich, Dave Cowens, Sam Lacey, John Johnson, Geoff Petrie, Jim McMillian, Calvin Murphy and Nate Archibald. Midway through the second round the expansion Cleveland Cavaliers took "Sunshine."

Things were rough in Cleveland in those days. The team was 15-67 in the first year, 23-59 in the second. Sorenson was sent to Philadelphia in his third year in the league, and they finished 9-73. "Dave's sweet hook shot and 17'-18' jumper were his strengths in the NBA," remembers Jim Cleamons, "but his footspeed and quickness hurt him in the corner."

Dave's fourth year he was invited to try-out with the Boston Celtics. "Camp went well, and I think I had a good shot to make the team," he recalls. "But it wasn't definite, and I didn't have a guaranteed contract. The Italians offered me a better deal, guaranteed, so I tried it. Eventually I was one of the three highest paid players in Italy, and had a car and housing paid for. I played for Valerio Bianchini, who coached Danny Ferry and Brian Shaw in 1990.

"I played in Europe for six years altogether. The fans were really fanatical. They loved basketball almost as much as soccer. Familiar names? Mitch Kupchack of North Carolina and Bob Morse of Pennsylvania. Bill Laimbeer (Detroit Piston) was there my last year."

After his varied professional basketball career, Dave Sorenson worked in sales and promotion for Converse. In late 1990 he and his partners arranged to purchase two businesses. He would be managing director of both a printing shop and a peanut processing plant. He lives in his hometown of Findlay, Ohio with his wife and family.

Sorenson's career in professional ball went much better than Buckeye teammate Jody Finney's. Jody was the first player taken in the fourth round of the draft. With 17 teams, that would equate to a late second round choice today.

He was taken by San Diego, but was the last man cut. Then he got a try-out with Atlanta but they had more players with no-cut contracts than they had roster positions. He was the 52nd ranked senior in the country at his craft — basketball — but he never played in the NBA.

Today Finney, his wife from college and their five children live in Springfield, Ohio. He has worked at Navistar in truck manufacturing for twenty years but says "What a person is is more important than what a person does." As a Christian Jody says "The great thrills of Ohio State were wonderful, but they don't compare to my personal relationship with Christ."

Dan Andreas taught and coached at Westland for three years after graduating from Ohio State, then returned to Ohio State. "I was in preliminary veterinary medicine for two years, because I wanted to become a vet. But it was tough to get into vet school and, despite Fred's help, I didn't make it."

That fact continues to irritate Fred Taylor today. "Here's a kid with all the qualities you could hope for in any field, a kid who works, sacrifices, competes, performs under pressure and they don't take him because his grades are just a shade low. Heck, he played varsity basketball when everyone else was studying. I just don't understand some people."

After two more years at Westland, Dan and his brother Bill formed a corporation and bought the family farm from their father ("One of the biggest milk farms in the state," says Mike Bordner). Dan couldn't be more pleased with the way things turned out. "It's a great way to raise a family," he says. "There's a slower pace of life, and I get to work as a vet on my own animals."

Craig Barclay became the lawyer everyone knew he would and is a partner with a law firm on E. Town St. in Columbus. His practice is limited to the prosecution of medical malpractice cases on behalf of patients.

Ed Smith, a strong defender, received his Masters in Guidance and Counseling at Ohio State. After teaching and coaching at South and East High Schools in Columbus, Smith is now Guidance Counselor at Eastmoor. He says "Antonio Watson needs to lift some weights, but he'll help the Buckeyes."

Jim Cleamons was taken in the first round by the Los Angeles Lakers, the thirteenth player selected in 1971. His first year the Lakers won 33 straight games on the way to 69 victories and an .841 winning percentage, all NBA records.

"I was like a fat rat in a cheese factory," says Jim today. "They played the game the way it should be played. I got to play against Jerry West every day in practice," truly learning from an all-time great.

West and Gail Goodrich were the starting guards, Flynn Robinson the third guard and Keith Erickson played guard and forward. That left very few minutes for a rookie. But West was expected to retire at the end of the year. "When he didn't, and L.A. had already drafted Jim Price of Louisville, they had too many guards," says Cleamons. "I was traded to Cleveland.

"L.A. put a 'W' on the board for every game scheduled with Cleveland. I was disappointed. But it worked out for me because Lenny Wilkens taught me to play pro point guard. I could lead a team on defense because I'm feisty. 'Cap' (Wilkens) had the knack to get guys to play offense together. He taught me to lead on offense. He is a great teacher of the game."

Cleamons played back-up to Wilkens in 1973 and 1974; in 1975 Wilkens went to Portland as player-coach and Cleamons became a regular. He played over 36 minutes a game, averaged 11.9 points and 5.1 assists per game, shot well and played a large role for a Cavalier team that just missed making the play-offs.

In 1976 Cleamons improved his personal statistics and sparked Cleveland to first place in the Central Division with a 49-33 record. He was the unquestioned leader of the Cavs and was selected to the second team All-Defensive team. Cleveland beat Washington 4-3, but lost 4-2 to John Havlicek and the eventual NBA champion Boston Celtics.

Clem was bothered by injuries in 1977 and was traded to New York for Hall-of-Famer Walt Frazier. After two seasons there he finished his nine year career with Washington. Remembering Jim Cleamons in the NBA Rick Barry says "He had no glaring weaknesses, and got the job done for a long time in that league. That is a tribute to him."

After his NBA career Jim Cleamons went into coaching. He was an assistant at Ohio State under Eldon Miller when Youngstown State offered their head coaching position. Before he could complete that turnaround he had an opportunity to become an assistant coach with the Chicago Bulls. Talk about a tough job, try teaching Michael Jordan how to play better. But Clem took the challenge, and the Bulls won the NBA title in June, 1991.

When watching the Bulls on television, remember some of the offensive plays Ohio State ran during The Golden Age. Chicago likes to send a guard down to screen for their center, who takes the pass at the foul line. Chicago's centers do not shoot the jump shot as often as Gary Bradds did, but the guard who sets the screen often gets the ball where Dick Ricketts and Dick Reasbeck did. The Bulls also love to pass the ball from one side of the court to the high post, for a pass to the other guard. It is the same "guard around" play Mark Minor and Allan Hornyak ran so well. Jim Cleamons says "Fred (Taylor) and Tex Winter (Bulls assistant) could be twins based on their offensive philosophies."

Mark Minor had an interesting journey to the National Basketball Association. "When we played Indiana in the Far West Classic my junior year John Havlicek came to the game," recalls Minor. "I had a fairly decent game, John noticed and remembered. He mentioned it to Red Auerbach. After my senior year there was a mix-up and Boston drafted Mark Wagar. He wasn't eligible since he was a junior, so Boston cleared it up with the league office.

"Our first day at camp Red said 'We're going to work on our turns.' Lots of guys didn't know how to do any of them, but they were second nature to an Ohio State player. I was in the top 12 but was let go when Boston went with 11 players," says Minor. He played four games for the Celtics.

Today Minor is in Contract Sales for Columbus Carpet Distributors in Columbus. As he meets people today, 20+ years after the title, he is asked "What did you get at Ohio State?" His answer is always the same: "$12.50 per quarter for Sunday meals," which is exactly what was allowed at the time. Minor enjoys coaching his son's team, and always tells them "Don't move without a change of direction" as he was told at Ohio State.

With a selection acquired from Phoenix the Cleveland Cavaliers took Allan Hornyak in the second round of the 1973 draft.

"They had Lenny Wilkens, Austin Carr, Clem, and Johnny Warren," Allan recalls. "With guards like that they didn't need me. When I was the last man cut they said I was doing too much. The next year Lenny Wilkens was player-coach at Portland and I got a try-out there. I cut back on my shooting and passed more. They cut me and they told me I didn't do enough.

"I always looked to be a scorer. I could have used better vision of the court. Like Ernie DiGregorio (Rookie of the Year in 1974). He knew where everybody was, I could have been better at that." Jim Cleamons remembers that "foot speed was what hurt Allan in the NBA. He had a great first step in college, and it was adequate as a pro. He needed a counter when a defender took that away from him."

The "Bellaire Bomber" is now back in the Valley with his wife and two daughters. When talking about one daughter playing basketball he is reminded of himself — "She puts it up; sometimes it goes in." He says "I stopped playing ball in my early 30's. Now I like to spend my time hunting and fishing." After working in the coal mines for several years, he now works for the county in the highway department.

Fred Taylor and I met at least 10 times as I researched this book. Often I would tell him I spoke to this player or that one. Usually I'd try to tell him a "new" story and he would finish it for me. After I mentioned talking with Allan, Fred said "What was that like?" It was the only time he asked that question.

"Fred," I said, "after we talked for a couple of minutes it was like I had known him all my life. Very straight forward, open, no hint of pretense. Just the kind of guy you would want for a friend. But it was clear he is quite independent. I'd rather be his friend than his supervisor." I saw a slight nod and we went back to talking about 1969, or 1963, or wherever we were that day.

The Cavaliers selected another Buckeye in the 1973 draft, Luke Witte in the fourth round. He "was a solid back-up" according to teammate Jim Cleamons, and played 118 games in three years.

Luke reflects that "I didn't appreciate Fred as much as I do now. He required you to be consistent and accountable. Kids need that, especially today."

262

Witte is embarking on a major career change, from banking to the ministry. Though he and his wife have three children, he is in a four year program to receive his Masters in Divinity from Asbury Theological Seminary in Kentucky. He says "My wife and I had been thinking about it for four years, but this year God opened the door." He is due to graduate in 1994, and is open to "pastoring a church, missions work or evangelism ... wherever the Lord leads." He has been a color man for Mid-American Conference games on the Sports Channel and hopes to continue doing that.

Dave Merchant became head coach at Elgin High School his first year out of college, then became assistant to Dick Harter at Oregon. He also coached at Robert Morris. As he was deciding college was "more business than coaching," he received a birth announcement from Buckeye teammate Gregg Testerman. Gregg, now a successful dentist in Lebanon, mentioned that Lebanon High School was looking for a head coach, Dave applied and got the job. "I've been here 14 years," he says.

Buckeye sixth man Bob Siekmann lives in Dublin and manages employee benefit programs — health plans, retirement plans — through The Siekmann Co. His comment about people in Columbus and the 1972 Minnesota game influenced the structure of this book. He said "When I meet someone and they find out I played at Ohio State they always want to talk about the fight. I wish that would just go away and leave the personal relationships and the basketball experiences."

Today Mark Wagar is President of HealthShare, "a consulting and marketing company specializing in managed health care services" in southern California.

"Ohio State basketball and Jimmy Crum had a lot to do with my choice of health care as a vocation," says Wagar today. "After The Fred Taylor Show on television, Fred, Jimmy and the players usually went to Children's Hospital. Later I went on my own. I remember an area for crippled children in particular, and the Burn Unit. There was one severely burned girl, 10-12 years old. It became very important to go see her, tell her about the games, ask how she was doing. The children were fascinated by talking with someone they had seen on television, and their spirit in spite of their problems had a profound effect on us.

"My wife and I later went to Children's as volunteers to feed the pre-mature babies. Sometimes we took another couple — it was an unusual way to spend a Friday night.

"Those kinds of experiences, and six months as an administrative resident at Children's, cemented in my mind that I liked health care. That led me to a Masters in Hospital Administration at Ohio State."

Wagar stays in touch with former classmates Merchant, Siekmann and Testerman. They have an "annual grudge golf match, the hogs against the weasels." Translated that means forwards Siekmann and Wagar (hogs) against guards Merchant and Testerman (weasels). The distinction between inside players and outside players, begun during OSU practices, continues. ("When I played, it was the 'hogs' and the 'mice'," says Gary Gearhart.)

* * * *

Children's Hospital visits directed Mark Wagar's career, and influenced several players who mentioned that experience as part of their days at Ohio State. Children's continues to work with athletes to help care for patients. January 14, 1991 Champions for Children — a group of 41 former and current athletes interested in helping Children's Hospital — was announced. The athletes will visit hospital patients and participate in or contribute to programs designed to boost the hospital's fund development and marketing activities. Fred Taylor, Bill Hosket, Coach Randy Ayers and recent Buckeye Jay Burson were charter members.

Appendix

Letter Winners of the Golden Age

*Ahijevych, Anatol	1964-65-66
Allen, James W.	1960-61
*Andreas, Daniel E.	1968-69-70
Apple, Harold R.	1961
*Barclay, Craig D.	1968-69-70
*Barker, David P.	1958-59-60
Barnard, Stephen C.	1967-68-69
Bauer, Ted C.	1968
*Bowman, William T.	1963-64
Bradds, Gary L.	1962-63-64
Brautigam, Darrell L.	1966-67
Brown, James D.	1963-64-65
Castilow, Henry C.	1963-64
Cedargren, John T.	1960
*Cleamons, James M.	1969-70-71
*DeVoe, Donald E.	1962-63-64
*Doughty, James E.	1962-63
*Dove, Robert L.	1964-65-66
*Finney, Jody R.	1968-69-70
Flatt,Donald H.	1962-63-64
Frazier, Curtis L.	1962-63-64
Furry, Donald L.	1961
*Furry, Richard L.	1958-59-60
*Gearhart, Gary L.	1960-61-62
Geddes, James L.	1968-70
Gregory, Marvin J.	1964-66
Halley, John W.	1968-69
Halley, William P.	1964
*Havlicek, John J.	1960-61-62
Haynes, Joel B.	1963-64
Heximer, Wendell	1971
*Hornyak, Allan J.	1971-72-73
*Hosket, Wilmer F.	1966-67-68
*Howell, John S.	1967-68-69
*Hoyt, Richard H.	1959-60-61
Kimble, Fred W.	1963
Kiracofe, Gary L.	1971-72
*Knight, Robert M.	1960-61-62
Landes, Jack T.	1960-61
Lane, Eugene	1962
Lee, Kenneth L.	1961
*Lucas, Jerry	1960-61-62
McDavid, John G.	1967-68
*McDonald, Doug G.	1961-62-63
Macknin, Michael L.	1970-71
*Meadors, Dennis D.	1967-68-69
*Merchant, David L.	1971-72-73
Miller, Jeffrey E.	1967-69
Miller, Nelson K.	1960-61
Milliken, Gary S.	1960-61
*Minor, Mark W.	1970-71-72
Moody, Curtis J.	1971-73
Newell, Joseph	1971
Noble, John L.	1961-62
Nourse, Howard F.	1959-60
*Nowell, Melvyn P.	1960-61-62
Painter, Michael L.	1971-72
*Peters, Albert L.	1964-65-66
Petty, John	1971
*Reasbeck, Richard F.	1961-62-63
Richardson, Delphis C.	1967
*Ricketts, Richard P.	1963-64-65
*Roberts, Joe C.	1958-59-60
*Rowley, Alan B.	1965-66-67
Sadelfeld, Joseph R.	1967
Schnabel, Bruce J.	1967-68-69
*Sepic, Ronald R.	1965-66-67
*Shaffer, James C.	1963-64-65
*Siegfried, Larry E.	1959-60-61
*Siekmann, Robert E.	1971-72-73
*Smith, Edward J.	1968-69-70
*Sorenson, David L.	1968-69-70
Spies, Thomas P.	1968-70
*Swain, Ralph M.	1966-67-68
Taylor, Richard S.	1962-63
Testerman, Gregg L.	1971-73
Thompson, Robert N.	1971
Tischer, Jerry A.	1965-66-67
*Wagar, Mark L.	1971-72-73
Walkey, John L.	1968
White, Albert M.	1963
*Witte, Luther E.	1971-72-73

*Interviewed for this book.

Outstanding College Programs

1960 — 1971

Team	W	L	% *	NCAA Champions	Runners-Up	Final Four
UCLA	291	55	.841	7	0	1
Cincinnati	249	81	.755	2	1	1
Ohio State	225	82	.733	1	2	1
Duke	250	86	.744	0	1	2
Kentucky	245	77	.761	0	1	0
North Carolina	228	87	.724	0	1	2
Houston	245	94	.723	0	0	2
Dayton	244	94	.722	0	1	0
Providence	238	83	.741	0	0	0
St. Bonaventure	218	78	.737	0	0	0

* Subjective weightings for value of NCAA success alter rank by percentages.
** St. Joseph's (.734) and Villanova (.729) not listed due to NCAA penalties during the time.

Coaching in the NCAA Tournament

During the Golden Age from 1960 — 1971, Ohio State and Fred Taylor went to five NCAA tournaments. Under today's 64 team format, the 1963, 1964, 1969 and 1970 teams would have qualified as well.

How does Taylor's coaching record in the "The Big Dance" compare to the best coaches of today? Based on records through the 1991 tournament, better than good.

Coach	School	W	L	%
Mike Krzyzewski	Duke	27	7	.794
* Fred Taylor	Ohio State	14	4	.778
Bob Knight	Indiana	31	12	.721
Jerry Tarkanian	UNLV	37	16	.698
Dean Smith	North Carolina	47	22	.681
Denny Crum	Louisville	32	15	.681
Rollie Massimino	Villanova	20	10	.667
Tom Davis	Iowa	12	6	.667
John Thompson	Georgetown	27	14	.659
Jud Heathcote	Michigan State	13	7	.650

*During the Golden Age, as Big Ten champion Ohio State played its first NCAA game in what is now called the "Sweet Sixteen". The advantage, compared to today, was that only four victories stood between the team and the NCAA title. For purposes of this comparison, however, this constituted a major disadvantage. Today a powerful team would likely defeat two weak opponents, maybe ranked #64 and #32 in the tournament, before the "Sweet Sixteen." Then Ohio State always played its first game against a team which, theoretically, as no worse than #16. Plus OSU's first opponent had always won an NCAA tournament game before the Buckeyes took the court. Without question the two extra games each year can result in upsets, but generally the games increase the winning percentages of the good coaches at the good schools.

Source: *The Sporting News*, March 18, 1991

"Fred-isms"

The players often mentioned "Fred-isms", phrases Coach Taylor used in teaching his teams — and occasionally a referee — the finer points of basketball. Here is a partial list, with a brief explanation in case one is needed.

- "Grab a root and growl" (Things may not get any better, so let's do all we can to help ourselves)

- "If that's not true I'll knit you a watch" (That's true)

- "Grandma was slow, but she was old" (Some people don't have much going for them)

- "They're just puppies — they aren't dogs until they've bitten somebody" (Potential is not as important as accomplishment; let the young team play a few games before deciding how great they are)

- "That team is in the pear tree" (They are in good position to challenge in the race)

- "Why don't you peel it and eat it?" (Do something constructive with the basketball)

- "Do you think he knows you're a senior? The captain? (We need leadership and you are elected)

- "They can't hurt you without the ball" (So move closer to the middle and help a teammate)

- "Move around before somebody walks up and ties a horse to you" (We need more movement in our offense)

- "There's a guy who never needed a new pair of shoes" (He is never active)

- "Get some guts" (Ref, you owe us several calls)

- "Did you ever think there might be a reason we want you to set that screen?" (Set better screens)

Final 1960 Ohio State Basketball Statistics

Name	G	FG	FGA	FG Pct.	FT	FTA	FT Pct.	Reb	PF	Pts	Avg.
Lucas, Jerry	27	283	444	.637	144	187	.770	442	71	710	26.3
Siegfried, Larry	28	145	311	.466	81	108	.750	107	76	371	13.2
Nowell, Mel	28	156	330	.473	56	73	.768	72	67	368	13.1
Havlicek, John	28	144	312	.461	53	74	.716	205	61	341	12.2
Roberts, Joe	28	135	281	.480	38	56	.678	194	57	308	11.0
Furry, Dick	28	61	134	.455	20	33	.606	92	35	142	5.1
Knight, Bob	21	30	74	.405	17	27	.629	42	25	77	3.7
Hoyt, Richie	23	22	52	.423	14	18	.778	19	21	58	2.5
Nourse, Howard	17	24	47	.511	5	5	1.000	46	28	53	3.1
Gearhart, Gary	19	21	52	.404	7	16	.437	22	26	49	2.6
Barker, Dave	16	11	27	.407	1	6	.166	13	6	23	1.4
Cedargren, John	13	7	12	.583	2	5	.400	14	6	16	1.2
Allen, Jim	7	1	9	.111	5	6	.833	2	3	7	1.0
Miller, Nelson	6	2	5	.400	1	3	.333	4	1	5	.8
Landes, J.T.	6	2	8	.250	0	2	.000	1	1	4	.7
Milliken, Gary	2	0	3	.000	0	0	.000	1	0	0	.0
(Team)								139			
Ohio State Totals	28	1044	2101	.497	444	619	.717	1415	484	2532	90.4
Opponent Totals	28	753	1941	.388	447	645	.693	1032	472	1953	69.7

Final 1961 Ohio State Basketball Statistics

Name	G	FG	FGA	FG Pct.	FT	FTA	FT Pct.	Reb	PF	Pts	Avg.
Lucas, Jerry	27	256	411	.623	159	208	.764	470	59	671	24.8
Siegfried, Larry	28	151	314	.481	123	143	.860	141	69	425	15.2
Havlicek, John	28	173	321	.539	61	87	.701	244	55	407	14.5
Nowell, Mel	28	155	317	.490	70	90	.778	80	64	380	13.6
Hoyt, Richie	28	60	140	.428	33	43	.767	80	67	153	5.4
Knight, Bob	28	54	136	.397	15	26	.577	77	65	123	4.4
Gearhart, Gary	24	25	66	.379	17	26	.654	24	43	67	2.8
Reasbeck, Dick	20	22	45	.489	6	11	.545	24	14	50	2.5
McDonald, Douglas	22	18	43	.418	4	12	.333	48	36	40	1.8
Lee, Kenneth	20	9	38	.237	9	10	.900	45	13	27	1.3
Landes, J.T.	13	6	17	.353	3	5	.600	8	6	15	1.1
Miller, Nelson	16	6	20	.263	1	2	.500	14	3	13	.8
Allen, James	7	1	5	.200	2	4	.500	1	4	4	.6
Furry, Donald	3	1	2	.500	1	2	.500	2	0	3	1.0
Apple, Raymond	8	1	6	.167	1	2	.500	4	3	3	.4
Noble, John	6	1	3	.333	0	0	.000	3	1	2	.3
Milliken, Gary	4	0	2	.000	0	0	.000	1	2	0	.0
(Team)								152			
Ohio State Totals	28	939	1886	.498	505	671	.753	1418	504	2383	85.1
Opponent Totals	28	690	1895	.364	460	691	.666	1053	485	1840	65.7

Final 1962 Ohio State Basketball Statistics

Name	G	FG	FGA	FG Pct.	FT	FTA	FT Pct.	Reb	PF	Pts	Avg.
Lucas, Jerry	28	237	388	.611	135	169	.799	499	52	609	21.7
Havlicek, John	28	196	377	.520	83	109	.761	271	55	475	16.9
Nowell, Mel	28	140	358	.391	72	92	.782	80	59	352	12.6
McDonald, Doug	28	92	180	.511	34	53	.642	99	55	218	7.8
Reasbeck, Dick	27	97	218	.445	19	29	.655	63	58	213	7.9
Bradds, Gary	26	50	72	.694	23	40	.575	72	26	123	4.7
Doughty, Jim	26	39	92	.424	23	31	.742	61	19	101	3.9
Gearhart, Gary	19	32	86	.372	21	36	.583	40	42	85	4.5
Knight, Bob	25	35	89	.393	9	11	.818	38	43	79	3.2
Taylor, Dick	22	9	24	.375	10	15	.667	12	20	28	1.3
Flatt, Don	25	9	28	.321	8	16	.500	18	11	26	1.0
Lane, Gene	18	8	23	.348	2	4	.500	16	11	18	1.0
Frazier, LeRoy	21	7	24	.292	1	5	.200	11	18	15	.7
Furry, Don	2	1	1	1.000	0	1	.000	0	0	2	1.0
Noble, John	5	0	0	.000	0	0	.000	2	0	0	.0
DeVoe, Don	5	0	1	.000	0	0	.000	1	2	0	.0
(Team)								108			
Ohio State Totals	28	952	1961	.485	440	611	.720	1391	471	2344	83.7
Opponent Totals	28	706	1848	.382	443	622	.712	971	468	1855	66.2

Final 1963 Ohio State Basketball Statistics

Name	G	FG	FGA	FG Pct.	FT	FTA	FT Pct.	Reb	PF	Pts	Avg.
Bradds, Gary	24	237	453	.523	198	248	.798	312	69	672	28.0
Reasbeck, Dick	24	158	363	.435	44	59	.746	84	82	360	15.0
Ricketts, Dick	24	87	184	.473	51	56	.911	73	47	225	9.4
Doughty, Jim	24	91	223	.408	40	84	.476	209	68	222	9.2
McDonald, Doug	24	79	195	.405	44	70	.629	123	62	202	8.4
Taylor, Dick	21	28	90	.311	15	24	.625	38	33	71	3.4
DeVoe, Don	17	18	46	.391	15	23	.652	41	19	51	3.0
Bowman, Tom	19	10	47	.213	6	13	.462	45	24	26	1.4
Shaffer, Jim	16	8	23	.348	5	11	.455	23	10	21	1.3
Flatt, Don	15	5	20	.250	5	8	.625	16	7	15	1.0
Brown, Jim	11	6	11	.545	0	0	.000	7	8	12	1.1
Frazier, LeRoy	8	2	9	.222	2	3	.667	7	6	6	.7
Castilow, Carter	3	0	3	.000	0	1	.000	1	1	0	.0
(Team)								123			
Ohio State Totals	24	729	1667	.437	425	600	.705	1102	436	1883	78.4
Opponent Totals	24	653	1531	.426	376	560	.671	983	452	1682	70.1

Final 1964 Ohio State Basketball Statistics

Name	G	FG	FGA	FG Pct.	FT	FTA	FT Pct.	Reb	PF	Pts	Avg.
Bradds, Gary	24	276	527	.523	183	231	.792	322	68	735	30.6
Ricketts, Dick	24	138	275	.502	60	76	.789	97	64	336	14.0
DeVoe, Don	23	96	202	.475	50	84	.595	116	64	242	10.5
Bowman, Tom	24	62	156	.397	49	74	.662	105	67	173	7.2
Shaffer, Jim	23	69	163	.423	14	29	.483	134	67	152	6.6
Dove, Bob	21	53	106	.500	15	25	.600	82	52	121	5.7
Peters, Al	18	29	72	.403	23	34	.676	40	32	81	4.5
Flatt, Don	20	25	70	.357	17	30	.567	52	24	67	3.3
Brown, Jim	18	19	49	.388	16	28	.571	16	24	54	3.0
Frazier, LeRoy	15	6	22	.273	1	4	.250	17	15	13	.8
Ahijevych, Andy	13	4	7	.571	3	5	.600	11	5	11	.8
others		0	4	.000	0	1	.000	2	1	0	.0
(Team)								128			
Ohio State Totals	24	777	1653	.470	431	621	.694	1122	483	1985	82.7
Opponent Totals	24	709	1712	.414	447	646	.692	1073	471	1865	77.7

Final 1968 Ohio State Basketball Statistics

Name	G	FG	FGA	FG Pct.	FT	FTA	FT Pct.	Reb	PF	Pts	Avg.
Hosket, Bill	29	228	422	.540	128	190	.674	332	108	584	20.1
Howell, Steve	29	217	428	.507	73	98	.745	157	71	507	17.5
Sorenson, Dave	29	196	329	.596	82	115	.713	289	85	474	16.3
Meadors, Denny	29	94	230	.409	82	112	.732	98	75	270	9.3
Finney, Jody	23	61	128	.477	32	46	.696	66	28	154	6.7
Swain, Mike	23	34	81	.420	24	37	.649	56	48	92	4.0
Smith, Ed	26	35	97	.361	15	46	.326	93	25	85	3.2
Schnabel, Bruce	23	25	48	.521	16	22	.727	14	31	66	2.8
Geddes, Jim	21	23	56	.411	12	27	.444	40	45	58	2.7
Andreas, Dan	22	18	47	.383	6	11	.545	39	14	42	1.9
Barclay, Craig	19	8	27	.296	12	18	.667	8	7	28	1.5
Spies, Tom	7	4	11	.364	4	7	.571	5	4	12	1.7
Barnard, Steve	9	3	9	.333	2	3	.667	14	7	8	.9
McDavid, Gary	2	2	2	1.000	0	0	.000	1	1	4	2.0
Bauer, Ted	3	1	2	.500	0	0	.000	0	1	2	.6
Others		0	4	.000	0	3	.000	4	1	0	.0
(Team)								164			
Ohio State Totals	29	949	1921	.494	488	735	.664	1380	551	2386	82.3
Opponent Totals	29	821	2035	.403	493	731	.674	1157	562	2135	73.6

Final 1971 Ohio State Basketball Statistics

Name	G	FG	FGA	FG Pct.	FT	FTA	FT Pct.	Reb	PF	Pts	Avg.
Hornyak, Allan	24	217	452	.480	114	147	.776	118	68	548	22.8
Witte, Luke	24	187	327	.572	82	127	.646	303	85	456	19.0
Cleamons, Jim	22	146	286	.510	93	126	.738	140	56	385	17.5
Minor, Mark	24	72	154	.468	29	41	.707	141	70	173	7.2
Siekmann, Bob	23	55	127	.433	51	61	.836	71	41	161	7.0
Wagar, Mark	24	55	139	.396	26	33	.788	103	71	136	5.7
Merchant, Dave	24	23	57	.404	26	34	.765	41	25	72	3.0
Macknin, Mike	14	11	23	.478	4	9	.444	33	14	26	1.9
Testerman, Gregg	6	1	8	.125	3	3	1.000	3	1	5	.8
Kiracofe, Gary	5	1	3	.333	1	2	.500	1	4	3	.6
Painter, Mike	7	1	5	.200	0	0	.000	0	2	2	.3
Petty, John	8	1	5	.200	0	1	.000	1	3	2	.2
Heximer, Wendell	5	0	4	.000	0	1	.000	1	3	0	.0
Others		0	4	.000	0	1	.000	1	0	0	.0
(Team)								148			
Ohio State Totals	24	770	1594	.483	429	586	.732	1105	443	1969	82.0
Opponent Totals	24	687	1670	.411	408	610	.669	1061	441	1782	74.2

Year-By-Year Scores (1960-1971)

1959-60

	OSU		OPP
12- 1	77	Wake Forest	69
12- 3	94	Memphis State	55
12- 5	94	Pittsburgh	49
12- 7	99	Butler	66
12-10	81	At St. Louis	74
12-18	96	At Butler	68
12-21	92	At Utah	97
12-22	91	At Brigham Young	79
12-28	93	At Kentucky	96
1- 4	97	Illinois	73
1- 9	96	Indiana	95
1-11	109	Delaware	38
1-16	81	Northwestern	64
1-23	85	At Purdue	71
1-30	111	Michigan State	79
2- 1	99	Michigan	52
2- 6	77	At Northwestern	58
2- 8	106	At Wisconsin	69
2-13	75	Iowa	47
2-15	109	At Illinois	81
2-20	84	At Michigan State	83
2-27	93	Wisconsin	68
2-29	83	At Indiana	99
3- 5	75	At Minnesota	66
3-11	98	Vs West. Kentucky#	79
3-12	86	Vs Georgia Tech#	69
3-18	76	Vs New York Univ.#	54
3-19	75	Vs California#	55

Won 25, Lost 3
Big Ten: 13-1 (1st)

(# = NCAA Tournament Game)

1960-61

	OSU		OPP
12- 1	85	At Ohio University	64
12- 5	81	St. Louis	66
12-10	103	Army	54
12-17	93	At Wichita	82
12-19	90	At Loyola (Chicago)	65
12-22	84	Detroit	73
12-27	97	Vs Seton Hall	57
12-29	70	Vs St. John's	65
12-31	84	Vs St. Bonaventure	82
1- 7	91	Illinois	65
1- 9	86	Evansville	59
1-14	79	At Northwestern	45
1-21	75	Minnesota	56
1-28	92	Purdue	62
1-30	100	At Wisconsin	68
2- 4	80	At Michigan	58
2- 6	100	Indiana	65
2-11	83	At Michigan State	68
2-13	89	Northwestern	65
2-18	62	At Iowa	61
2-20	73	At Indiana	69
2-25	97	Wisconsin	74
3- 4	91	Michigan State	83
3-11	95	At Illinois	66
3-17	56	Vs Louisville#	55
3-18	87	Vs Kentucky#	74
3-24	95	Vs St. Joseph's#	69
3-25	65	Vs Cincinnati# (OT)	70

Won 27, Lost 1
Big Ten: 14-0 (1st)

(# = NCAA Tournament Game)

Year-By-Year Scores (1960-1971)

1961-62

	OSU		OPP
12- 2	72	Florida State	57
12- 6	99	At Pittsburgh	79
12- 8	85	Wichita	62
12- 9	84	At Wake Forest	62
12-16	92	Loyola (Chicago)	72
12-18	61	At St. Louis	48
12-23	92	Penn State	49
12-27	59	Vs Washington	49
12-28	105	Vs UCLA	84
12-30	76	Vs S. California	66
1- 6	85	At Northwestern	62
1-13	89	Michigan	64
1-20	90	At Minnesota	76
1-22	91	Purdue	65
1-29	94	At Purdue	73
2- 3	97	Northwestern	61
2- 5	89	Iowa	63
2-10	91	Minnesota	66
2-12	72	At Michigan	57
2-17	80	At Michigan State	72
2-24	102	Illinois	79
2-26	72	At Iowa	62
3- 3	67	At Wisconsin	86
3-10	90	Indiana	65
3-16	93	Vs W. Kentucky#	73
3-17	74	Vs Kentucky#	64
3-23	84	Vs Wake Forest#	68
3-24	59	Vs Cincinnati#	71

Won 26, Lost 2
Big Ten: 13-1 (1st)

(# = NCAA Tournament Game)

1962-63

	OSU		OPP
12- 1	62	Utah State	50
12- 3	84	St. Louis	59
12- 5	70	Virginia	46
12- 8	76	West Virginia	69
12-15	74	Texas Christian	62
12-22	101	At Detroit	66
12-27	66	At Butler	62
12-29	54	At Wichita	71
12-31	97	Brigham Young	91
1- 5	78	Minnesota	76
1- 7	78	At Illinois	90
1-12	68	Michigan	66
1-19	74	At Iowa	81
1-26	78	Creighton	73
1-28	72	Northwestern	70
2- 2	97	At Purdue	93
2- 9	94	Wisconsin	70
2-16	75	At Michigan	68
2-18	87	Michigan State	77
2-23	83	Iowa	70
2-25	50	At Northwestern	45
3- 2	95	Purdue	75
3- 4	85	At Minnesota	65
3- 9	85	At Indiana (OT)	87

Won 20, Lost 4
Big Ten: 11-3 (1st, 2-way tie)

Year-By-Year Scores (1960-1971)

1963-64

	OSU		OPP
11-30	68	California-Davis	42
12- 2	74	Butler	68
12- 6	75	Vs Duke	76
12- 7	66	Vs St. John's	64
12-11	73	Davidson	95
12-13	74	Missouri	85
12-21	78	Wichita	60
12-23	79	Houston	62
12-28	66	At Utah State	79
12-31	89	At St. Louis (2-OT)	91
1- 4	101	At Wisconsin	85
1-11	85	Minnesota	73
1-18	64	At Michigan	82
1-25	98	Purdue	87
1-27	99	At Michigan State	102
2- 3	86	Michigan	85
2- 8	98	At Indiana (OT)	96
2-10	110	Illinois	92
2-15	92	Wisconsin	74
2-17	99	At Iowa	82
2-22	72	At Northwestern	61
2-29	73	Indiana	69
3- 2	86	At Illinois	74
3- 7	80	Michigan State	81

Won 16, Lost 8
Big Ten: 11-3 (1st, 2-way tie)

1964-65

	OSU		OPP
12- 2	86	South Dakota	54
12- 3	70	St. Louis	79
12- 5	84	At Texas Christian	79
12- 7	77	At Houston	69
12- 9	67	Butler	66
12-19	64	At Davidson	87
12-22	71	At Brigham Young	112
12-28	90	Dartmouth	59
12-30	89	Duke (2-OT)	94
1- 2	73	Georgia Tech	68
1- 9	64	At Purdue	71
1-16	72	Indiana	84
1-23	77	At Minnesota	97
1-30	98	Wisconsin	86
2- 6	73	At Wisconsin	71
2- 8	71	Illinois	86
2-13	81	Iowa	82
2-16	72	At Illinois	95
2-20	61	At Michigan	100
2-22	101	Michigan State	90
2-27	100	Northwestern	87
3- 1	90	At Indiana	110
3- 6	97	At Michigan State	75
3- 8	93	Michigan	85

Won 12, Lost 12
Big Ten: 6-8 (6th)

Year-By-Year Scores (1960-1971)

1965-66

	OSU		OPP
12- 1	76	At Missouri	74
12- 3	66	At UCLA	92
12- 6	72	North Carolina	82
12- 8	75	At Butler	74
12-18	58	At St. Louis	83
12-20	87	Iowa State	70
12-23	68	Kansas	81
12-28	88	Wake Forest	81
12-31	78	West Texas	53
1- 8	78	Michigan	83
1-15	64	At Michigan State	80
1-22	79	Northwestern	73
1-24	89	At Iowa	98
1-29	72	Hardin-Simmons	64
1-31	87	Wisconsin (OT)	81
2- 5	77	At Illinois	78
2-12	68	Purdue	54
2-14	61	At Indiana	81
2-19	80	Iowa	86
2-21	102	At Minnesota	98
2-26	77	At Northwestern	78
2-28	79	Michigan State	98
3- 5	94	Minnesota	89
3- 7	86	At Purdue	92

Won 11, Lost 13
Big Ten: 5-9 (8th)

1966-67

	OSU		OPP
12- 1	74	Butler	67
12- 3	79	At Iowa State	77
12- 5	70	At Kansas	94
12-10	73	Washington State	63
12-20	84	Texas Christian	78
12-23	61	Army	59
12-29	83	Vs Duke	82
12-30	82	Vs North Carolina	105
1- 7	78	At Minnesota	65
1-14	80	Indiana	81
1-16	73	At Georgia Tech	84
1-21	60	Minnesota	67
1-23	82	Purdue	72
1-30	77	At Northwestern	100
2- 4	90	At Wisconsin	84
2- 6	80	Northern Michigan	74
2-11	72	Iowa	73
2-13	66	At Purdue	86
2-18	97	At Michigan	85
2-20	80	Michigan State	64
2-25	82	Northwestern	95
2-27	63	At Michigan State	74
3- 4	56	At Iowa	90
3- 6	100	Illinois	79

Won 13, Lost 11
Big Ten: 6-8 (7th, 2-way tie)

Year-By-Year Scores (1960-1971)

1967-68

	OSU		OPP
12- 1	95	Calif.-Davis	52
12- 4	76	Florida State	69
12- 9	97	South Dakota	54
12-19	78	New Mexico State	75
12-22	71	At Butler	69
12-27	60	Vs Marquette	64
12-29	85	Vs Bradley	62
12-30	76	At Hawaii	80
1- 6	108	Purdue	80
1-13	72	At Iowa (OT)	74
1-20	103	Michigan	70
1-22	66	Georgia Tech	55
1-27	95	At Michigan	92
1-29	64	Cornell	76
2- 3	86	Wisconsin	64
2- 5	78	At Indiana	77
2-10	90	Michigan State	62
2-12	78	At Wisconsin	86
2-17	79	At Minnesota	83
2-20	87	Northwestern	67
2-24	72	At Purdue	93
2-26	95	Illinois	75
3- 2	107	Indiana	93
3- 4	67	At Illinois	64
3-12	85	Vs Iowa (Playoff)	81
3-15	79	Vs E. Tennessee#	72
3-16	82	Vs Kentucky#	81
3-22	66	Vs North Carolina#	80
3-23	89	Vs Houston#	85

Won 21, Lost 8
Big Ten: 10-4 (1st, 2-way tie)

(# = NCAA Tournament Game)

1968-69

	OSU		OPP
11-30	85	Ohio University	77
12- 6	73	UCLA	84
12-14	89	Harvard	74
12-16	75	At Washington State	74
12-21	84	Washington State	69
12-23	74	Butler	71
12-27	93	At Florida State	86
12-30	59	Washington	64
1- 4	90	At Indiana	82
1-11	84	Wisconsin	69
1-18	98	At Michigan	85
1-20	73	Vs Georgia Tech	66
1-24	96	Vs Cornell	78
1-28	76	Illinois	67
2- 1	85	At Purdue (OT)	95
2- 8	73	At Wisconsin	77
2-11	88	Purdue	85
2-15	58	Minnesota	41
2-18	57	At Illinois	73
2-22	88	Iowa	81
2-25	83	At Northwestern	86
3- 1	72	At Michigan State	85
3- 4	108	Indiana	86
3- 8	95	Michigan	86

Won 17, Lost 7
Big Ten: 9-5 (2nd, 2-way tie)

Year-By-Year Scores (1960-1971)

1969-70

	OSU		OPP
12- 1	96	At Wake Forest	92
12- 6	112	At Butler	89
12- 8	106	Northern Illinois	99
12-13	80	Ohio University	82
12-20	96	At Alabama	68
12-22	87	At Tulane	74
12-27	84	Fresno State	77
12-29	89	At Texas Christian	80
1- 3	78	Minnesota	71
1-10	59	At Illinois	77
1-13	103	Michigan	95
1-17	93	Northwestern	67
1-19	84	West Virginia	70
1-24	76	At Minnesota	77
1-26	74	Georgia Tech	71
1-31	68	At Northwestern	64
2- 7	85	Purdue	88
2-10	89	At Michigan State	66
2-14	100	At Indiana	83
2-21	89	Iowa	97
2-24	98	At Wisconsin	86
2-28	80	Michigan State	82
3- 3	92	At Iowa	113
3- 7	96	Wisconsin	87

Won 17, Lost 7
Big Ten: 8-6 (3rd, 2-way tie)

1970-71

	OSU		OPP
12- 1	89	At Utah State	95
12- 5	71	E. Tennessee State	63
12- 7	74	Alabama	58
12-12	64	Pennsylvania	71
12-21	96	Butler	77
12-28	74	Vs Stanford (OT)	78
12-29	103	Vs Harvard	87
12-30	77	Vs Indiana	85
1- 2	95	Yale	75
1- 9	97	At Iowa	76
1-13	83	At West Virginia	74
1-16	83	Wisconsin	69
1-23	68	At Minnesota	66
1-30	70	Michigan State	82
2- 6	87	At Michigan State	76
2- 9	69	At Purdue	67
2-13	92	Illinois	72
2-16	79	At Wisconsin	71
2-20	84	Northwestern	72
2-23	80	Iowa	71
2-27	91	At Michigan	85
3- 2	84	Minnesota	70
3- 6	68	At Northwestern	67
3- 9	91	Indiana	75
3-18	60	Vs Marquette#	59
3-20	78	Vs W. Kentucky# (OT)	81

Won 20, Lost 6
Big Ten: 13-1 (1st)

(# = NCAA Tournament Game)